Transforming Chaplaincy

Transforming Chaplaincy

The George Fitchett Reader

Edited by
STEVE NOLAN
and ANNELIEKE DAMEN

Foreword by Wendy Cadge

PICKWICK *Publications* · Eugene, Oregon

TRANSFORMING CHAPLAINCY
The George Fitchett Reader

Pickwick Publications
An Imprint of Wipf and Stock Publishers
199 W. 8th Ave., Suite 3
Eugene, OR 97401

www.wipfandstock.com

PAPERBACK ISBN: 978-1-7252-9451-6
HARDCOVER ISBN: 978-1-7252-9452-3
EBOOK ISBN: 978-1-7252-9453-0

Cataloguing-in-Publication data:

Names: Fitchett, George, 1948–, author. | Nolan, Steve, editor | Damen, Annelieke, editor | Cadge, Wendy, foreword writer

Title: Transforming chaplaincy : the George Fitchett reader / edited by Steve Nolan and Annelieke Damen.

Description: Eugene, OR: Pickwick Publications, 2021 | Series: Transforming Chaplaincy | Includes bibliographical references and index.

Identifiers: ISBN 978-1-7252-9451-6 (paperback) | ISBN 978-1-7252-9452-3 (hardcover) | ISBN 978-1-7252-9453-0 (ebook)

Subjects: LCSH: Fitchett, George, 1948– | Chaplains, Hospital | Medicine—Religious aspects | Pastoral care | Pastoral counseling | Pastoral theology | Spiritual life | Models, Theoretical | Counseling

Classification: BL65.M4 F58 2021 (paperback) | BL65.M4 (ebook)

09/30/21

For the next generation who are transforming chaplaincy

Contents

Tables and Figures

TABLES

FIGURES

Permissions

American Psychological Association

G. Fitchett, B. D. Rybarczyk, G. A. DeMarco, and J. J. Nicholas. 1999. "The Role of Religion in Medical Rehabilitation Outcomes: A Longitudinal Study." *Rehabilitation Psychology* 44:4, 333–53.

Journal of Pastoral Care and Counseling

G. Fitchett, P. Meyer, and L. A. Burton. 2000. "Spiritual Care in the Hospital: Who Requests It? Who Needs It?" *Journal of Pastoral Care and Counseling* 54:2, 173–86.

SAGE

G. Fitchett, P. E. Murphy, J. Kim, J. L. Gibbons, J. R. Cameron, and J. A. Davis. 2004. "Religious Struggle: Prevalence, Correlates and Mental Health Risks in Diabetic, Congestive Heart Failure, and Oncology Patients." *International Journal of Psychiatry in Medicine* 34:2, 179–96.

Oxford University Press

A. L. Canada, P. E. Murphy, G. Fitchett, and K. Stein. 2016. "Re-examining the Contributions of Faith, Meaning, and Peace to Quality of Life: A Report from the American Cancer Society's Studies of Cancer Survivors–II (SCS–II)." *Annals of Behavioral Medicine* 50:1, 79–86.

Journal of Supervision and Training in Ministry

G. Fitchett. 1998–1999. "CPE and Spiritual Growth." *Journal of Supervision and Training in Ministry* 19:130–46. Reprinted in *Expanding the Circle: Essays in Honor of Joan Hemenway* edited by C. F. Garlid, A. A. Zollfrank, and G. Fitchett, 213–34. Decatur, GA: Journal of Pastoral Care, 2009.

Taylor & Francis

G. Fitchett. 2011. "Making Our Case(s)." *Journal of Health Care Chaplaincy* 17:1–2, 3–18.

Taylor & Francis

G. Fitchett and D. Grossoehme. 2012. "Health Care Chaplaincy as a Research-Informed Profession." In *Professional Spiritual and Pastoral Care: A Practical Clergy and Chaplain's Handbook* edited by S. Roberts, 387–406. Woodstock, VY: SkyLight Paths.

The George Washington Institute for Spirituality and Health

G. Fitchett and P. A. Roberts. 2003. "In the Garden with Andrea: Spiritual Assessment in End of Life Care." In *Walking Together: Physicians, Chaplains and Clergy Caring for the Sick* edited by C. M. Puchalski, 23–31. Washington, DC: The George Washington Institute for Spirituality and Health.

Journal of Pastoral Care and Counseling

G. Fitchett and J. Risk. 2009. "Screening for Spiritual Struggle." *Journal of Pastoral Care and Counseling* 63:1–2, 1–12.

Mary Ann Liebert

G. Fitchett, A. L. H. Pierson, C. Hoffmeyer, D. Labuschagne, A. Lee, S. Levine, S. O'Mahony, K. Pugliese, and N. Waite. 2019. "Development of the PC-7, a Quantifiable Assessment of Spiritual Concerns of Patients Receiving Palliative Care Near the End of Life." *Journal of Palliative Medicine.*

Foreword

IT WAS JULY OF 2016 and we were in a conference room at Rush University. We were surrounded by chaplains from across the country in the process of becoming chaplaincy researchers. The first cohort of eight Transforming Chaplaincy Fellows had just finished their first year of research-based master's degree programs and the second cohort would be starting in the fall. Gathered for a conference, we were tired after a long day and looking forward to dinner.

George was putting away the small black clock he uses to keep time during conference panels. Rather than packing up and heading outside for some fresh air, many of us clustered in small groups working on projects. I remember thinking that this "break" looked more like a study-hall, and then realizing that this cohort of people, passionate about using research to improve the work of chaplains, was doing exactly what George and I envisioned when we wrote the grant proposal that funded the first phase of the Transforming Chaplaincy Project. We were building a stronger research-base for the field, creating a leadership pipeline to support it, and collaborating all along the way.

What I most remember about this scene, though, is George. Not sitting with any one group, he moved among us because we all wanted his attention and needed his help. He suggested references to one group, looked at rough drafts of tables with another, and brainstormed with a third—the leading chaplaincy researcher and teacher doing his craft.

George's journey to this role was far from linear. He was an undergraduate sociology major at Rutgers University, interested in research and advised by the department chair in the mid-1960s to join the Society for the Scientific Study of Religion. He was a staff chaplain and then ACPE Supervisor at Rush University Medical Center, reading articles by Ken Pargament about religious coping in the *Journal for the Scientific Study of Religion* and going to grand rounds sponsored by the Department of Psychology and the Department of Psychiatry, where it was taken for granted that research improved clinical practice.

In 1990, new leadership in the Department of Religion, Health and Human Values at Rush made it possible for George to begin to do research half-time in collaboration, with experienced health psychologists he knew from clinical work there. He encouraged them to add questions about religion and spirituality to the surveys they conducted with patients with serious illnesses, and he began to develop measures and contribute to the growing field of psycho-oncology. With the mentoring of Rush colleagues, Lynda Powell, a psychologist in the Department of Preventive Medicine, and Carlos Mendes de Leon, an epidemiologist in the Institute for Aging, George continued to do research and received a National Institutes of Health Career Development (K) Award that enabled him, in 2007, to complete a PhD at the University of Illinois-Chicago's School of Public Health in Epidemiology, focused on religion and cardiovascular health.

George was the first chaplain to get a research-focused PhD, and his work has become central to the field of chaplaincy research. Support from the Department of Religion, Health and Human Values at Rush was essential—this was not a field that could be built by chaplains with full-time jobs in their "free" time at night and on the weekends—as were collaborations with colleagues in psychology, sociology, and medicine both locally and nationally. As George remembers, there was an immense amount of doubt along the way, which made collaborations with colleagues all the more important.

As we gather some of George's most influential papers in this volume, it is all too easy to forget the collegiality and circuity that have shaped George's personal and professional journey. It is this journey, both George's and those of the chaplaincy-researchers gathered in July of 2016, which continues to shape chaplaincy-research as an emerging profession, one critical to the soulful and ethical practice of healthcare in the twenty-first century.

Thank you, George, for your curiosity, your persistence along this untrod path, and your colleagueship. We, who have been on this journey with you, are better for it, as are the patients, family members and students in our care.

Wendy Cadge
Brandeis University
Waltham, MA
February 2020

Acknowledgments

THE EDITORS ARE GRATEFUL to Kristen Schenk and Christa Chappelle for their assistance in preparing the text for this book.

Introduction

—Steve Nolan and Annelieke Damen

Retrospectives have long been a feature of major art galleries and afford rare opportunities to view, review, and assess the life's work of a creative personality. Wander through a well-curated retrospective and you are gifted the chance to look back over that individual's development, see their work in its various contexts, and come to a fresh appreciation of what the artist has achieved and contributed.

This book is most definitely *not* a retrospective. It has not been our intention to provide an insight into George Fitchett's intellectual development, nor is it an homage to a man who has done more than most to develop his profession. As the "curators" of this collection we do understand the depth of Fitchett's contribution to professional chaplaincy. As a chaplain-researcher, Fitchett has been at the leading edge, not only of chaplaincy research but of influencing chaplaincy thinking about a number of issues pertinent to the profession over the last twenty-five years. This is clear from the appreciation shown by his peers and is witnessed to by the many national and international awards his work has garnered, among them the American Psychiatric Association's Oskar Pfister Award (2019) and an Honorary Doctorate from the University for Humanistic Studies, Utrecht, The Netherlands (2019).

But more important than the acclamation of colleagues is the fact that, as this collection of ten of his most important papers demonstrates, Fitchett has spoken with clarity on issues that will continue to challenge chaplaincy in the coming phases of its development. The ambition of this collection is, therefore, twofold: first, to make the essence of Fitchett's contribution easily available to the next generation of chaplains and chaplain-researchers and, second, to enable his insights to continue to inform debates that will continue to be important to the profession. For these reasons, the publication of this collection is timely, as it facilitates a new generation of chaplain-researchers to engage with Fitchett's work.

The challenge, in compiling this collection, has been, first, to identify key themes in Fitchett's work and then to single out papers that best represent those themes, highlight his contribution and, crucially, have things to say to the profession going forward.

We began by thematically reviewing Fitchett's more than 120 scientific papers, articles, and book chapters, reducing these to a short list of seven themes and twenty-one papers—enough material for a volume twice the size of the present one. In consultation with Fitchett himself, we settled on the present list of ten papers, which we believe crystallize around three important themes: the relationship between religion/spirituality and health; chaplain education and research literacy; spiritual care, screening and assessment. Categories are, of course, artificial. Fitchett did not set out to pursue the themes as we have identified them; they emerged organically as his interests, concerns and opportunities developed through his career. Nevertheless, it is convenient to structure the collection and thereby aid readers in accessing the papers. The papers are presented here as originally published, expect for minor corrections and updating of web addresses.

RELIGION/SPIRITUALITY AND HEALTH

Article 1 *The Role of Religion in Medical Rehabilitation Outcomes: A Longitudinal Study (1999)*

Fitchett's interest in research developed over a number of years, and he had already published several award-wining, peer-reviewed papers[1] prior to the publication of this paper. The question of whether and to what extent religion (beliefs and practices) may have a positive role in aiding patients' health had been the subject of much interest at the time. In this longitudinal study of medical rehabilitation inpatients, Fitchett's team at Rush University Medical Center set out to investigate whether religion may have a protective role (i.e., preventing health problems; aiding recovery; supporting health adjustments) and/or a consoling role (i.e., enabling patients to cope better with illness or stress). The study had a third aim, which was to identify any religious beliefs or practices that may predict

1. Emblen, Fitchett, Farran and Burck (1992), received the 1987 Research Award, of the Joint Council on Research in Pastoral Care and Counseling; Fitchett and Gray (1994), received the 1996 Researcher of the Year Award, Association for Clinical Pastoral Education; Fitchett, Burton and Sivan (1997), received the 1997 Research Award, Commission on Research in Pastoral Care and Counseling of COMISS.

poor rehabilitation outcomes in these patients, thereby allowing clinicians to develop items to screen for spiritual risk that would impact negatively on their medical outcome. Although Fitchett and his colleagues found little evidence to support either the protective or the consolatory claims for religion, they did find evidence to support the idea that negative religious coping (for example, feeling abandoned by God or, rarely, being angry at God) was predictive of recovery of somatic autonomy. As Fitchett notes, this finding was a surprise, but it did inform what became an important theme in his later research (see Articles 3 and 9).

Article 2 *Spiritual Care in the Hospital: Who Requests It? Who Needs It? (2000)*

From as early as 1988 Fitchett had been publishing papers and articles on spiritual assessment (Fitchett, Quiring-Emblen, Farran and Burck 1988; Farran, Fitchett, Quiring-Emblen and Burck 1989; Fitchett and Burck 1990; Fitchett 1993) and in 1993 he wrote the first book-length treatment of the subject by a chaplain (Fitchett 1993/2002). This interest, in what continues to be a vital topic for chaplains, was given further stimulus by the findings reported in Article 1. The study reported in this article, a survey of 202 general medical and surgical patients, was an attempt to understand what proportion of patients might actually want to have a chaplain. As Fitchett records, this study uncovered the surprising discovery that those who may have the greater need for spiritual care were not, in fact, those who were likely to request it. In his introduction to this article, Fitchett notes the limitations of this small study, but notes that findings from the study, combined with those reported in Article 1, added to the sense that there needed to be some way to screen for those patients who would be most in need of chaplain care (see Articles 8, 9, and 10).

Article 3 *Religious Struggle: Prevalence, Correlates and Mental Health Risks in Diabetic, Congestive Heart Failure, and Oncology Patients (2004)*

The research reported in Article 1, which had highlighted the impact of negative religious coping on medical outcome, found resonance at the time with other investigations that were drawing attention to the negative effects of religious struggle, in particular, on quality of life and emotional wellbeing. In this paper, Fitchett and his team reported on a cross-sectional study developed with the intention of extending what was known about this issue. Specifically, they aimed to describe both the prevalence and the correlates of religious struggle. To this end, the team examined religious struggle in three groups of medical patients (diabetic and congestive heart failure outpatients, and oncology inpatients). In total, 238 participants completed a bank of questionnaires, key among which was the Brief RCOPE measure (Pargament, Smith, Koenig and Perez 1998), in which religious struggle is understood largely in terms of the patient's sense of abandonment or punishment by God, or their anger at God. Although the levels of negative religious coping were generally low—52% reported no negative religious coping; 15% responded "quite a bit" or "a great deal"— levels were higher in younger patients and patients with congestive heart failure, and were understood to be likely to be associated with higher levels of depressive symptoms and emotional distress.

Article 4 Re-examining the Contributions of Faith, Meaning, and Peace to Quality of Life: A Report from the American Cancer Society's Studies of Cancer Survivors-II (SCS-II) (2016)

The final article in this section shows how the use of a measure of spiritual well-being, in this case the Functional Assessment of Chronic Illness Therapy—Spiritual Well-being Scale (FACIT—Sp), led to a new understanding of how meaning, peace and faith contribute to cancer patients' quality of life. The research team had noted that previous research had misinterpreted the role played by faith, meaning, and peace—dimensions of spiritual wellbeing—in mediating quality of life. To investigate this, they hypothesized that faith would have a significant effect on a cancer survivor's functional quality of life, and that this would be mediated through meaning and/or peace. The research team used data from the American Cancer Society's Study of Cancer Survivors–II, and conducted mediation analyses using the FACIT—Sp. They confirmed an indirect effect of faith through meaning on mental functioning, and an indirect effect of faith through meaning and peace on physical functioning. Both were significant findings, and suggested that religion/spirituality can make an important contribution to the way survivors cope with cancer.

CPE AND RESEARCH LITERACY

Article 5 CPE and Spiritual Growth (1998–1999)

Of all Fitchett's published papers, this is perhaps the most personal, revealing, as it does, his struggles with faith as he journeyed from Calvinism to Quakerism. Fitchett's personal journey has relevance to the profession insofar as it gives particular expression to the experience of many contemporary chaplains. As this article makes clear, Clinical Pastoral Education (CPE) frequently plays a role in enabling aspiring chaplains to process their faith and so better equip themselves to offer spiritual care in the pluralist context that is contemporary healthcare. As Fitchett explained, at the time he wrote this essay he was very interested in theories of faith development, and his article is particularly informed by the thinking of John Westerhoff (1976). For Westerhoff, the pilgrimage of faith proceeds through four styles: experienced faith; affiliative faith; searching faith; and owned faith. Fitchett used this schema to understand his own journey of faith as well as that of the CPE students whom he was supervising.

Article 6 Making Our Case(s) (2011)

The idea that chaplains might write up and publish case studies of their work, for the purpose of developing the profession through teaching and research, may seem obvious now, but this is only so because of visionary work initiated by Fitchett. In 2009, he began a collaborative project, nurturing a group of experienced chaplains to write and publish the first chaplain case studies. This work has since been taken up by others and has grown to be an international project, issuing in numerous individual journal articles and several book length collections (to date: Fitchett and Nolan 2015; Fitchett and Nolan 2018; Kruizinga et al. 2020; Wirpsa, & Pugliese, 2020). This is the germinal article in which Fitchett presented the case for why chaplains' case studies are important, not only for developing the profession but also as a base on which to ground meaningful research. The paper is important, not only for its account of why chaplains' case studies matter but because it clearly articulates what a good case study would look like.

Article 7 Health Care Chaplaincy as a Research-Informed Profession (2012)

Fitchett has played a significant role in shaping what he describes as "the broad consensus emerging in the U.S. supporting a research-informed or evidence-based approach to chaplaincy." There can be little doubt that this consensus is changing the shape of contemporary chaplaincy, literally transforming chaplaincy. This article does more than simply reiterate the vision of chaplaincy as a research-informed profession, it sets out a series of steps by which that vision may mature into reality. Building on a foundation of good chaplain case studies, the chapter articulates five steps to achieving that vision. While not offering a strategy for the profession's further development towards becoming more thoroughly research-informed, this essay does offer a program for chaplaincy groups to use in developing their own research literacy and awareness.

SPIRITUAL CARE, SCREENING AND ASSESSMENT

Article 8 In the Garden with Andrea: Spiritual Assessment in End-of-Life Care (2003)

As already noted, spiritual assessment has been a theme of Fitchett's work for over thirty years. For many years, his book, *Assessing Spiritual Needs* (1993/2002) filled the void in chaplaincy literature, and offered some direction in an aspect of care that has been claimed as a chaplaincy specialty—despite the lack of professional consensus on what it is or how it might be done well. This article emerged from CPE supervision, specifically, a verbatim shared by a then resident about her work with a female patient. The jointly written article, which includes the resident's verbatim report, achieves two purposes. Primarily, the article illustrates Fitchett's 7x7 model for spiritual assessment, walking readers through the seven dimensions of holistic assessment followed by the seven dimensions of spiritual assessment, and offering a sample summary assessment that might be shared with members of the care team in a chart note. In a secondary sense, the article also illustrates how case study material may be used for the purpose of educating chaplains.

Article 9 Screening for Spiritual Struggle (2009)

In this 2009 article, Fitchett and Jay Risk responded to both the accumulating research around the harmful effects of religious/spiritual struggle and the increasing awareness that clinicians needed some way to screen patients for religious/spiritual struggle. The article reports on a pilot study that set out to test the efficacy of simple spiritual screening tool or protocol that could be administered by non-chaplain healthcare professionals in an acute medical rehabilitation unit. Despite the challenge the chaplain-researchers faced in finding clinical colleagues who would consistently administer the protocol to all new medical rehab patients, the article reports that the protocol had a positive predictive value of 92%, and led to only one false positive case of spiritual struggle. Although this was a small-scale pilot study ($N =$ 170), the "Rush Spiritual Screening Protocol," has subsequently been used in both in- and out-patient clinical care settings.

Article 10 Development of the PC–7, a Quantifiable Assessment of Spiritual Concerns of Patients Receiving Palliative Care Near the End of Life (2019)

The final paper in this collection brings Fitchett's work up to date, with a reappraisal and fresh direction to his work on spiritual assessment. Growing out of an interdisciplinary palliative education project, Fitchett's team addressed perceived weaknesses in many current approaches to spiritual assessment, specifically, the limited evidence for their validity and reliability, or their clinical usefulness, as well as their lack of clinical specificity. With that in mind, the project aimed at developing an evidence-based and quantifiable model for assessing unmet spiritual concerns, in this instance in palliative care patients near the end of life. The report describes a two-phase project. The researchers first examined the published literature in the field and consulted with chaplains on their clinical practice. In this way, they identified seven key spiritual care concerns of palliative care patients: need for meaning in the face of suffering; need for integrity, a legacy; concerns about relationships; concern or fear about dying or death; issues related to treatment decision making; R/S struggle; and other concerns. From these, the team developed indicators of those concerns and focused on developing inter-rater reliability to score patients' unmet spiritual needs. In this, the team was informed by work on the Spiritual Distress Assessment Tool (Monod et al. 2012; Monod, Rochat, Büla and Spencer 2010). Fitchett's team report that their PC–7 achieved high levels of inter-rater reliability, but acknowledge the need for further research.

THREE COMMENTARIES

A characteristic of Fitchett's approach to research has been his openness to challenge, discussion and debate. In that spirit, we invited three chaplaincy professionals, well-positioned to understand and evaluate Fitchett's contribution, to offer suggestions for the direction others may take his work in the future.

Writing from within the Australian context, Cheryl Holmes, Chief Executive Officer for the Spiritual Health Association, considers how Fitchett's work has influenced the way chaplains think about fundamental questions of concern to the profession—what we do, how we do it, and the difference it makes to the people who receive our care—particularly given the trend for people to self-identify as having "no religion" or as being "spiritual but not religious." She acknowledges that Fitchett's work has helped to give chaplains a language and a voice within health care, but she argues that chaplains need now to adapt, and she proposes that the language of spiritual care, as distinct from religious care, offers chaplaincy a way, not only to "rebrand ourselves" but "to carve out a broader remit . . . [and] lay claim to a domain of care essential to whole person care." Key in this respect, Holmes argues, is the use of language, including definitions and terminology.

Martin Walton, professor emeritus of Spiritual Care and Chaplaincy Studies at the Protestant Theological University, Groningen, The Netherlands, also addresses the theme of the use of language but in a different direction. Whereas Holmes essentially argues that chaplaincy needs to adopt the discourse of spirituality to communicate more effectively, Walton posits the need for a new hermeneutic to facilitate more effective communication between religion/chaplaincy and science/evidence-based healthcare: as he puts it "a hermeneutic for relating stories and statistics." Referencing in particular, Fitchett and Grossoehme (2012) (Article 7 in this volume), Walton highlights chaplains' multi-linguality, and poses the question of how chaplains can avoid speaking two unreconciled and independent languages. As a possible solution, he proposes a number of subtle but significant shifts in vocabulary that could facilitate greater exposition of answers to Holmes' questions about what chaplains do, how we do it, and the difference that makes—concerns that are central in Fitchett's work. It is interesting to observe how Holmes and Walton diverge in their willingness to use the term "spirituality," with Walton's preferred term being "meaning" (the term widely used to further define and clarify the meaning of "spirituality").

Based in New York City, David Fleenor is, among other things, Director of Education for the Center for Spirituality and Health at Mount Sinai where he oversees Mount Sinai's Clinical Pastoral Education (CPE) programs. From that perspective, he reflects on Fitchett's 1998–1999 paper on CPE (Article 5 in this volume). Fleenor's experience mirrors that of Fitchett, and he notes how, as a second year Master of Divinity student at a Pentecostal seminary in Tennessee, CPE prompted him to pose the same question posed by Holmes and Walton: what do chaplains do? He comments that in exploring this question he had, without knowing it or planning it, become a researcher. Twenty years on, Fleenor notes the contemporary challenges to addressing the educational requirements for today's chaplains. Fleenor draws inspiration from Fitchett's career as an example for the profession, specifically, seeing in Fitchett's experience of transitioning through "searching faith" an embodiment of the profession's own transition and transformation to becoming spiritually mature and evidence-based. In making his own contribution to that process, Fleenor shares a vision of what such education and training might look like. To that end, he describes his "unrealistic" vision for educating health care chaplains in a way that retains CPE's focus on spiritual growth and integrates it with evidence-based practice. A particular focus for his critique is the Master of Divinity degree, which insufficiently equips the increasing number of non-Christian students who wish to become chaplains. As with Holmes and Walton, Fleenor comments on the role language plays in communicating what it is that chaplains do, and he goes as far as suggesting that Clinical Pastoral Education should be rebranded as Spiritual Care Education.

ORIENTATION TO STATISTICAL TERMS AND QUANTITATIVE RESEARCH

Because several articles in this collection assume a degree of familiarity with quantitative research and statistical analysis, we have included a brief orientation to some of the statistical terms used in these articles. This orientation is not intended as a primer in statistics. It is offered simply to facilitate readers new to quantitative research to engage more effectively with what they are reading in this collection and perhaps to engage with the wider literature.

FINALLY

Two themes that are characteristic of, and very identifiable in, Fitchett's work are his willingness to collaborate with other researchers and his desire to encourage chaplains who are new to chaplaincy and spiritual care research. Although we claimed above that this book is not an homage to Fitchett, we might be permitted at this point to express our own personal thanks (and perhaps the thanks of numerous other chaplain-researchers) to George for the support and encouragement he has given us. George's commitment to fostering and developing emerging researchers is nowhere more evident than in what is his legacy project, Transforming Chaplaincy, which he co-founded with Wendy Cadge. Initially funded by the John Templeton Foundation, Transforming Chaplaincy began as a scholarship scheme aiming to provide, among other things, professional academic training for aspiring chaplain-researchers. Before morphing into a think tank of research-based chaplaincy practice and education, the original time-limited project produced two cohorts of research-literate chaplains, many of whom have become actively engaged in research. No title more aptly encapsulates the spirit of George's work and vision than "Transforming Chaplaincy," and for that reason this book bears that title.

REFERENCES

Emblen, J. Q., Fitchett, G., Farran, C. J., and Burck, J. R. 1992. Identifying Parameters of Spiritual Need. *The CareGiver Journal* 8:2, 44–50.

Farran, C. J., Fitchett, G., Quiring-Emblen, J., and Burck, J. R. 1989. Development of a Model for Spiritual Assessment and Intervention. *Journal of Religion and Health* 28:3, 185–94.

Fitchett, G. 1993/2002. *Assessing Spiritual Needs: A Guide for Caregivers* (Original edition: Minneapolis: Augsburg, 1993), Reprint edition Lima, Ohio: Academic Renewal, 2002.

Fitchett, G. 1993. A Functional Approach to Spiritual Assessment. In *The Future of Pastoral Counseling*, edited by J. McHolland, 139–44. Fairfax, VA: American Association of Pastoral Counselors.

Fitchett, G. and Burck, J. R. 1990. A Multi-dimensional, Functional Model for Spiritual Assessment. *Caregiver* 7:1, 43–62.

Fitchett, G., Burton, L. A., and Sivan, A. B. 1997. The Religious Needs and Resources of Psychiatric In-patients. *Journal of Nervous and Mental Disease* 185.5, 320–26.

Fitchett, G., and Gray, G. T. 1994. Evaluating the Outcome of Clinical Pastoral Education: A Test of the Clinical Ministry Assessment Profile. *Journal of Supervision and Training in Ministry* 15:3–22.

Fitchett, G. and Grossoehme, D. 2012. "Health Care Chaplaincy as a Research-Informed Profession." In *Professional Spiritual and Pastoral Care: A Practical Clergy and Chaplain's Handbook* edited by S. Roberts, 387–406. Woodstock, VY: SkyLight Paths.

Fitchett, G. and Nolan, S. eds. 2015. *Spiritual Care in Practice: Case Studies in Healthcare Chaplaincy*. London and Philadelphia: Jessica Kingsley.

Fitchett, G. and Nolan, S. eds. 2018. *Case Studies in Spiritual Care: Healthcare Chaplaincy Assessments, Interventions and Outcomes.* London and Philadelphia: Jessica Kingsley.

Fitchett, G., Quiring-Emblen, J., Farran, C., and Burck, R. 1988. A Model of Spiritual Assessment. *Caregiver* 5:144–54.

Kruizinga, R., Korver, J., den Toom, N., Walton, M., and Stoutjesdijk, M. eds. 2020. *Learning from Case Studies in Chaplaincy: Towards Practice Based Evidence and Professionalism.* Utrecht: Eburon.

Monod, S., Martin, E., Spencer, B., Rochat, E. and Büla, C. 2012. Validation of the Spiritual Distress Assessment Tool in Older Hospitalized Patients. *BMC Geriatrics* 12:13. doi.org/10.1186/1471-2318-12-13

Monod, S., Rochat, E., Büla, C. and Spencer, B. 2010. The Spiritual Needs Model: Spirituality Assessment in the Geriatric Hospital Setting. *Journal of Religion, Spirituality and Aging* 22:4, 271–82. doi: 10.1080/15528030.2010.509987

Pargament, K. I. 1997. *The Psychology of Religion and Coping: Theory, Research, Practice.* New York: Guilford.

Pargament, K. I., Smith, B. W., Koenig, H. G. and Perez, L. 1998. Positive and Negative Religious Coping with Major Life Stressors. *Journal for the Scientific Study of Religion* 37:710–24.

Westerhoff, J. H. III. 1976. *Will Our Children Have Faith?* New York: Seabury.

Wirpsa, M. J. and Pugliese, K. eds. 2020. *Chaplains as Partners in Medical Decision-Making: Case Studies in Healthcare Chaplaincy.* London and Philadelphia: Jessica Kingsley.

Part I

KEY PAPERS

ARTICLE 1

The Role of Religion in Medical Rehabilitation Outcomes

A Longitudinal Study[1]

—GEORGE FITCHETT
Rush-Presbyterian-St. Luke's Medical Center, Chicago, IL

—BRUCE D. RYBARCZYK
Rush-Presbyterian-St. Luke's Medical Center, Chicago, IL

—GAIL A. DEMARCO
Rush-Presbyterian-St. Luke's Medical Center, Chicago, IL

—JOHN J. NICHOLAS
Temple University School of Medicine, Philadelphia

THE RESEARCH PROGRAM IN the Department of Religion, Health and Human Values began in 1990. In 1996 the Fetzer Institute issued a request for proposals to examine the role of religion/spirituality for patients in medical rehabilitation. I had become familiar with the developing research about religion

1. G. Fitchett, B. D. Rybarczyk, G. A. DeMarco, and J. J. Nicholas. 1999. "The Role of Religion in Medical Rehabilitation Outcomes: A Longitudinal Study." *Rehabilitation Psychology* 44:4, 333–53. https://doi.org/10.1037/0090-5550.44.4.333

and health, including coping with illness, and approached Bruce Rybarczyk about submitting a proposal. Bruce, a clinical psychologist and experienced researcher, was interested in the role of religion in medical rehabilitation. Our proposal was funded and Bruce guided the data collection. None of our hypotheses about religion's contributions to better rehabilitation outcomes were supported by the data. But to our surprise we found that higher levels of religious struggle (e.g., anger with God) were associated with poorer recovery of activities of daily living. This was one of the first reports of the harmful effects of religious struggle in a sample of medical patients. In the following years this finding was confirmed in many studies with diverse clinical samples and it became an important theme in our research (see Articles 3 and 9).

ABSTRACT

Objective:

To investigate the protective and consolation models of the relationship between religion and health outcomes in medical rehabilitation patients.

Design:

Longitudinal study, data collected at admission, discharge and 4 months postadmission.

Measures:

Religion measures were public and private religiosity, acceptance, positive and negative religious coping, and spiritual injury. Outcomes were self-report of activities of daily living (ADL), mobility, general health, depression, and life satisfaction.

Participants:

96 medical rehabilitation inpatients; diagnoses included joint replacement, amputation, stroke, and other conditions.

Results:

The protective model of the relationship between religion and health was not supported; only limited support was found for the consolation model. In regression analyses, negative religious coping accounted for significant variance in follow-up ADL (5%) over and above that accounted for by admission ADL, depression, social support, and demographic variables. Subsequent item analysis indicated anger with God explained more variance (9%) than the full negative religious coping scale.

Conclusions:

Religion did not promote better recovery or adjustment, although it may have been a source of consolation for some patients who had limited recovery. Negative religious coping compromised ADL recovery. Although anger with God was rare, it may be useful in screening for patients who are spiritually at risk for poor recovery.

In recent years a considerable body of research has emerged regarding the relationship between religion and health (Koenig 1995; Larson 1993; Levin 1989, 1994a, 1994b, 1996; Levin and Schiller 1987; Matthews and Larson 1995; Matthews, Larson and Barry 1993; Matthews and Saunders 1997). Matthews et al. (1998) reviewed a number of studies which indicate that religious beliefs and practices had a positive effect on preventing illness, on recovery from surgery, on reducing mental illness, and on coping with illness. However, participants in a recent national conference concluded that more research is needed that addresses the role of religion for persons with disabilities and rehabilitation patients (Underwood-Gordon, Peters, Bijur and Fuhrer 1997).

Three different associations between religion and health have been proposed. Religion may play a protective role in health, preventing health problems or aiding in recovery or adjustment to health problems, leading to positive associations between measures of religion and health. These effects have been shown for a wide variety of groups, including community samples (Strawbridge, Cohen, Shema and Kaplan 1997), older adults (Zuckerman, Kasl and Ostfeld 1984), heart surgery patients (Oxman, Freeman and Manheimer 1995), transplant patients (Harris et al. 1995), dialysis patients (O'Brien 1992), and general medical patients (Koenig et al. 1992; Koenig, George and Peterson 1998; Koenig, Pargament and Nielsen 1998).

In other cases, religion may play a more consoling role and be mobilized to cope with illness or stress, leading to negative associations between measures of religion and health (Ferraro and Koch 1994; Idler 1995; Krause and Van Tran 1989). In some studies, the combination of both religion's protective and consolation effects have led to different dimensions of religion having opposite correlations with the same health variable (Levin, Chatters and Taylor 1995). Finally, some religious beliefs and practices may be associated with poorer coping with negative life events (Pargament 1997).

These different findings and models indicate that religion is a complex, multi-dimensional construct. Separate dimensions of religion that have been identified include the following: attending public worship and participation in religious group activities, private devotional activities, religious social support, religious beliefs, and positive and negative religious coping (Williams 1994; Pargament 1997). Religion may exert a protective effect on health in several different ways, including better health practices (e.g., avoiding substance abuse) and greater social support (Ellison 1994; Strawbridge et al. 1997). Religion may also provide a sense of meaning which may aid in coping with stressful life events (Pargament 1997). On a cognitive level, religious beliefs may provide a sense of self-efficacy in the face of stress or a way to positively reframe negative events (Ellison 1993; Krause and Van Tran 1989; Pargament 1997). The preceding examples illustrate two types of positive religious coping. Believing that a stressful event is a sign of abandonment or punishment by God is an example of negative religious coping (Pargament 1997). Recent research has shown that positive and negative religious coping activities predict adjustment to a variety of life stresses over and above measures of religious belief and practice and nonreligious coping (Pargament 1997).

Two studies point to the importance of religion for rehabilitation patients. In a study of 37 inpatients with spinal cord injury, Salisbury, Ciulla and McSherry (1989) report that 65% identify themselves as religious. Anderson, Anderson and Felsenthal (1993) report that 57% of a sample of 152 former rehabilitation inpatients rated their religious beliefs as important to them and "regularly thought of them." This is comparable to Gallup's report (1996) that 58% of people in the general population indicate that religion is "very important" in their lives. It is also consistent with Koenig's report (1997) that 75% of medical patients report using religion to a large extent to help them cope when they are ill.

These studies point as well to the possibility of problematic religious coping among medical rehabilitation patients. Specifically, Anderson et al. (1993) found that 23% of their respondents believed God was punishing them, and 27% were losing purpose in life. Salisbury et al. (1989) reported that 25% of their patients were angry with God, and a similar proportion were asking why God allowed them to suffer.

A study by Pressman, Lyons, Larson and Strain (1990) with 30 women who underwent hip replacement surgery was one of the first empirical studies of the role of religion in the recovery and adjustment of medical rehabilitation patients. They reported that, at discharge, more religious patients had greater ambulation and less depression. Idler (1995) studied 146 patients at a rehabilitation clinic and found that 62% of the patients reported that religion helped them with their health problems. Consistent with the consolation model, she found that patients with higher levels of disability were more likely to report seeking help from religion. She also found that more religious patients had better self-rated health, pointing to the important role of religion in helping patients maintain a subjective sense of health and well-being in the midst of a disability. Finally, Riley et al. (1998) recently examined different types of spiritual well-being in 216 cancer and medical rehabilitation inpatients. Cluster analysis identified three groups: patients whose religious beliefs provided meaning, patients with an existential sense of meaning, and a third group who had no sense of meaning, either religious or existential. Patients in the third group had lower quality of life and life satisfaction than those in the other two groups.

There are several important limitations in the existing research on religion in medical rehabilitation patients. With the exception of Pressman et al. (1990), the studies have been cross-sectional, limiting tests of hypotheses about the role of religion in recovery from and adjustment to disability. The studies have used limited measures of religion, focusing mainly on self-reported levels of religiousness, religious beliefs, and meaning and purpose in life. None of the studies have used measures of religious coping, which have been shown to predict adjustment to a variety of life stresses over and above measures of religious belief and practice and nonreligious coping (Pargament 1997). Further, and of potential greatest interest for clinicians, none of the studies examined the potential negative effects of religious beliefs or practices on recovery and adjustment for medical rehabilitation patients.

The present study was designed to further our understanding of the role of religion in medical rehabilitation patients. It had three specific aims. The first aim was to study the religious protection hypothesis, comparing cross-sectional and longitudinal analyses. Specifically, we hypothesized that higher levels of spiritual and religious beliefs, practices, acceptance, and positive religious coping and lower levels of negative religious coping and spiritual injury would have a positive impact on the recovery and adjustment of rehabilitation patients. The second aim was to test the religious consolation hypothesis. Specifically, we hypothesized that patients who did not show improvement in functioning over the course of the study would report higher levels of private religiosity and positive religious coping at the end of the study. The third aim was to identify any religion items which predicted poor rehabilitation outcomes in these patients. This would allow clinicians to develop items to screen for spiritual risk. Similar to other risk factors, spiritual risk assesses the potential contribution of religion to poor medical outcome.

METHOD

Sample and Procedure

Study participants were recruited between April 1997 and January 1998 from consecutive admissions to the inpatient medical rehabilitation units of a large Midwestern medical center. Unlike other medical rehabilitation patients, patients admitted to the medical rehabilitation unit with a diagnosis of Parkinson's disease were generally not experiencing a major change in their health status and were excluded from the study. Patients' cognitive impairment was assessed, via their orientation to time, place, and person, by the nursing staff and confirmed by the study interviewer. Approximately 20% of the patients screened for inclusion in the study were eliminated on the basis of not being oriented in all three spheres or not having English as a primary language. Potential study participants were interviewed by a research assistant who described the purpose of the study and its procedures. Patients who chose to participate in the study signed an informed consent form.

One hundred and twenty-one patients were approached to participate in the study, and 114 consented (94%). Study participants were interviewed within 5 days of admission to the unit and as close as possible to discharge from the unit. A follow-up telephone interview was completed 4 months after admission. Additional diagnostic data were obtained from the patient's medical record. The average length of the participant's inpatient hospitalization was 14.51 days (SD=7.37). Of the 114 patients who completed admission interviews, 96 completed 4–month follow-up interviews (84%). Of the 18 patients who did not complete follow-up surveys, 11 could not be reached, 5 declined to participate, and 2 showed signs of cognitive impairment. The average time between these two interviews was 133.35 days (SD=15.17).

The study participants ranged in age from 29 to 86 years (M=65.2 years, SD=11.6). Sixty-seven percent of the participants were female, 68%

were Caucasian, and 26% were African American. Thirty-seven percent of the participants were married, and 27% were widowed. The mean educational level was 12.9 years. Forty-nine percent of the patients had a hip or knee joint replacement. The remaining patients had various diagnoses, including stroke (17%), amputation (17%), deconditioning (6%), neuromuscular weakness (3%), laminectomy (3%), multiple sclerosis (2%), spinal tumor (1%), broken pelvis (1%), and arm infection (1%).

Forty-three percent of the subjects identified themselves as Catholic; 42%, as Protestant; 5%, as Jewish; and 2%, as having no religious affiliation. Eight study participants identified other religious affiliations: Jehovah's Witness (*n*=1), Mormon (*n*=1), Unitarian-Universalist (*n*=1), Moslem (*n*=1), Orthodox Christian (*n*=1), and unspecified (*n*=3). The distribution of religious affiliations of the study participants was consistent with all admissions to the medical center and with the general population of the county in which the study was conducted (Brady, Green, Jones, Lynn and McNeil 1992).

Measures

Index of Religiosity

This four-item measure consists of two 2-item subscales, public and private religiosity. These items have been widely used in epidemiological studies (Idler 1987; Idler and Kasl 1992; Zuckerman et al. 1984). Public religiosity measures frequency of attendance at public worship and the number of people one knows at one's place of worship. Private religiosity measures the extent of the respondent's perceived religiosity and the level of strength and comfort which come from religion. Table 1.1 reports the scale properties and Cronbach alpha coefficients obtained for the religion measures used in the study.

Table 1.1 **Scale Properties of Admission Religion Measures**

Variable	No of items	Potential range	Cronbach's α
Public religiosity	2	2–10	.73
Private religiosity	2	2–7	.69
Positive religious coping	10	0–30	.89
Negative religious coping	7	0–21	.45
Spiritual injury	6	6–24	.55
Acceptance	5	5–30	.56

Brief Religious Coping Scale (Brief RCOPE)

The Brief RCOPE represents a further stage in the work of Pargament and colleagues to develop a broad measure of religious coping (Pargament 1997; Pargament, Smith, Koenig and Perez 1998). The instrument has two subscales that assess positive and negative religious coping. Individuals are asked to rate how much they used these activities to cope with their disability on a 4-point Likert scale ranging from *not at all* (0) to *a great deal* (3). For the present study, we modified the original 21-item scale, selecting 17 items that were appropriate for a study of coping with disability. An example of an item measuring positive religious coping is "I look to God for things like strength, support, and guidance in this situation." An example of an item measuring negative religious coping is "I wonder whether God has abandoned me." In the original 21-item Brief RCOPE, the positive and negative coping scales had alpha coefficients of .87 and .78, respectively.

Spiritual Injury Scale

The Spiritual Injury Scale (Berg 1994) consists of eight items that assess an individual's sense of being troubled by guilt, resentment, or disbelief in God. The items are scored with a 4-point Likert scale ranging from *never* (1) to *very often* (4). A sample item is "How often does anger or resentment block your peace of mind?" In a sample of male veterans in a substance abuse program, the alpha coefficient for the scale was .79 with significant positive and negative associations with other measures of religious beliefs and activities in the expected directions (Lawson, Drebing, Berg, Jones and Penk, 1998). In the present study, which included another measure of depression, the two items measuring grief and hopelessness were omitted to reduce respondent burden.

Acceptance

The spiritual component of acceptance was defined as the ability to find meaning in life despite disability, or the sense that one's value as a person transcended one's physical abilities. It was measured with five items taken from Linkowski's Acceptance of Disability Scale (1971). The items were chosen by five expert judges (psychologists and chaplains) who compared all of the items from the Linkowski scale with the just-noted definition of the spiritual dimension of acceptance. Patients were asked to rate, on a 6-point Likert scale, how much they agreed with statements about meaning and satisfaction in life. A sample item is "Though I am disabled or ill, my life is full."

Self-Rated Health

Previous research has found that one-item measures of self-rated health are highly predictive of scores on larger self-report measures of health (Stewart, Hayes and Ware 1992) and mortality (Idler and Kasl 1991). Patients were asked to indicate their current health in general on a 5-point scale ranging from *excellent* (1) to *poor* (5). For the analysis and this report, these were reversed so that the higher value indicated better self-rated health.

Somatic Autonomy and Mobility Control

Patients' ratings of their functional level was assessed with the 17-item Somatic Autonomy subscale and the 12-item Mobility Control subscale from the Sickness Impact Profile (SIP–68; Post, de Bruin, de Witte and Schrijvers 1996). We used the Somatic Autonomy subscale as a measure of activities of daily living (ADL), including such activities as transferring, bathing, dressing, and eating. The SIP–68 was developed from the larger 136 item SIP and has been shown to be a valid and reliable measure of functional level in rehabilitation patients (Post et al. 1996).

Brief Depression Scale

Depression was measured with the Brief Depression Scale (Koenig, Cohen, Blazer, Meador and Westlund 1992), an 11-item measure with a yes-no response format. It was developed for use with medically ill patients and has demonstrated adequate validity (Koenig, Pargament and Nielsen 1998). Scores on the scale range from 0 to 11, with a threshold of 3 indicating the presence of depression. For the present study, the alpha coefficient for this measure at the admission interview was .57.

Satisfaction with Life Scale

Adjustment was also measured with the Satisfaction with Life Scale (Diener, Emmons, Larsen and Griffin 1985). This 5-item scale measures the cognitive-judgmental aspects of general life satisfaction. Respondents indicate their level of agreement on a 7-point Likert scale. The instrument has been shown to be a valid and reliable measure of life satisfaction in a wide range of age groups, including older adults (Diener et al. 1985; Pavot, Diener, Colvin and Sandvik 1991).

Perceived Social Support

To control for its important role in rehabilitation recovery and coping with illness, we included a measure of perceived social support in the study. The measure we used was adapted by Rybarczyk, Nyenhuis, Nicholas, Cash and Kaiser (1995) from Cohen, Mermelstein, Karmarck and Hoberman (1985). It consists of 6 items rated on a 4-point Likert scale ranging from *definitely true* (1) to *definitely false* (4). Assuming that perceived social support was stable, we assessed this variable only at the 4-month follow-up.

Analysis

The analysis focused on data obtained from the admission and 4-month follow-up interviews for two reasons. First, there was little change in the religion measures between admission and discharge, the correlations for the measures at these two times ranging from .50 to .91. Second, it was assumed that the short average length of participants' hospitalization (14.51 days) was an insufficient time to permit the effects of religion on recovery and adjustment to become evident. (Discharge data are available from George Fitchett.)

Zero-order correlations were used to identify the religion variables that might have a protective effect on recovery and adjustment. Multivariate regression equations, with controls for baseline measures and other significant variables, were used to test the protection hypothesis. The consolation hypothesis was tested by comparing the mean follow-up scores on private religiosity and positive religious coping for patients with no recovery and patients with recovery in mobility and somatic autonomy. Private religiosity and positive religious coping were selected for this test because they are good measures of the mobilization of religious beliefs and activities in the face of stress.

RESULTS

Characteristics of the Sample and Study Measures

Table 1.2 reports descriptive statistics for the study variables. Eighty-five percent of the study participants described themselves as fairly or deeply religious, and 78% reported they received a great deal of strength and comfort from religion. Thirty-five percent of the respondents reported that, in the previous year, they usually attended public worship once a week or more. The average score for positive religious coping (15.7) fell near the mid-point of the potential range, and the scores were normally distributed. Negative religious coping scores ranged from 0 to 9 (potential range: 0 to 21), with a mean of 1.5. Two thirds of the participants scored 0 or 1, and another 20% scored only 2 or 3. The mean spiritual injury score (8.7) was also low relative to the potential range (6–24).

Table 1.2 **Mean Scores, Standard Deviations, and Correlations for All Measures at Admission and Follow-Up**

Variable	Admission		Follow-up		Correlation: Admission and Follow-Up
	M	*SD*	*M*	*SD*	
Independent					
Public religiosity	6.1	2.4	5.7	2.5	.84
Private religiosity	5.9	1.2	5.8	1.3	.73
Positive religious coping	15.7	8.0	15.8	8.2	.82
Negative religious coping	1.5	2.0	1.3	2.0	.66
Spiritual injury	8.7	2.3	8.1	2.3	.52
Acceptance	21.1	5.3	22.0	6.1	.48
Dependent					
Mobility control	1.8	1.7	4.4	3.4	
Somatic autonomy (activities of daily living)	8.9	4.0	14.3	3.7	
General health	2.7	1.1	3.2	1.1	
Depression	2.7	1.9	2.3	2.1	
Life satisfaction	23.8	6.9	23.0	6.7	
Control					
Social support[a]			21.1	3.1	

Note. All correlations were significant at p<.001.

[a] Follow-up only

As can be seen from Table 1.3, the correlations among the measures of religion at admission were weak to moderate (rs=-.22 to .60), suggesting that these variables measured distinct dimensions of religion. The stability of the measures of spirituality and religiosity used in the study was also examined. As can be seen from Table 1.2, three of the measures—public religiosity, private religiosity, and positive religious coping—had moderately high correlations between baseline and the 4-month follow-up (rs=.73 to .84). For the other three measures—negative religious coping, spiritual injury, and acceptance—there was more change between baseline and follow-up scores, as can be seen in the lower correlations, ranging from .48 to .66.

Table 1.3 Admission Correlations

Variable	1	2	3	4	5	6	7	8	9	10	11
1. Public religiosity	—										
2. Private religiosity	.53***	—									
3. Positive religious coping	.51***	.60***	—								
4. Negative religious coping	-.34***	-.31**	-.31**	—							
5. Spiritual injury	-.22*	-.14	-.03	.56***	—						
6. Acceptance	.17	.13	.12	-.14	-.19	—					
7. General health	.23*	.23*	.17	-.06	-.07	.36***	—				
8. Somatic autonomy	.09	.13	.09	-.08	-.09	.32**	.25**	—			
9. Mobility control	.01	-.11	.13	.10	.09	.14	.15	.40***	—		
10. Depression	-.15	-.13	-.19	.21*	.48***	-.20*	-.26**	-.21*	-.15	—	
11. Life satisfaction	.11	.13	.04	-.02	-.33**	.07	.21	.21	.15	-.34**	—

Note. n = 94 to 96 except for correlations with life satisfaction, where *n* = 75 or 76.
*p ≤.05. **p ≤.01. ***p ≤.001.

At baseline, the participants in the study had moderate somatic autonomy (M=8.9) and low mobility control (M=1.8). Only 16% percent could not walk at all, but a large majority needed assistance with bathing (76%), and many needed assistance with getting dressed (47%). At the 4-month follow-up, most of the subjects had achieved a high level of somatic autonomy (M=14.3) but the overall level of mobility control was still quite low (M=4.4). At admission, nearly half (45%) of the subjects rated their general health as poor or fair; at the 4-month follow-up, this proportion had decreased to 28%. Paired t tests indicated that the change in all three of these measures was significant.

Hip and knee joint replacement patients had higher levels of follow-up somatic autonomy than stroke patients and patients with other diagnoses (Ms=15.7, 11.8, and 11.4, respectively), $F_{(4, 90)}$=5.89, p<.001. Joint replacement patients (M=5.3), patients with deconditioning (M=6.0), and patients with amputations (M=4.4) all had better follow-up mobility control than stroke patients (M=1.2), $F_{(4, 91)}$=5.68, p<.001. At the 4-month follow-up, education was positively associated with mobility control (r=.22, p=.03). Race was associated with somatic autonomy, $F_{(3, 91)}$=3.31, p=.02); White patients having higher levels than Black patients (M=15.0 vs 12.5). Age, gender, and marital status were not associated with any differences in recovery or adjustment.

The recommended threshold score of 3 was used for a diagnosis of depression (Koenig, Cohen, Blazer, Meador and Westlund 1992); at admission, 47% of the participants in the study reported three or more symptoms of depression. This was slightly higher than the rates that have been reported in other rehabilitation populations (Nanna, Lichtenberg, Buda-Abela and Barth 1997; Rybarczyk et al. 1995; Rybarczyk, Winemiller, Lazarus, Haut and Hartman 1996). At the 4-month follow-up, the proportion of subjects with three or more symptoms of depression dropped to 37%. A paired t test revealed that this change was not significant. Joint replacement patients had lower levels of depression than stroke patients and patients with other diagnoses (Ms=1.4, 3.2 and 3.7, respectively), $F_{(4, 87)}$=5.16, p<.001.

Religion as a Correlate and Predictor of Recovery and Adjustment

Table 1.4 presents the correlations between religion and recovery and adjustment at follow-up. Table 1.5 presents the correlations between admission religion measures and follow-up recovery and adjustment.

Table 1.4 Correlations of Religion Measures with Recovery and Adjustment at Follow-Up

Variable	Public religiosity	Private religiosity	Positive religious coping	Negative religious coping	Spiritual injury	Acceptance
Somatic autonomy (activities of daily living)	.00	-.02	-.15	-.13	-.11	.19
Mobility control	.01	-.05	-.10	.01	-.19	.26**
General health	.15	.13	.11	.01	.10	.24**
Depression	-.20	-.14	.01	.21*	.36***	-.56***
Life satisfaction	.31**	.27**	.24*	-.18	-.30**	.55***

Note. n = 89 to 96.
*p ≤.05. **p ≤.01. ***p ≤.001.

Table 1.5 Correlations of Admission Religion Measures with Follow-Up Recovery and Adjustment

Variable	Public religiosity	Private religiosity	Positive religious coping	Negative religious coping	Spiritual injury	Acceptance
Somatic autonomy (activities of daily living)	.05	-.07	-.09	-.24*	-.10	.17
Mobility control	-.06	-.20*	.00	-.11	-.11	.20
General health	.15	.09	.08	.10	-.04	.06
Depression	-.09	-.03	-.06	.20*	.33***	-.27**
Life satisfaction	.28**	.18	.28**	-.22*	-.32**	.37***

Note. n = 91 to 96.
*p ≤.05. **p ≤.01. ***p ≤.001.

In those cases where there were significant correlations between admission religion and follow-up recovery and adjustment, we followed up with regression analyses, controlling for important covariates. Controls for race and diagnostic group were included because of significant differences in somatic autonomy associated with these variables. Previous research has pointed to the importance of controls for depression (Nanna et al. 1997) and social support (Rybarczyk et al. 1995).

Table 1.6 reports the only significant results from these analyses. After controlling for admission somatic autonomy, race (recoded into two groups: Black and other), diagnostic group, social support, and admission depression, negative religious coping at admission was a significant negative predictor of follow-up somatic autonomy. The inclusion of negative religious coping in the analysis produced an R^2 increase of .05 (p=.02).

Table 1.6 **Hierarchial Regression Analysis of Follow-Up Somatic Autonomy (ADL)**

Variable	Step 1	Step 2	Step 3
Admission somatic autonomy (ADL)	.246*	.192	.198*
Race (1 = Black, 2 = other)		.204*	.231*
Diagnostic group (1 = other, 2 = joint replacement)		-.286**	-.256*
Social support		.032	-.006
Admission depression		-.060	-.012
Admission negative coping[a]			-.229*
R^2	.060	.224	.271
Adjusted R^2	.050	.179	.220
R^2 change	.060	.164	.047
Significance of R^2 change	.018	.002	.022

Note. Variable values are standardized betas. *ADL* = activities of daily living.
[a] Entered via the stepwise method.
*$p \leq$.05. **$p \leq$.01.

Religious Consolation and Poor Recovery

Differences between admission and follow-up measures of somatic autonomy and mobility control were used to divide the study participants into two groups: those who had no change or showed a decrease in functioning and those who showed any improvement in functioning. Using paired t tests, we compared the mean scores for follow-up private religiosity and positive religious coping for these two groups. Differences in improvement in somatic autonomy were not associated with any differences in the two religion measures. Differences in improvement in mobility control were associated with a difference in positive religious coping. Participants whose mobility control had not changed or had worsened ($n = 30$) had higher positive religious coping than those whose mobility control had improved ($Ms = 18.41$ and 14.57, respectively), $t(92) = 2.15$, $p = .03$).

Selecting Religion Screening Items

The significant relationship between baseline negative religious coping and follow-up somatic autonomy suggested that further analysis be conducted to determine which negative coping items might be predictive of poor recovery. A stepwise regression analysis entering all seven negative religious coping items was performed, with baseline somatic autonomy entered first. Only the item "I express anger at God for letting this happen," entered the equation ($\beta = -.295$, $p = .003$). The addition of this item to a regression equation with baseline somatic autonomy produced an R^2 change of .09 ($p = .003$). Figure 1.1 illustrates the minimal ADL recovery for the 6 participants with any level of anger with God at admission.

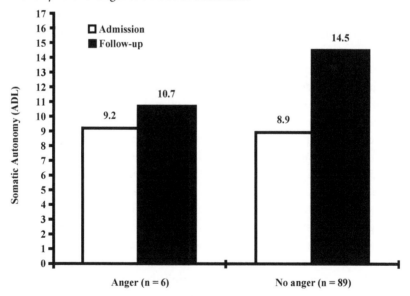

Figure 4.1 Hypothesized Model for Mediation

DISCUSSION

The correlational data in the present study are consistent with the protective model of religion as a resource for medical rehabilitation patients and persons with disabilities. At admission (Table 1.3), public and private religiosity and acceptance were positively associated with self-rated general health, and acceptance was inversely associated with depression. At follow-up (Table 1.4), public religiosity, private religiosity, positive religious coping, and acceptance were positively associated with life satisfaction. Acceptance was also positively associated with mobility control and general health and negatively correlated with depression. Further, admission scores on public religiosity, positive religious coping, and acceptance were positively associated with follow-up life satisfaction, and acceptance was inversely associated with follow-up depression (Table 1.5).

Although the correlational data from this study appear to lend support to the protective model, the results of the regression analyses controlling for baseline levels of each dependent measure and other important covariates found that religion made no positive contribution to recovery or adjustment for this sample. That is, the present study did not confirm the protective model of the relationship between religion and health. Several factors may have played a role in this result. The longitudinal design of our study and the use of multivariate analyses, controlling for the effects of important covariates, permitted a more rigorous test of the protection hypothesis than found in most previous studies of the contribution of religion to the recovery and adjustment of medical patients. Our findings suggest that religion may be better understood as a covariate than a cause of better health and adjustment. Furthermore, religion may function differently for persons who are facing long-term disability (e.g., stroke or amputation) than those who are facing short-term impairment but long-term improvement (e.g., patients with joint replacement). The diagnostic heterogeneity of our sample may have introduced differences in the role of religion in recovery and adjustment that yielded no significant protective effects. Further research, especially longitudinal studies, will be needed to clarify religion's possible protective role in the recovery and adjustment of medical patients. Studies that explore the role of religion in homogeneous groups of patients with diseases that have different courses and outcomes will be especially helpful.

The results of this study did provide limited support for the consolation hypothesis. Participants who suffered a loss of mobility control or who had no recovery had higher positive religious coping compared to those who had improvement in mobility control. However, the study design did not include a measure of stress or pre-illness measures of religiosity. Both would be required for a more rigorous test of the consolation hypothesis.

The present study also demonstrated that some negative forms of religious coping, while uncommon, can compromise recovery. Correlational analysis revealed that negative religious coping and spiritual injury were associated with poor adjustment cross-sectionally and longitudinally. However, in the regression analysis, when controls for baseline values were included, these findings were not significant. In contrast, in regression analyses, negative religious coping predicted poorer recovery of somatic autonomy even with controls for baseline values, accounting for 5% of the variance.

Although small, the amount of variance explained by negative religious coping is noteworthy for several reasons. It exceeded the predictive value of any other psychosocial variable in this study and baseline ADL and was nearly equal to the variance explained by diagnostic category (Table 1.6). Further, although negative religious coping was significant as a predictor of only one out of three of the recovery variables (ADL), there was less change in the other two recovery variables, thereby reducing the likelihood of significant associations with any predictor. Finally, it should be noted that in a comparable study two psychological variables, depression and cognitive status, also predicted similar change in ADL (7%) but not change in mobility (Nanna et al. 1997).

It is difficult to explain why negative religious coping would have an impact on measures of recovery but not adjustment. Different forms of coping have been shown to influence medical outcomes through a variety of pathways (Stone and Porter 1995). These influences can occur through both behavioral and cognitive/affective pathways. It may be that negative religious coping impacts outcomes through strictly behavioral pathways (e.g., decreased compliance, problem solving, or motivation) or influences other cognitive/affective pathways not measured in this study (e.g., hope, anxiety, learned helplessness, or anger).

The finding that anger with God predicted poorer recovery appears to run counter to the idea that feelings of anger, whether anger with God or other angry feelings, are a potentially constructive dynamic in adjustment to illness or disability. However, it is consistent with other recent work on negative religious coping and religious red flags (i.e., religious or spiritual problems involving risk for compromised recovery). Among older medically ill patients, negative religious coping has been associated with higher levels of depression and lower quality of life (Koenig, Pargament and Nielsen 1998). In a study of church members and college students who had experienced negative life events, anger with God was one of the strongest predictors of poor adjustment among 11 types of ineffective religious coping (Pargament, Zinnbauer et al. 1998). Finally, among primary caregivers of hospice patients, appraisals of God as punishing unfairly or as not caring were infrequent but significantly correlated with depression and anxiety (Mickley, Pargament, Brant and Hipp 1998).

Why did patients who were angry with God have poorer recovery? One possibility is that some patients may focus long-standing generalized anger and resentment on God at a time of crisis. In the present study, anger with God at admission was positively associated with an item about generalized anger from the Spiritual Injury Scale: "How often does anger or resentment block your peace of mind?" ($r=.35$, $p<.001$). However, in a regression equation, generalized anger at admission was not a significant predictor of follow-up independence in ADL ($\beta=-.160$, $p=.78$), whereas anger with God was significant ($\beta=-3.056$, $p=.001$), suggesting that the negative effect of anger with God on recovery cannot be explained by the effects of generalized anger.

Another possibility is that some patients who feel angry with God are conflicted about this feeling and find it difficult to express or work through their anger (Pargament, Zinnbauer et al. 1998). In contrast, there may be another group of patients who feel angry with God, are able to express and resolve that emotion, and invest in their recovery (Pargament 1997; Pargament, Smith et al. 1998). Data from the present study make it clear that anger with God is not associated with lack of interest in religion; all six patients who endorsed this item described themselves as "fairly" or "deeply" religious. Further research is needed to help determine whether there are different types of anger with God and identify those patients for whom it may compromise recovery from or adjustment to illness or disability.

The present study has several limitations. First, the sample includes patients with diagnoses that have different prognoses for improved mobility—specifically, joint replacement patients, stroke patients, and persons with amputations—but subgroups were not sufficiently large to permit separate analysis. The diversity of this sample may have obscured some of the role of religion in adjustment and recovery for these patients.

Second, the significant findings for negative religious coping occurred in only one of the five of the recovery and adjustment measures. This raises questions about whether negative religious coping has a broader impact on outcomes. However, it should be noted that somatic autonomy showed the greatest amount of change among the outcome measures over 4 months (see Table 1.2). Similarly, in the Nanna et al. (1997) study, depression and cognitive status predicted ADL but not mobility outcome.

Third, three of the measures of religion used in this study had low coefficients of internal reliability (see Table 1.1). This raises the possibility that the null findings are a consequence of measurement limitations.

Finally, the main outcome variables used were patients' self-reports of functional ability and adjustment rather than clinician ratings with a standardized instrument (i.e., Functional Independence Measure; Granger and Hamilton 1993). Unfortunately, the rehabilitation unit where the study was conducted was in the process of adopting a new rehabilitation staff rating scale, so clinician rating data were not available for use in this study. Clinician ratings of functional status and depression would have provided an important comparison with patient self-reports.

Two findings from the study should be of interest to psychologists and other clinicians working in medical rehabilitation. First, at discharge, participants were asked if they had received any counseling from a psychologist during their hospitalization. Twenty-nine participants (30%) reported that they had received counseling. Six of these participants also reported they had discussed spiritual issues with the psychologist. In comparison with those who did not discuss spiritual issues, participants who reported discussing spiritual issues with the psychologist were more likely to evaluate the counseling they received as very helpful (29% vs. 67%). Medical rehabilitation patients may welcome a psychologist's inquiry about their religious beliefs and practices as part of a comprehensive assessment.

Second, the finding that anger with God was predictive of poor recovery of functional ability should be of interest to psychologists, chaplains, and other clinicians working in medical rehabilitation. At present, there are no reliable instruments that enable clinicians to screen rehabilitation patients to determine those who may have religious red flags. The finding in the present study suggests that consideration should be given to including a question about feeling angry with God in comprehensive initial screening of medical rehabilitation patients. Further assessment should be conducted to determine if patients who express anger with God have long-standing problems with anger, personality disorders, or other problems that require psychological treatment. Consideration should also be given to referring such patients to a chaplain or pastoral counselor for more in-depth spiritual assessment (Fitchett 1993a, 1993b) and for pastoral counseling. Interested clinicians who have not received any training in addressing the religious dimension of their patient's lives can find information in a variety of resources (e.g., see Eiesland 1994; Fitchett 1993a, 1993b; Pargament 1997; Shafranske 1996; see also *Journal of Religion, Disability, and Health*) that will assist them in integrating an understanding of the religious and spiritual dimensions of life into their clinical practice.

ACKNOWLEDGEMENT

This research was supported in part by the Fetzer Institute, Kalamazoo, MI.

REFERENCES

Anderson, J. M., Anderson, L. J. and Felsenthal, G. 1993. "Pastoral Needs and Support within an Inpatient Rehabilitation Unit." *Archives of Physical Medicine and Rehabilitation* 74:574–78.

Berg, G. E. 1994. "The Use of the Computer as a Tool for Assessment and Research in Pastoral Care." *Journal of Health Care Chaplaincy* 6:1, 11–25.

Brady, M. B., Green, N. M. Jr., Jones, D. E., Lynn, M. and McNeil, L. 1992. *Churches and Church Membership in the United States 1990*. Atlanta, Georgia: Glenmary Research Center.

Cohen, S., Mermelstein, R., Karmarck, T. and Hoberman, H. 1985. "Measuring the Functional Components of Social Support." In *Social Support: Theory, Research and Applications*, edited by I. G. Sarason and B.R. Sarason, 73–94. The Hague: Martinus Nijhoff.

Diener, E., Emmons, R.A., Larsen, R.J. and Griffin, S. 1985. "Satisfaction with Life Scale." *Journal of Personality Assessment* 49:71–75.

Eiesland, N.L. 1994. *The Disabled God: Toward a Liberatory Theology of Disability*. Nashville, TN: Abingdon.

Ellison, C.G. 1993. "Religious Involvement and Self-perception among Black Americans." *Social Forces* 71:1027–55.

Ellison, C. G. 1994. "Religion, the Life Stress Paradigm, and the Study of Depression." In *Religion in Aging and Health: Theoretical Foundations and Methodological Frontiers*, edited by J. S. Levin, 78–121. Thousand Oaks, CA: Sage.

Ferraro, K. F. and Koch, J. R. 1994. "Religion and Health among Black and White Adults: Examining Social Support and Consolation." *Journal for the Scientific Study of Religion* 33:362–75.

Fitchett, G. 1993a. *Assessing Spiritual Needs: A Guide for Caregivers* (Original edition: Minneapolis: Augsburg, 1993). Reprint edition, Lima, OH: Academic Renewal, 2002.

Fitchett, G. 1993b. *Spiritual Assessment in Pastoral Care: A Guide to Selected Resources*. Decatur, GA.: Journal of Pastoral Care Publications.

Gallup, G. H., Jr. 1996. *Religion in America, 1996*. Princeton, NJ: Princeton Religion Research Center.

Granger, C. V. and Hamilton, B. B. 1993. "The Uniform Data System for Medical Rehabilitation Report of First Admissions for 1991." *American Journal of Physical Medicine and Rehabilitation* 72:33–38.

Harris, R. C., Dew, M. A., Lee, A., Amaya, M., Buches, L., Reetz, D. and Coleman, G. 1995. "The Role of Religion in Heart-Transplant Recipients' Long-term Health and Well-being." *Journal of Religion and Health* 34:17–32.

Idler, E. L. 1987. "Religious Involvement and the Health of the Elderly: Some Hypotheses and an Initial Test." *Social Forces* 66:226–38.

Idler, E. L. 1995. "Religion, Health, and Nonphysical Senses of Self." *Social Forces* 74:683–704.

Idler, E. L. and Kasl, S. 1991. "Health Perceptions and Survival: Do Global Evaluations of Health Status Really Predict Mortality?" *Journal of Gerontology: Social Sciences,* 46, S55–S65.

Idler, E. L. and Kasl, S. 1992. Religion, Disability, Depression and the Timing of Death. *American Journal of Sociology* 97:1052–79.

Koenig, H. G. 1995. *Research on Religion and Aging: An Annotated Bibliography.* Westport, CT: Greenwood.

Koenig, H. G. 1997. "Use of Religion by Patients with Severe Medical Illness." *Mind/ Body Medicine* 2:31–36.

Koenig, H. G., Cohen, H. J., Blazer, D. G., Meador, K. G. and Westlund, R. 1992. "A Brief Depression Scale for Use in the Medically Ill." *International Journal of Psychiatry in Medicine* 22:183–95.

Koenig, H. G., Cohen, H. J., Blazer, D. G., Pieper, C., Meador, K. G., Shelp, F., Goli, V. and DiPasquale, R. 1992. "Religious Coping and Depression among Elderly, Hospitalized Medically Ill Men." *American Journal of Psychiatry* 149:1693–1700.

Koenig, H. G., George, L. K. and Peterson, B. L. 1998. "Religiosity and Remission of Depression in Medically Ill Older Patients." *American Journal of Psychiatry* 155:536–42.

Koenig, H. G., Pargament, K. I. and Nielsen, J. 1998. "Religious Coping and Health Status in Medically Ill Hospitalized Older Adults." *Journal of Nervous and Mental Disease* 186:513–21.

Krause, N. and Van Tran, T. 1989. "Stress and Religious Involvement among Older Blacks." *Journal of Gerontology: Social Sciences* 44, S4–S13.

Larson, D. B. 1993. *The Faith Factor: Vol. 2. An Annotated Bibliography of Systematic Reviews and Clinical Research on Spiritual Subjects.* Rockville, MD: National Institute of Healthcare Research.

Lawson, R., Drebing, C. E., Berg, G., Jones, S. and Penk, W. 1998. *The Spiritual Injury Scale: Validity and reliability.* Paper presented at the annual meeting of the American Psychological Association, San Francisco, CA.

Levin, J. S. 1989. "Religious Factors in Aging, Adjustment, and Health: A Theoretical Overview." In *Religion, Aging and Health: A Global Perspective*, edited by W. M. Clements, 133–46. New York: Haworth.

Levin, J. S. 1994a. "Religion and Health: Is There an Association, Is It Valid, and Is It Causal?" *Social Science in Medicine* 38:1475–82.

Levin, J. S. ed. 1994b. *Religion in Aging and Health: Theoretical Foundations and Methodological Frontiers.* Thousand Oaks, CA: Sage.

Levin, J. S. 1996. "How Religion Influences Morbidity and Health: Reflections on Natural History, Salutogenesis and Host Resistance." *Social Science in Medicine* 43:849–64.

Levin, J. S., Chatters, L. M. and Taylor, R. J. 1995. "Religious Effects on Health Status and Life Satisfaction among Black Americans." *Journal of Gerontology: Social Sciences* 50B, S154–S163.

Levin, J. S. and Schiller, P. L. 1987. "Is There a Religious Factor in Health?" *Journal of Religion and Health* 26:9–36.

Linkowski, D. C. 1971. "A Scale to Measure Acceptance of Disability." *Rehabilitation Counseling Bulletin* 14:236–44.

Matthews, D. A. and Larson, D. B. 1995. *The Faith Factor: An Annotated Bibliography of Clinical Research on Spiritual Subjects, Vol. 3: Enhancing Life Satisfaction.* Rockville, MD: National Institute for Healthcare Research.

Matthews, D. A., Larson, D. B. and Barry, C. P. 1993. *The Faith Factor: An Annotated Bibliography of Clinical Research on Spiritual Subjects.* Rockville, MD: National Institute for Healthcare Research.

Matthews, D. A., McCullough, M. E., Larson, D. B., Koenig, H. G., Swyers, J. P. and Milano, M. G. 1998. "Religious Commitment and Health Status: A Review of the Research and Implications for Family Medicine." *Archives of Family Medicine* 7:118–24.

Matthews, D. A. and Saunders, D. M. 1997. *The Faith Factor: An Annotated Bibliography of Clinical Research on Spiritual Subjects, Vol. 4. Prevention and Treatment of Illness, Addictions, and Delinquency.* Rockville, MD: National Institute for Healthcare Research.

Mickley, J. R., Pargament, K. I., Brant, C. R. and Hipp, K. M. 1998. "God and the Search for Meaning among Hospice Caregivers." *Hospice Journal* 13:4, 1–17.

Nanna, M. J., Lichtenberg, P. A., Buda-Abela, M. and Barth, J. T. 1997. "The Role of Cognition and Depression in Predicting Functional Outcome in Geriatric Medical Rehabilitation Patients." *Journal of Applied Gerontology* 16:120–32.

O'Brien, M. E. 1982. "Religious Faith and Adjustment to Long-term Hemodialysis." *Journal of Religion and Health* 21:68–80.

Oxman, T. E., Freeman, D. H. Jr. and Manheimer, E. D. 1995. "Lack of Social Participation or Religious Strength and Comfort as Risk Factors for Death after Cardiac Surgery in the Elderly." *Psychosomatic Medicine* 57:5–15.

Pargament, K. I. 1997. *The Psychology of Religion and Coping: Theory, Research, Practice.* New York: Guilford.

Pargament, K. I., Smith, B. W., Koenig, H. G. and Perez, L. 1998. "Positive and Negative Religious Coping with Major Life Stressors." *Journal for the Scientific Study of Religion* 37:710–24.

Pargament, K. I., Zinnbauer, B. J., Scott, A. B., Butter, E. M., Zerowin, J. and Stanik, P. 1998. "2 Red Flags and Religious Coping: Identifying Some Religious Warning Signs among People in Crisis." *Journal of Clinical Psychology* 54:77–89.

Pavot, W., Diener, E., Colvin, C. R. and Sandvik, E. 1991. "Further Validation of the Satisfaction with Life Scale: Evidence for the Cross-method Convergence of Well-being Measures." *Journal of Personality Assessment* 57,1:149–61.

Post, M. W. M., de Bruin, A., de Witte, L. and Schrijvers, A. 1996. "The SIP68: A Measure of Health-related Functional Status in Rehabilitation Medicine." *Archives of Physical Medicine and Rehabilitation* 77:440–45.

Pressman, M. A., Lyons, J. S., Larson, D. B. and Strain, J. J. 1990. "Religious Belief, Depression, and Ambulation Status in Elderly Women with Broken Hips." *American Journal of Psychiatry* 147:758–60.

Riley, B. B., Perna, R., Tate, D. G., Forchheimer, M., Anderson, C. and Luera, G. 1998. "Types of Spiritual Well-being among Persons with Chronic Illness: Their Relation to Various Forms of Quality of Life." *Archives of Physical Medicine and Rehabilitation* 79:258–64.

Rybarczyk, B. D., Nyenhuis, D. L., Nicholas, J. J., Cash, S. M. and Kaiser, J. 1995. "Body Image Perceived Social Stigma, and the Prediction of Psychological Adjustment to Leg Amputation." *Rehabilitation Psychology* 40:95–110.

Rybarczyk, B. D., Winemiller, D. R., Lazarus L. W., Haut, A. and Hartman, C. 1996. "Validation of a Depression Screening Measure for Stroke Inpatients." *American Journal of Geriatric Psychiatry* 4:131–39.

Salisbury, S. R., Ciulla, M. R. and McSherry, E. 1989. "Clinical Management Reporting and Objective Diagnostic Instruments for Spiritual Assessment in Spinal Cord Injury Patients." *Journal of Health Care Chaplaincy* 2:35–64.

Shafranske, E. ed. (1996). *Religion and the Clinical Practice of Psychology.* Washington, DC: American Psychological Association.

Stewart, A. L., Hays, R. D. and Ware, J. E. 1988. "The MOS Short-form General Health Survey: Reliability and Validity in a Patient Population." *Medical Care* 26:724–35.

Stone, A. A. and Porter, L. S. 1995. "Psychological Coping: Its Importance for Treating Medical Problems." *Mind/Body Medicine* 1:46–53.

Strawbridge, W. J., Cohen, R. D., Shema, S. J. and Kaplan, G. A. 1997. "Frequent Attendance at Religious Services and Mortality Over 28 Years." *American Journal of Public Health* 87:957–61.

Underwood-Gordon, L., Peters, D. J., Bijur, P. and Fuhrer, M. 1997. "Roles of Religiousness and Spirituality in Medical Rehabilitation and the Lives of Persons with Disabilities." *American Journal of Physical Medicine and Rehabilitation* 76:255–57.

Williams, D. R. 1994. "The Measurement of Religion in Epidemiological Studies: Problems and Prospects." In *Religion in Aging and Health: Theoretical Foundations and Methodological Frontiers*, edited by J. S. Levin, 125–48. Thousand Oaks, CA: Sage.

Zuckerman, D. M., Kasl, S. and Ostfeld, A. M. 1984. "Psychosocial Predictors of Mortality among the Elderly Poor: The Role of Religion, Well-being, and Social Contacts." *American Journal of Epidemiology* 119:410–23.

ARTICLE 2

Spiritual Care in the Hospital
Who Requests It? Who Needs It?[1]

—GEORGE FITCHETT

Associate Professor and Director of Research, Department of Religion, Health, and Human Values, Rush-Presbyterian-St. Luke's Medical Center Chicago, IL

—PETER M. MEYER

Assistant Professor and Director of the Section of Biostatistics, Department of Preventive Medicine, Rush-Presbyterian-St. Luke's Medical Center Chicago, IL

—LAUREL A. BURTON

Bishop Anderson Professor of Religion and Medicine, Chairperson, Department of Religion, Health, and Human Values, Rush-Presbyterian-St. Luke's Medical Center Chicago, IL

AT THE TIME WE undertook this study little was known about the proportions of patients who would want to receive a chaplain visit. We were interested to know more and were surprised to discover that those who have the greater need for spiritual care were not those who were likely to request it. In retrospect our measures of potential spiritual, medical or social need were limited. However, findings from this study, combined with findings from our study of medical rehabilitation patients (Article 1) on the harmful effects of religious

1. G. Fitchett, P. Meyer, and L. A. Burton. 2000. "Spiritual Care in the Hospital: Who Requests It? Who Needs It?" *Journal of Pastoral Care and Counseling* 54:2, 173–86. https://doi.org/10.1177/002234090005400207

struggle, strengthened our view that some method of screening was needed to identify patients who might be most in need of, and likely to benefit from, chaplain care (see Article 9).

ABSTRACT

Reports the results of a survey of general medical and surgical patients ($N = 202$) who were asked if they wanted to have a chaplain talk with them, have a chaplain pray with them, and/or receive the sacrament of communion. Discusses the implications of the findings for hospital chaplains.

How do hospital chaplains and managers of hospital spiritual care departments decide which patients should receive a visit from a chaplain? In some hospitals the answer is simple, there are enough people in the department, staff chaplains, students, or volunteers, so that all newly admitted patients receive a visit from a chaplain or a representative from the pastoral care department.

But in most hospitals the answer is not so simple. In most hospitals there are not enough chaplains to see all the patients who might want to or need to receive a visit from a chaplain. In this situation, how do chaplains set priorities about who to visit? Knowing who would like a chaplain to visit could help the chaplain set priorities, especially when customer satisfaction is an important goal. Knowing who needs to receive a chaplain's visit could also help the chaplain set priorities, especially when demonstrating the contribution of the chaplain to documentable patient outcomes is an important goal.

This research project was designed to answer four questions related to chaplain's decisions about which patients to visit: What percent of general medical/surgical patients request spiritual care? How do care requesters differ from non-requesters? Do patients who need spiritual care request it? Are patients with greater spiritual risk—that is patients with high levels of spiritual, psychosocial and/or medical need or distress and low levels of religious resources—more likely to request spiritual care?

METHOD

Structured interviews were administered to patients on one general medical and one general surgical unit of an urban tertiary care medical center over a ten week period in the summer of 1993. The interviews, which typically lasted ten minutes, were conducted within 24 to 48 hours of the patient's admission. Additional information was obtained from the patient's medical records. The interviewer was a second year medical student.

Two major areas were covered in the interviews: aspects of the patient's religious and spiritual life, and the patient's social support and risk factors related to their social support. The patients were also asked if they wanted any of the following three spiritual care services: to talk with a chaplain, to have a chaplain pray with them, and/or to receive the sacrament of communion. Patient's requests for spiritual care were referred to the appropriate chaplain.

Following the suggestion of Schiller and Levin (1988), the study attempted to gather information on several different dimensions of religion and spirituality which were assumed to be related to health. A fifteen item, multi-dimensional Initial Spiritual Assessment Inventory was developed for the study. The items in the Inventory were taken from existing measures used in previous research on religion and health (Greeley 1984; Idler 1987; Berg 1998; Pargament et al. 1988; Kass et al. 1991). The dimensions included in the Inventory and the sources of the questions employed to measure them are shown in Table 2.1. Patients were also asked to identify any specific religious affiliation.

Table 2.1 **Initial Spiritual Assessment Inventory**

Dimension	Number of Items	Source of Items
Religious affiliation	1	
Public religiousness		Idler
Private religiousness	3	Idler, Kass
Spiritual experience	2	Kass
Image of God	2	Kass, Greeley
Religious coping style	3	Pargament
Spiritual injury	2	Berg

The study also included a four-item assessment of social support and changes or risks associated with it. Social support was measured with one item modified from the perceived social support scale of Blumenthal and colleagues, "I can count on my family or friends when things go wrong" (Blumenthal et al. 1987). Changes and risks in social support were assessed by asking if in the past two years there had been any of the following: change in marital or domestic status; death of a friend or family member; verbal or psychological abuse, physical beating or injuries caused by someone close.

Medical risk was assessed by asking if the patient had increased their use of alcohol or drugs in the past two years. In addition, from the patient's medical record, we collected information about their diagnosis, their acuity code—a measure of the level of nursing care the patient needed each 24 hours[2]—and demographic information. Information about the average length of stay for each diagnostic code represented in the study (ALOS/DRG) was obtained from the medical center's information services department. Information about the patient's actual length of stay (LOS) was obtained from the daily census.

The statistical analysis proceeded in four stages. Descriptive statistics were used to answer the first question regarding the proportion of patients who requested spiritual care. The determination of patient characteristics associated with requests for spiritual care began with bi-variate tests of association between each demographic, religious, or medical variable and requests for spiritual care. When the variable was continuous (e.g., age), we used t-tests to compare means between those who did and did not request care. When the variable was categorical (e.g., sex or marital status) we used the chi-square statistic. In those cases where there were too few patients in certain categories to permit the use of the chi-square statistic, Fishers Exact test was used for this analysis. Variables that were significantly associated with requests for spiritual care in the bi-variate analysis were then entered in a logistic regression equation with any request for spiritual care as the dependent variable. This procedure enabled us to determine which variables were significantly associated with requests for spiritual care when the effects of the other variables in the equation were taken into account.

To examine the possible effects of spiritual risk on requests for spiritual care we used the existing data to create several new variables. A total index of religious resources was created by adding together the values of the eight items in the dimensions of: have any religious affiliation (yes/no), public religiousness, private religiousness, and spiritual experience. By dividing the sample in half at the median score for this index, we created two equal size groups, one high and the other low on religious resources. In a similar fashion we created an index of potential spiritual, social, or medical need or distress by adding the values of the two spiritual injury items, the four social risk items, the substance abuse item, and the average length of stay for the patient's diagnosis. (For purposes of the study we assumed that patients who had a higher average length of stay for their diagnosis had a more serious condition than patients whose diagnosis had a lower average length of stay.

---

2. The acuity code was developed by the division of nursing to measure the level of nursing care required by each patient. Three of the activities included in the assessment are: vital signs every hour, wound management, activities of daily living with partial assistance. Each activity is weighted. The acuity code is the total of the weighted activities. It is employed here as an approximate measure of the patient's current illness.

The patient's acuity score was not employed here because temporarily high acuity codes, for surgical patients for example, might have misrepresented the seriousness of the patient's condition.) Again we created two groups, one with high and the other with low potential need, by dividing the sample at the mid-point of this index. A new variable was then created classifying the patients into one of the following four groups: low need and low resources, low need and high resources, high need and low resources, and high need and high resources. We used the chi-square statistic to test for any association among these groups and requests for spiritual care.

FINDINGS

Sample

Four hundred and seventy-one patients were admitted to the two study units during the study period. Of this population, interviews were completed with 202 (43%). Thirty-two percent of those admitted were not available for interview for various reasons including other staff being with them or being out of their room for a test, surgery or other procedure. An additional 19% of the patients were not interviewed due to limitations in the interviewer's schedule. The remaining 6% were not interviewed for other reasons. Only five patients refused to be interviewed for the study.

Data on two variables, acuity and length of stay (LOS), were available with which to compare the patients who were interviewed and those who were not interviewed. There were significant differences in both acuity and LOS between the patients who were interviewed and those not interviewed. Interviewed patients required fewer hours of nursing care per 24 hours (mean acuity score 36.3 compared to 42.9, $t (60.7)= -2.83$, $p=.006$), and had an average length of stay two days shorter (mean LOS 6.2 compared to 8.4, $t (472)= -3.23$, $p=.001$) than those who were not interviewed.

The average age of the patients in the study was 54.5 years (standard deviation 7.63, range 18 to 93). Fifty-six percent of the patients were women, 54% were White, 39% were Black, and 49% were married. There were slightly more medical patients (59%) than surgical patients in the study. The patients in the study had a wide variety of diagnoses, with 94 different diagnostic codes.

Over two-thirds of the patients (68%) reported having a religious affiliation: 42% were Protestant, 35% Roman Catholic, 3% Jewish, 4% other, and 16% reported no affiliation. One third of the patients (34%) reported attending worship at least once a week. Two-thirds (66%) reported spending time on some private religious practice at least weekly. Almost three-fourths (72%) reported that religion was the source of a great deal of comfort and strength for them. A similar proportion (72%) reported having an experience that convinced them that God exists.

Who Requests Spiritual Care?

As can be seen from Table 2.2, 35% of the patients requested one or more of the three spiritual care services that were offered. Over half of those who requested spiritual care (59%) requested all three types of care. About one third (31%) of those who requested care requested only one type of care, including 20% who only requested communion.

Table 2.2 **Medical/Surgical Patients' Requests for Spiritual Care** (*N* = 202)

	Number	Percent
Request any spiritual care	70	35%
(request one or more of the following)		
Communion minister to bring the sacrament	57	29%
Chaplain to pray with you	52	26%
Chaplain to talk with you	50	25%

We examined the differences in age, gender, race, and marital status between those who requested spiritual care and those who did not request spiritual care. As can be seen from Table 2.3, those who requested spiritual care were likely to be older, and non-White. While women were somewhat more likely to request spiritual care than men, this difference was not statistically significant. Additionally, the differences in requests for spiritual care associated with marital status were not statistically significant.

Table 2.3 **Association Between Demographic Factors, Religious Affiliation and Requests for Spiritual Care (Percent Who Requested Care)**

	Talk with Chaplain	Pray with Chaplain	Receive Communion	Any Request
Mean age				
Requester	61 years	60 years	59 years	60 years
Non requester	52 years	52 years	53 years	52 years
t-test	$t = 3.01^{**}$	$t = 2.91^{**}$	$t = 2.33^{*}$	$t = -3.30^{***}$
Race				
White	14%	16%	25%	27%
non-White	38%	38%	34%	44%
Chi-square	15.5^{***}	12.8^{***}		6.8^{***}
Gender				
Female	27%	28%	32%	39%
Male	22%	24%	25%	29%
Marital status				
Single	25%	25%	14%	30%
Married	22%	25%	34%	34%
Separated	40%	40%	40%	40%
Divorced	14%	19%	25%	29%
Widowed	38%	34%	34%	45%
Have religious affiliation				
Yes	27%	27%	32%	38%
No	19%	23%	23%	28%
Religious affiliation				
Protestant	31%	31%	27%	38%
Catholic	24%	25%	40%	41%
Jew	0%	0%	0%	0%
Other	14%	14%	0%	14%
None	18%	18%	18%	17%

$^{*}p<=.05.$ $^{**}p<=.01.$ $^{***}p<=.001.$

We examined the association between religious affiliation and requests for spiritual care. Religious affiliation was assessed two different ways, with a yes/no response, and with specific affiliation. As can also be seen from Table 2.3, patients who said they had a religious affiliation were somewhat more likely to request spiritual care, but this difference was not statistically significant. While Table 2.3 indicates some differences in requests for spiritual care associated with religious affiliation, these differences were not statistically significant. Jews did not request any spiritual care. A small proportion of those who reported no specific religious affiliation (17%) still requested spiritual care.

As can be seen from Table 2.4, requests for spiritual care were significantly associated with the items in four of the dimensions of religion in the Initial Spiritual Assessment Inventory. Patient's images of God were not associated with differences in requests for spiritual care. Patients who favored an image of God as King or Judge were as likely to request spiritual care as those who favored an image of God as a Friend or Lover (40% and 38% versus 38% and 38% respectively). Patients who requested one or more type of spiritual care had higher religious resource index scores than those who did not request spiritual care (mean religious resources index scores 21.4 versus 19.2, t (182)= -3.11, p=.002).

Table 2.4 **Religious Factors Associated with Requests for Spiritual Care**

	Number	Request any Spiritual Care (percent yes)	Chi-square
Public religiousness			
Attend public worship			
Never/yearly	89	31%	9.2**
Bi- to semi-monthly	43	21%	
At least weekly	69	48%	
Know people in the congregation			
None/few	107	28%	4.4*
Many/all	95	42%	
Private religiousness			
How religious are you			
None/little	33	12%	8.6**
Fairly/deeply	168	39%	
How much strength and comfort from religion			
None/little	56	14%	14.7***
A great deal	144	43%	
Frequency of private religious practice			
Monthly or less	32	12%	14.5***
At least monthly	34	21%	
At least weekly	131	44%	
Religious experience			
How close feel to God			
Not very/somewhat	71	21%	9.1**
Extremely	122	43%	
Had experience which convinced that God exists			
No	53	19%	8.8**
Yes	139	42%	
Religious coping style			
Deferring			
Low	10	21%	9.1**

High	41	47%	
Collaborative			
Low	8	19%	8.4**
High	42	44%	
Self-directing			
Low	41	46%	6.8**
High	11	23%	

*$p<=.05$. **$p<=.01$. ***$p<=.001$.

Who Needs Spiritual Care?

Measures of social or medical stress or distress, and of spiritual injury, were employed as measures of potential need or distress. As can be seen from Table 2.5, most of these sources of distress were rare. As can also be seen from Table 2.5, while there were some differences in requests for spiritual care associated with higher levels of stress, none of these differences were statistically significant. However, there was one exception to this pattern. Patients whose diagnostic group had a higher average length of stay were more likely to request one or more type of spiritual care than patients whose diagnosis had a lower average length of stay (mean ALOS/DRG 6.8 for care requesters versus 5.7 for non-requesters, $t(189)= -3.09$, $p=.002$).

Table 2.5 **Spiritual, Social or Medical Stress and Requests for Spiritual Care**

	Number	Request any Spiritual Care (percent yes)
Spiritual injury (how often feel)		
Life has no meaning or purpose		
Often/very often	7	43%
Sometimes/never	195	34%
Despair or hopeless		
Often/very often	8	50%
Sometimes/never	194	34%
Medical risk		
Substance abuse		
Yes	3	33%
No	197	34%
Social risk		
Change in marital status		
Yes	9	22%
No	191	36%
Death of family or friends		
Yes	85	34%
No	117	35%
Abusive relationship		
Yes	6	50%
No	196	34%
Someone to count on		
No	12	42%
Yes	105	28%

None of the differences in need in this table were associated with statistically significant differences in requests for spiritual care.

Patients who requested one or more type of spiritual care had higher total potential need scores than those who did not request spiritual care (mean total potential need 12.2 for care requesters *versus* 10.7 for non-requesters, t (106.7)= -3.23, p=.002). However, when ALOS/DRG was omitted from the total need index, the difference between those who did and did not request spiritual care was not statistically significant. That is, aside from ALOS/

DRG, none of the other measures of potential need or distress, either singly or combined, was associated with requests for spiritual care.

Multi-variate Analysis of Who Requests and Needs Spiritual Care

The above bi-variate analyses indicated that age, race, religiosity, and ALOS/DRG were all associated with requests for spiritual care. However, other research indicates that several of these variables may be strongly associated with each other. For example, older adults have been found to be more religious, as have Blacks when compared with Whites, and in some cases people's religious commitment or private devotional activities increase when they are ill (Gallup 1996; Levin 1989; Levin, Taylor and Chatters 1994). Logistic regression is the statistical test that permitted us to test which of the variables associated with requests for spiritual care were significant when the effects of the other variables were taken into account. In our logistic regression equation we included the patient's age, race (coded as White or non-White), the ten statistically significant religion items from the dimensions of public and private religiousness, spiritual experience, and religious coping style, and ALOS/DRG. The logistic regression analysis indicated that four of these items were significant predictors of who requests spiritual care: age, frequency of private religious practices, how religious the patient described him or herself to be, and ALOS/DRG.

Spiritual Risk and Spiritual Care

Simple measures of spiritual injury, or medical or social stress, may be an inadequate method of determining which patients should receive a chaplain's visit, since such measures do not take into account the religious or spiritual resources which patients may have available to cope with such stress. Patients with low levels of spiritual resources and high levels of spiritual injury or other stress might be described as having a high level of spiritual risk for poor coping with illness or recovery from illness. Conversely, patients with high levels of spiritual resources and low levels of spiritual injury or other stress might be described as having low levels of spiritual risk for poor recovery or coping with illness.

As described earlier, we created several variables that permitted us to classify the patients into one of four groups according to their potential needs and religious resources: low need and low resources, low need and high resources, high need and low resources, and high need and high resources. As can be seen from Table 2.6, there were significant differences in the proportion of patients who requested spiritual care associated with these four groups. As the patient's level of potential need increased, their likelihood of requesting spiritual care increased. However, at each level of potential need, compared to those with high religious resources, those with low religious resources were significantly less likely to request spiritual care.

Table 2.6 **Spiritual Risk and Requests for Spiritual Care (percent who request spiritual care)**

		Religious Resources	
		Low	High
Potential	Low	9%	35%
Need	High	31%	59%

Chi-square = 21.19, $p < .001$

DISCUSSION

How Many Patients Request Spiritual Care?

As this is the first published study we are aware of that has asked patients while they were in the hospital about their preferences for spiritual care, it is not possible to make a direct comparison between the results of this study and previous research. However, in an earlier study of 51 psychiatric and 50 medical/surgical in-patients we found two-thirds reported that having a chaplain visit and pray was important or very important to them (Fitchett, Burton and Sivan 1997). Among 142 medical rehabilitation patients surveyed after discharge, Anderson and colleagues (1993) reported that 54% desired pastoral visitation. In a national survey of 484 former hospital patients, 51% reported receiving one or more visits from a hospital chaplain (VandeCreek et al. 1991). Compared to these studies, the proportion of patients who requested spiritual care in the present study is a little low.

One factor that may have affected this is that patients who were interviewed for this study tended to be healthier than those who were not interviewed. Requests for spiritual care were associated with length of stay. Those who requested spiritual care had longer hospitalizations than those who did not request care (mean LOS 7.5 days *versus* 5.6 days, $t(199) = -2.81$, $p = .005$). Given this difference, it is possible that if we had interviewed all patients admitted to these units the proportion who requested spiritual care would be higher than the 35% reported here.

Who Requests Spiritual Care?

Some stereotypes about who would be interested in spiritual care were confirmed by the study, but other stereotypes were confounded. Patients who requested spiritual care were more likely to be older, non-White, and more religious compared to those who did not request spiritual care. This is consistent with other research that indicates greater levels of religious commitment among older adults and Blacks (Gallup 1996; Levin, Taylor and Chatters 1994). It is also consistent with Parkum's (1985) report that among 432 patients in six hospitals, older patients reported more use of chaplains.

However, in contrast to these findings, while national surveys also indicate that women are more religious than men (Gallup 1996; Levin, Taylor and Chatters 1994), they were not significantly more likely than men to request spiritual care. This is consistent with Parkum's (1985) finding that men and women had similar ratings of chaplains' helpfulness. However, it differs from Martin and colleagues' (1978) finding that women were more likely than men to report spiritual needs. In addition, compared to those who report having a religious affiliation, patients who reported they had no religious affiliation were not significantly less likely to request spiritual care.

Requests for spiritual care were also associated with longer ALOS/DRG. This is consistent with other research that finds people mobilize their faith to help them cope with stressful situations (Pargament 1997). This research also offers an explanation for the finding that more religious patients are more likely to request spiritual care. That is, more religious people are likely to be more familiar with spiritual care services and to welcome them as a resource in a stressful time.

To Him (or Her) Who Has, Will More Be Given

Because more religious patients are more likely to request spiritual care, it is possible that a considerable proportion of the patients who request services from the hospital's pastoral care department will also be receiving spiritual care from their own clergy and congregation. The present study did not permit a test of this possibility. However, such a pattern was observed in Vande-Creek and colleagues' (1991) study of 484 former hospital patients, in which 56% of those who reported a visit from a chaplain also reported visits from their local clergy. In a recently completed study of 96 medical rehabilitation patients we also found a similar pattern. Sixty-four percent of the patients who reported visits from a chaplain also reported receiving spiritual care from their pastor or a member of their congregation (Fitchett et al. 1999).

In the interests of good stewardship of their limited time, chaplains may wish to carefully consider which patients are receiving adequate spiritual care from their local clergy and/or congregation and which patients require additional care from the chaplain.

Finding Lost Sheep

In contrast to the patients who may receive spiritual care from both the chaplain and the local congregation are patients who do not receive any spiritual care. As the findings from the present study indicated, compared to patients with higher religious resources, patients with multiple stresses who had lower religious resources were less likely to request spiritual care. Some patients in this subgroup may not be at greater risk for poor recovery or coping with their illness. They may be well-adjusted people, with many personal and social resources, for whom religion is not important. However, given the consistently small proportion of people in the United States who report they do not believe in God (5%) (Gallup 1996), it is more likely that these are people for whom religion is underdeveloped, problematic, or conflicted.[3]

Chaplains may need to be more intentional in developing methods of screening for patients who we might think of, metaphorically, as lost sheep. These are patients with spiritual risk, those with high needs and limited religious resources. As the present study demonstrates, these patients are not likely to self-refer to the pastoral care department. Their low religious resources suggest it is unlikely they will be referred by their local clergy. If one of the cues used by nurses in making referrals to chaplains is obvious signs of a patient's religiosity, it is also likely that these patients will not be referred by a nurse.

Having Needs, Reporting Needs, and Requesting Help

The relationship between having needs, being aware of them, and requesting help for them appears to be a complex one. As the findings from the present study show, people who had greater spiritual, social, and medical needs, were generally not more likely to request spiritual care. In Anderson and

3. For helpful studies of the effects of problematic religious coping see: Pargament, *The Psychology of Religion and Coping*; Pargament, Smith, Koenig, and Perez, "Patterns of Positive and Negative Religious Coping," 710–24; Pargament et al., "Red Flags and Religious Coping," 77–89; and Mickley, Pargament, Brant, and Hipp, "God and the Search for Meaning," 1–17.

colleagues' (1993) study of medical rehabilitation patients, 27% reported feeling they were losing a sense of purpose in life, 23% reported feeling that God was punishing them, and 9% reported a need for hope. Unfortunately, we do not know from that study if any of these were among the 54% who desired a pastoral visit, but based on the present study, we might conclude that many of them would not be.

In our study of the psychiatric and medical/surgical in-patients, 46 patients, approximately half, when asked a general question about having any spiritual needs, reported they were not aware of any. However, when we asked the patients to rate of the importance of eight specific religious needs (e.g., knowledge of God's presence), only two of these 46 patients did not rate one or more of these needs as important or very important to them (Fitchett et al. 1997). When the survey question was about specific religious needs it appeared to generate more awareness of need in comparison to a general question about awareness of religious or spiritual need. Further study is called for to help us understand the complex relationship between having needs, religious, spiritual or otherwise, being aware of them, and requesting help for them.

Limitations

The results of this study should be interpreted in light of its limitations. First among them is the limitation of the sample. The patients in the study were hospitalized in a tertiary care institution, in a major mid-Western metropolitan area. Caution should be used in generalizing from this study about the proportion of patients who will request spiritual care in other types of hospitals, in other size communities, in other regions of the nation. Similar caution should be used in generalizing about patients in other medical services, such as obstetrics, psychiatry, pediatrics, or intensive care.

A second limitation is the proportion of total patients admitted to the study units who were interviewed for the study (43%). As we have noted, the sample was biased toward the healthier patients admitted to the study units, perhaps underestimating the proportion of general medical/surgical patients who would request spiritual care. Efforts should be made to increase the proportion of eligible patients who participate in future studies.

The small proportion of patients who reported problems with substance abuse, domestic violence, social support, and spiritual injury raises questions about the willingness of the patients to disclose such information. In-depth clinical and spiritual assessments would provide more reliable measures of need and risk. Validated scales that assessed social support, psychological distress, and spiritual injury or negative religious coping, would also strengthen the assessment of need and risk.[4] Validated scales are also needed for assessing spiritual needs.

While the patients may have understated their needs or risks, social desirability may have contributed to some overstatement of their religious commitment. As the levels of religious commitment of the patients in the study are similar to those reported in other studies, we do not believe there was any serious distortion here. However, a more rigorous study would include controls for social desirability.

Future Research

It would be helpful if future studies of who requests spiritual care were conducted in a variety of hospitals, including religiously affiliated hospitals, in a variety of settings and regions, with a variety of patients. Studies that help us understand which patients are aware of their spiritual need, and the factors associated with requesting help for those needs will also be important.

Catholic chaplains who responded to a 1996 survey reported that 38.4% of their contacts came from visits to every patient. Comparing this statistic to earlier surveys, the authors of the report wrote, "because of time constraints and greater acuity, fewer and fewer departments are seeing every patient. Pastoral care will increasingly rely on others to refer those who find themselves in spiritual distress" (Catholic Health Association of the United States 1997, 14). Some important progress has been made in developing instruments that can be used by chaplains or their professional colleagues in screening for spiritual risk.[5] However, additional studies to

4. For measures of social support see: Blumenthal et al., "Social Support, Type A Behavior," 331–40; and Rybarczyk et al., "Body Image," 95–110. For measures of psychological distress see: Zabora, "Screening Procedures," 653–61. For measures of spiritual injury see: Berg, "A Statement on Clinical Assessment," 42–50; and Lawson et al., "The Spiritual Injury Scale." For measures of negative religious coping see: Pargament, Smith, Koenig, and Perez, "Patterns of Positive and Negative Religious Coping," 710–24; and Pargament, *The Psychology of Religion and Coping*.

5. Resources for chaplains interested in screening for spiritual risk include: Fitchett, and Handzo, "Spiritual Assessment," 790–808; the 1998 symposium "Clinical Pathways for Pastoral Care: Which Way Are We Going?", edited by George Handzo, *Chaplaincy Today* 14:2, 2–50, and especially the articles: Handzo, "An Integrated System," 30–37, and Berg, "A Statement on Clinical Assessment," 42–50; Palmer, VandeCreek, "Religious Evaluation," 9–19; and Larry VandeCreek's research including: VandeCreek, "Identifying the Spiritually Needy," 38–47; VandeCreek, and Smith, "Measuring the Spiritual Needs," 46–52; and VandeCreek, Ayers, and Bassham, "Using INSPIRIT," 83–89.

help develop valid and reliable screening instruments are becoming increasingly important.

Clinical Implications

Three findings from the study have direct relevance for the work of the chaplain. To ensure high levels of customer satisfaction with spiritual care services among general medical/surgical patients, chaplains should target their spiritual care to older, more religious patients, who have diagnoses associated with longer hospitalizations. The findings from the present study indicate that if given an opportunity, these are the patients who are most likely to request spiritual care. Meeting the spiritual needs of these patients not only has inherent value, but may be associated with greater customer satisfaction and continued use of that hospital.[6]

At the same time, chaplains should be mindful of the possibility that those patients who expect or request spiritual care may not be the ones who need spiritual care the most. As we have seen, patients with high levels of need and low levels of religious resources were far less likely to request spiritual care than patients with high levels of religious resources. However, identifying such patients and providing them with spiritual care is more likely to have a measurable effect on their recovery or adjustment to their illness than similar care provided to patients with high levels of spiritual resources. It perhaps cannot be emphasized enough that chaplains who wish to make documentable differences in patients' recovery and adjustment should concentrate their efforts on identifying patients with spiritual risk. The development of valid and reliable spiritual screening tools will be essential in helping chaplains identify such patients soon after admission.[7]

Finally, it is important to note that the patients did not object to participation in an extended spiritual and psychosocial screening interview. They accepted the extended social and religious assessment of the study as part of their total initial assessment. Only 5 patients (2%) refused to participate in the assessment interview and in most of those cases the patients indicated that they did not object to the content of the interview, but were feeling too ill to participate. Chaplains and other health professionals are

6. For studies of patient and family satisfaction with spiritual care see: VandeCreek, Jessen, Thomas, Gibbons, and Strasser, "Patient and Family Perceptions," 455–67; and VandeCreek, and Lyon, *Ministry of Hospital Chaplains.*

7. For a discussion of screening for spiritual risk and suggested resources, see Fitchett, "Screening for Spiritual Risk." 2–12; and Fitchett, "Selected Resources for Screening for Spiritual Risk," 13–26.

sometimes reluctant to ask about patient's religious needs and resources. Our experience with this study supports other recent research that indicates that patients welcome an opportunity to talk about their faith with members of the health care team.[8]

CONCLUSION

When the chaplain's time is limited, difficult decisions must be made about which patients will receive spiritual care. Many chaplains will identify with the colleague who reports using prayer to help him decide which patients to visit, "I ask God to lead me to the ones who need me" (Kallaos 1998, 7). The findings in the present study may be used to supplement these supplications. They suggest that, if given an opportunity, older, more religious patients with more serious health problems would request spiritual care. By making it a priority to offer spiritual care to such patients, chaplains should maintain high levels of customer satisfaction. However, the study findings suggest that patients who potentially have greater needs for spiritual care are not likely to request it. Chaplains may need to work with health care colleagues to institute some method of screening for spiritual risk or need in order to facilitate early identification and referral of these patients. Based on our experience in this study, patients would have no objection to answering questions about their spiritual needs and resources required in such a screening process.

8. For recent studies about patients' willingness to talk about their religion and spirituality see: Ehman et al., "Pulmonary Patients' Attitudes"; King, and Bushwick, "Beliefs and Attitudes of Hospital Inpatients," 349–52; and Maugans, and Wadland, "Religion and Family Medicine," 210–13.

REFERENCES

Anderson, J. M., Anderson, L. J. and Felsenthal, G. 1993. "Pastoral Needs and Support Within an Inpatient Rehabilitation Unit." *Archives of Physical Medicine and Rehabilitation* 74:574–78.

Berg, G. E. 1998. "A Statement on Clinical Assessment for Pastoral Care." *Chaplaincy Today* 14:2, 42–50.

Blumenthal, J. A. Burg, M. M. Barefoot, J. Williams, R. B. Haney, T. and Zimet, G. 1987. "Social Support, Type A Behavior, and Coronary Artery Disease." *Psychosomatic Medicine* 49:331–40.

Catholic Health Association of the United States, The. 1997. *Chaplaincy: Moving Toward the Next Millennium.* St. Louis, MO: The Catholic Health Association of the United States.

Ehman, J. W., Ott, B. B., Ciampa, R. C., Hansen-Flaschen, J. and Short, T. H. 1997. "Pulmonary Patients' Attitudes Concerning Physician Inquiry about Spiritual/ Religious Beliefs." Accessed August 17, 2020, http://www.uphs.upenn.edu/pastoral/resed/summary.html

Fitchett, G. 1999. "Screening for Spiritual Risk." *Chaplaincy Today* 15:1, 2–12.

Fitchett, G. 1999. "Selected Resources for Screening for Spiritual Risk." *Chaplaincy Today* 15:1, 13–26.

Fitchett, G., Burton, L. A. and Sivan, A. B. 1997. "The Religious Needs and Resources of Psychiatric Inpatients." *Journal of Nervous and Mental Disease* 185:5, 320–26.

Fitchett, G. and Handzo, G. 1998. "Spiritual Assessment, Screening, and Intervention." In *Psycho-oncology*, edited by J. C. Holland, 790–808. New York: Oxford University Press.

Fitchett, G., Rybarczyk, B. D., DeMarco, G. A., and Nicholas, J. J. 1999. "The Role of Religion in Medical Rehabilitation Outcomes: A Longitudinal Study." *Rehabilitation Psychology* 44:4, 333–53. [Article 1 in this volume]

Gallup, G. H. 1996. *Religion in America*. Princeton, NJ: The Princeton Religion Research Center.

Greeley, A. 1984. "Religious Imagery as a Predictor Variable in the General Social Survey." A paper presented to the Society for the Scientific Study of Religion.

Handzo, G. 1998. "An Integrated System for the Assessment and Treatment of Psychological, Social and Spiritual Distress." *Chaplaincy Today* 14:2, 30–37.

Idler, E. L. 1987. "Religious Involvement and the Health of the Elderly: Some Hypotheses and an Initial Test." *Social Forces* 66:1, 226–38.

Kallaos, T. (1998). "Agents of Healing Glad to Do More." *News Leader*, April 19.

Kass, J. D., Friedman, R., Leserman, J., Zuttermeister, P. C. and Benson, H. 1991. "Health Outcomes and a New Index of Spiritual Experience." *Journal for the Scientific Study of Religion* 30:2, 203–11.

King, D. E. and Bushwick, B. 1994. "Beliefs and Attitudes of Hospital Inpatients about Faith Healing and Prayer." *Journal of Family Practice* 39:4, 349–52.

Lawson, R., Drebing, C. E., Berg, G., Jones, S. and Penk, W. 1998. "The Spiritual Injury Scale: Validity and Reliability." Paper presented at the annual meeting of the American Psychological Association, San Francisco, CA.

Levin, J. S. 1989. "Religious Factors in Aging, Adjustment and Health: A Theoretical Overview." In *Religion, Aging and Health: A Global Perspective*, edited by W. M. Clements, 133–46. New York: Haworth.

Levin, J. S., Taylor, R. J. and Chatters, L. M. 1994. "Race and Gender Differences in Religiosity among Older Adults: Findings from Four National Surveys." *Journal of Gerontology: Social Sciences* 49:3, S137–S145.

Martin, C., Burrows, C. and Pomilio, J. 1978. "Spiritual Needs of Patients Survey." In *Spiritual Care: The Nurse's Role*, edited by S. Fish and J. A. Shelly, 150–66. Downers Grove, IL: InterVarsity.

Maugans, T. A. and Wadland, W. C. 1991. "Religion and Family Medicine: A Survey of Physicians and Patients." *Journal of Family Practice* 32:2, 210–13.

Palmer C. L. and VandeCreek, L. 1996. "Religious Evaluation of Lung Transplant Patients." *The Caregiver Journal* 12:3, 9–19.

Pargament, K. I. 1997. *The Psychology of Religion and Coping: Theory, Research, Practice.* New York: Guilford.

Pargament, K. I., Kennell, J., Hathaway, W., Grevengoed, N., Newman, J. and Jones, W. 1988. "Religion and the Problem-solving Process: Three Styles of Coping." *Journal for the Scientific Study of Religion* 27:1, 90–104.

Pargament, K. I., Smith, B. W., Koenig, H. G. and Perez, L. 1998. "Patterns of Positive and Negative Religious Coping with Major Life Stressors." *Journal for the Scientific Study of Religion* 37:4, 710–24.

Parkum, K. H. 1985. "The Impact of Chaplaincy Services in Selected Hospitals in the Eastern United States." *Journal of Pastoral Care* 39:3, 262–69. Reprinted 1995 in *Spiritual Needs and Pastoral Services: Readings in Research*, edited by L. VandeCreek, 325–33. Decatur, GA: Journal of Pastoral Care Publications.

Rybarczyk, B. D., Nyenhuis, D. L., Nicholas, J. J., Cash, S. M. and Kaiser, J. 1995. "Body Image, Perceived Social Stigma, and the Prediction of Psychological Adjustment to Leg Amputation." *Rehabilitation Psychology* 40:2, 95–110.

Schiller, P. L. and Levin, J. S. 1988. "Is There a Religious Factor in Health Care Utilization? A Review." *Social Science in Medicine* 27:12, 1369–79.

VandeCreek, L. 1991. "Identifying the Spiritually Needy Patient." *The Caregiver Journal* 8:3, 38–47.

VandeCreek, L., Ayers, S. and Bassham, M. 1995. "Using INSPIRIT to Conduct Spiritual Assessments." *Journal of Pastoral Care* 49:4, 83–89.

VandeCreek, L., Jessen, A., Thomas, J., Gibbons, J. and Strasser, S. 1991. "Patient and Family Perceptions of Hospital Chaplains." *Hospital and Health Services Administration* 36:3, 455–67. Reprinted 1995 in *Spiritual Needs and Pastoral Services: Readings in Research*, edited by L. VandeCreek, 343–56. Decatur, GA: Journal of Pastoral Care Publications.

VandeCreek, L. and Lyon, M. 1997. *Ministry of Hospital Chaplains: Patient Satisfaction.* New York: Haworth Pastoral.

VandeCreek, L. and Smith, D. 1992. "Measuring the Spiritual Needs of Hospital Patients and their Families." *The Journal of Pastoral Care* 46:1, 46–52.

ARTICLE 3

Religious Struggle

Prevalence, Correlates and Mental Health Risks in
Diabetic, Congestive Heart Failure, and Oncology
Patients [1]

—George Fitchett
Rush University Medical Center

—Patricia E. Murphy
Rush University Medical Center

—Jo Kim
Evanston Northwestern Health Care

—James L. Gibbons
Advocate Health Care

—Jacqueline R. Cameron
General Theological Seminary of the Episcopal Church

1. G. Fitchett, P. E. Murphy, J. Kim, J. L. Gibbons, J. R. Cameron, and J. A. Davis. 2004. "Religious Struggle: Prevalence, Correlates and Mental Health Risks in Diabetic, Congestive Heart Failure, and Oncology Patients." *International Journal of Psychiatry in Medicine* 34:2, 179–96. https://doi.org/10.2190/UCJ9-DP4M-9CoX-835M

—JUDY A. DAVIS
Rush University Medical Center

AS WE WERE REPORTING our findings about the harmful effects of religious struggle in medical rehabilitation patients (Article 1) other investigators began to report findings of the negative effects of religious struggle on quality of life, emotional well-being, and other factors in other clinical samples. Consequently, as we designed new studies of the role of religion and spirituality in coping with illness in diverse clinical populations, we made a point of including the negative religious coping subscale from Ken Pargament's Brief RCOPE, the best short measure of religious struggle available at that time. By 2000 we had collected data on religious struggle in a sample of out-patients with diabetes and had collaborated with colleagues who had included the measure in a study of patients newly diagnosed with congestive heart failure and a study of inpatients on an oncology unit. This paper shows how we were able to combine data from the three samples to examine the prevalence and correlates of religious struggle in this diverse clinical sample.

ABSTRACT

Objectives:

For some people, diagnosis with a serious illness or other adverse life events can precipitate a period of religious struggle. While evidence of the harmful effects of religious struggle is accumulating, less is known about its prevalence or correlates. The aim of this study was to examine the prevalence and correlates of religious struggle in three groups of medical patients.

Methods:

Study participants included diabetic outpatients ($n = 71$), congestive heart failure (CHF) outpatients ($n = 70$), and oncology inpatients ($n = 97$). Participants completed questionnaires which included several measures of religion, including religious struggle, emotional distress or well-being, and demographic characteristics.

Results:

Half of the total sample (52%) reported no religious struggle, while 15% reported moderate or high levels. In a multi-variate analysis, younger patients ($p<0.001$) and CHF patients ($p<0.05$) had higher levels of religious struggle. Those with higher levels of positive religious coping also reported higher levels of religious struggle ($p<0.01$), while those who attended worship most frequently had lower levels of religious struggle ($p<0.05$). Religious struggle was associated with higher levels of depressive symptoms and emotional distress in all three patient groups.

Conclusions:

While further research is needed to help clarify the sources, additional correlates, and course of religious struggle, the findings in this study confirm the association between religious struggle and emotional distress in these three groups of medical patients. Clinicians should be attentive to signs of religious struggle. Where patient's responses indicate possible religious struggle, clinicians should consider referral to a trained, professional chaplain or pastoral counselor.

Key words: Religion; Diabetes mellitus; Congestive heart failure; Cancer; Depression

INTRODUCTION

Diagnosis with a serious illness or other adverse life events can precipitate a time of emotional turmoil. In such situations, some people may turn to religious beliefs and practices for consolation (Ellison and Taylor 1996; Ferraro and Kelley-Moore 2000). Some may find the consolation they seek, but others may not (Albrecht and Cornwall 1989; Ingersoll-Dayton, Krause and Morgan 2002; Taylor, Outlaw, Bernardo and Roy 1999; Pargament 1997). For example, a woman in her fifties with advanced cancer told a chaplain, "Why? Why me? I just can't figure it out. And I get so depressed that I just want to give up on life altogether, you know? And I'm so very angry at God. So angry. I refuse to speak to Him. You know what I mean?" (Fitchett and Roberts 2003 [Article 8 in this volume]). As people attempt to integrate the reality of grave illness or other adverse life events into their pre-existing religious beliefs, they may ask, "God, why did you let this happen to me?" (Bradshaw and Fitchett 2003). For some, this period of religious struggle may be brief, for others it can be quite protracted. It may lead to growth and transformation for some people and to distress and despair for others (Ingersoll-Dayton, Krause and Morgan 2002; Carpenter, Brockopp and Andrykowski 1999).

There has been little investigation of religious struggle precipitated by serious illness or other adverse life events. Why do some people pass through it while others get stuck? Why does it lead to growth for some and turmoil for others? What role, if any, do factors such as age, gender, prior religiousness, or the specific nature of the adverse event play in this process?

While little is known about the factors that may be associated with religious struggle, evidence of its adverse effects has been accumulating over the past few years. In a study of medical rehabilitation patients, higher levels of religious struggle were associated with less recovery of independence in activities of daily living (Fitchett, Rybarczyk, DeMarco and Nicholas 1999). Further analysis revealed that anger with God was the feature of religious struggle that most accounted for this effect.

In a study of hospitalized, medically ill older patients, Koenig and colleagues (1998) found that some aspects of religious struggle were associated with poorer physical health, worse quality of life, and greater depressive symptoms. In a two-year follow-up of this sample, Pargament and colleagues (2001) reported that religious struggle was a significant predictor of increased risk for mortality, even after controlling for demographic, physical health, and mental health variables. These and other studies (Berg 1994; Berg, Fonss, Reed and VandeCreek 1995; Kaldjian, Jekel and Friedland 1998; Trenholm, Trent and Compton 1998) suggest that some types of religious struggle may contribute to poor physical or mental health outcomes for clinical samples. Evidence of the adverse effects of religious struggle in community samples has also been reported (Exline, Yali and Lobel 1999; Exline, Yali and Sanderson 2000; Strawbridge et al. 1998).

The aim of the present research was to examine religious struggle in three groups of medical patients, diabetic outpatients, congestive heart failure (CHF) outpatients, and oncology inpatients. Specifically, we sought to: 1) describe the prevalence of religious struggle in these patients and to describe the differences in the level of religious struggle, if any, among the three patient groups; and 2) to describe the demographic and religious correlates of religious struggle. In addition, to confirm whether the associations observed in other reports held true for these patients, a secondary aim of this research was to describe any associations between religious struggle and emotional distress.

METHODS

Design

We conducted separate studies to investigate these aims in three groups of medical patients. The studies were conducted at three different institutions located in a large Midwestern metropolitan area. Diabetic patients were recruited from an outpatient clinic at a community hospital, CHF patients were recruited from an outpatient clinic at another community hospital, and oncology patients were recruited from an inpatient oncology unit at a major academic medical center. For the diabetic and CHF samples, all patients who attended the clinic on days when the study was being conducted were invited to participate. For the oncology sample, all consecutive admissions on days when study personnel were present on the unit were approached. Persons who were under age 18 or who were non-English-speaking were not considered as potential participants. Each study was approved by the institutional review board of the institution in which it was conducted and all the study participants provided written informed consent.

Participation rates for the diabetic and oncology studies were 67% and 88%, respectively, and approximately 50% for the CHF study. The most common reason for non-participation in all three studies was feeling ill. Other frequently cited reasons for not participating included feeling under too much stress or being too busy. In the diabetic and CHF samples, most participants completed the questionnaires themselves and returned them either during their clinic visit or by mail. In several cases, questionnaires were interviewer-administered at the participants' request. Among the cancer patients, all questionnaires were interviewer-administered. The total sample with non-missing data on the study measures was 238; diabetic outpatients ($n = 71$), CHF outpatients ($n = 70$), and oncology inpatients ($n = 97$).

Measures

Religious Struggle

The measure of religious struggle employed for all three studies was the seven-item negative religious coping subscale from the Brief RCOPE (Pargament, Smith, Koenig and Perez 1998). The Brief RCOPE was developed by Pargament and colleagues to provide a broad measure of religious coping. The items are shown in Table 3.2. Pargament and colleagues (1998) reported an alpha coefficient of 0.69 for negative religious coping in a sample of 551 hospitalized medical patients. Negative religious coping scores were correlated in the expected directions with other measures of physical and emotional health. Individuals were asked to rate how much they used these activities to cope on a 4-point Likert scale (0 "not at all" to 3 "a great deal"). The present study used the sum of the responses to the seven items, a score with a potential range from 0 to 21. In the present study, among the patients in all three samples, the alpha coefficient for the negative religious coping subscale was 0.77.

Other Religion Measures

Two additional religion measures were employed in each of the three studies. The first was the positive religious coping subscale from the Brief RCOPE (Pargament, Smith, Koenig and Perez 1998). It is also a well-validated measure, with an alpha coefficient of 0.87 in a sample of hospitalized medical patients. Like the negative religious coping subscale, this is also a seven-item scale. It assesses coping activities such as drawing closer to God, working with God to address one's problems, and seeking forgiveness. A sample item is, "I looked for a strong connection with God." The present study used the sum of the responses to the seven items, a score with a potential range from 0 to 21. In the present study, among the patients in all three samples, the alpha coefficient for the positive religious coping subscale was 0.90.

Participants in all three studies were also asked about their frequency of attendance at public worship, coded into four levels (never, rarely, monthly, or weekly or more). This is a widely used measure in studies of religion and health (Idler 1987; Idler and Kasl 1992; Oxman, Freeman and Manheimer 1995).

Mental Distress

Each of the three studies included well-developed measures of several dimensions of emotional distress or well-being such as depressive symptoms, psychological distress, or emotional well-being. The specific measures employed differed in each of the patient groups.

DIABETES-RELATED DISTRESS (PAID)

In the diabetic sample, diabetes-related psychosocial distress was measured with the Problem Areas in Diabetes Survey (PAID) (Polonsky et al.

1995; Welch, Jacobson and Polonsky 1997). This 20-item survey assesses several areas of diabetes-related distress, including anger, interpersonal distress, and frustration with aspects of the diabetic regimen. Each item is rated on a 6-point Likert scale (from 1 "no problem" to 6 "serious problem"). Original psychometric data was reported for a study of 451 females with type I and type II diabetes. In the present study, the alpha coefficient for the PAID was 0.91.

Minnesota Living with Heart Failure Questionnaire (LHFQ)

Emotional distress in the CHF sample was assessed using the emotional symptom subscale of the LHFQ. The LHFQ measures patients' perceptions of the impact of symptoms of heart failure on their lives in the past month (Rector, Frances and Cohn 1987; Rector, Kubo and Cohn 1987). The 5-item emotional symptom sub-scale includes items about feeling worried, depressed, and believing one is a burden. The instrument has been used in a number of studies of the impact of CHF on quality of life (Gorkin et al. 1993; Bennett, Baker and Huster 1998; Murberg, Bru, Torbjorn and Svebak 1998). In the present study, the alpha coefficient for the emotional symptom subscale of the LHFQ was 0.75.

Functional Assessment of Cancer Therapy — General (FACT—G)

The FACT-G is a widely-used, well-validated measure of four domains of cancer patients' quality of life (QOL): physical, functional, social/family, and emotional (EWB) (Cella et al. 1993). In the current study, the 6-item EWB subscale, which assesses mood and emotional response to illness, was used to assess the emotional well-being of participants in the oncology sample. The alpha coefficient for the EWB subscale in the present study was 0.68.

Chicago Multiscale Depression Inventory (CMDI)

The CMDI was used in the diabetic sample to assess depression. The CMDI was developed to provide a measure of depression in medical patients that would distinguish the psychological and vegetative aspects of depression in this population (Nyenhuis et al. 1998). We employed the 9-item mood subscale to assess non-vegetative symptoms of depression. Respondents were asked to rate how much each item described their feelings in the past week on a 5-point scale (from 1 "not at all" to 5 "extremely"). In the present study, the alpha coefficient for the CMDI mood sub-scale was 0.94.

PROFILE OF MOOD STATES (POMS-SF)

The depression, anxiety and hostility subscales of the POMS-SF were employed in the CHF and oncology samples to assess the respondents' emotional adjustment to living with their illness. The POMS-SF is a widely used, well-validated measure of emotional distress in medical samples (McNair, Lorr and Droppleman 1992). For the CHF and oncology samples the alpha coefficients for the anxiety, depression, and hostility subscales ranged from 0.82 to 0.89.

Demographic

Standard measures of demographic variables were also included in all three studies. In the bi-variate analysis we created 10-year age categories to examine the association with negative religious coping. Age was treated as a continuous variable in the multi-variate analysis. Race and marital status were treated as dichotomous variables, white vs. other and married vs. other, respectively. Three categories for education were created: less than a high school diploma, high school diploma or some college, and college degree or more.

Analysis

We created frequency distributions for each item to examine the prevalence of negative religious coping. We also examined the proportion of patients who responded "not at all" to all seven items, as well as the proportion who responded "quite a bit" or "a great deal" to two or more items.

Differences in the level of religious struggle among the three patient groups or in association with the demographic or religious factors were initially tested in bi-variate analyses and then in a multi-variate analysis. A preliminary analysis indicated there were non-linear relationships between negative religious coping and both positive religious coping and worship attendance. We transformed the continuous positive religious coping measure into five approximately equal size groups and we created dummy variables for this and the worship attendance variable. These dummy variables were employed in both the bi-variate and multi-variate analyses. Due to the skewed nature of the negative religious coping scores, non-parametric statistics were employed for the bi-variate analyses. For variables with more than two categories we employed the Kruskal-Wallis chi-square statistic. For variables with two categories we employed the Mann-Whitney z-score.

Multiple regression was employed for the multi-variate analysis with negative religious coping as the dependent variable. We employed a transformation (the opposite of the inverse of the negative religious coping score) to address the skewness of the negative religious coping variable. This type of transformation does not change the rank order of responses to the scale. Because distance between items on Likert scales is arbitrary, a change of distance between scores without changing rank provides the same information as the original scale.

We determined partial correlations for the transformed negative religious coping score and the mental health measures, controlling for age and gender. All analyses were conducted using SPSS 10.0 for Windows.

RESULTS

Table 3.1 summarizes key demographic characteristics for each of the three patient groups. There were several significant differences between the groups. The CHF patients were older than the diabetic and oncology patients. In addition, the CHF patients were less likely not to have completed high school and more likely to have at least a college degree than the diabetic or oncology patients. There were also significant differences in worship attendance and positive religious coping among the three patient groups. The groups did not differ significantly with respect to gender, race, or marital status.

Table 3.1 **Demographic and Religious Characteristics of the Three Patient Groups** ($N = 238$)

	Diabetic Outpatients	CHF Outpatients	Oncology Inpatients	Comparison
Sample size	$n = 71$	$n = 70$	$n = 97$	
Age, mean (*SD*)	59.4 (13.5)	68.3 (10.6)	56.9 (12.6)	$F = 18.1^{***}$
Percent female (vs. male)	63%	44%	59%	$x^2 = 5.8$
Percent married (vs. other)	48%	64%	59%	$x^2 = 4.0$
Percent White (vs. other)	58%	74%	73%	$x^2 = 5.9$
Education				$x^2 = 13.01^{**}$
Less than high school	24%	4%	13%	
High school diploma or some college	52%	56%	57%	
College degree or more	24%	40%	30%	
Worship attendance				$x^2 = 35.7^{***}$
Never	3%	13%	29%	
Rarely	31%	29%	8%	
Monthly	17%	11%	6%	
Weekly or more	49%	47%	57%	
Positive religious coping score (quintiles)				$x^2 = 19.4^{*}$
0–5	10%	19%	25%	
6–9	32%	27%	13%	
10–14	20%	21%	13%	
15–18	20%	21%	21%	
19+	18%	11%	28%	

$^{*}p<0.05.$ $^{**}p<0.01.$ $^{***}p<0.001.$

Prevalence of Negative Religious Coping

As can be seen from Table 3.2, a very high proportion of patients (76.5%–92.4%) responded "not at all" to the seven negative religious coping items. The proportion of patients who responded "quite a bit" or "a great deal" to each item ranged from 3.7% for "I wondered whether my church had abandoned me," to 13.5% for the item, "I questioned the power of God." When we examined responses to all seven items we found that slightly more than half of the total sample (52%) reported no negative religious coping, while 15% responded "quite a bit" or "a great deal" to two or more of the items.

Table 3.2 **Distribution of Negative Religious Coping Item Responses** (*N* = 238)

Item	Not at all (%)	Somewhat (%)	Quite a bit (%)	A great deal (%)
I wondered whether God had abandoned me.	76.5	12.6	5.5	5.5
I felt punished by God for my lack of devotion.	79.4	11.3	4.6	4.6
I wondered what I did for God to punish me.	79.4	11.8	3.4	5.5
I questioned God's love for me.	81.9	9.7	2.1	6.3
I wondered whether my church had abandoned me.	92.4	3.8	0.8	2.9
I decided the devil made this happen.	88.2	6.7	1.7	3.4
I questioned the power of God.	79.0	7.6	5.9	7.6

As can be seen from Table 3.3, for the total sample the mean total negative religious coping score was 2.2 (*SD* 3.4). Total negative religious coping scores ranged from 0–19 (the maximum possible score was 21).

Table 3.3 **Total Negative Religious Coping Score (Mean, SD) and Sample Characteristics**

Variable	Values	N	Mean	SD	Comparison[a]
All subjects		238	2.2	3.4	
Patient group	Diabetes	71	1.8	2.8	1.21
	CHF	70	2.7	4.1	
	Oncology	97	2.1	3.4	
Age	40 or less	18	4.1	4.4	15.46**
	41–50	32	2.9	3.9	
	51–60	58	2.1	3.2	
	61–70	68	2.1	3.6	
	71–80	53	1.7	3.0	
	81–90	9	0.3	0.7	
Gender	Male	105	2.6	4.0	−1.37
	Female	133	1.8	3.0	
Marital status	Married	142	2.3	3.5	−.01
	Other	106	2.2	3.4	
Race	White	164	2.2	3.5	−.21
	Other	74	2.1	3.3	
Education	Less than HS	33	2.2	2.7	.26
	HS diploma or some college	131	2.1	3.4	
	College degree or more	74	2.3	3.8	
Attend worship	Never	39	2.4	3.0	10.65*
	Rarely	50	3.3	4.6	
	Monthly	26	2.9	3.4	
	Weekly or more	123	1.5	2.9	
Positive Religious Coping Score	0–5	44	1.7	3.6	6.82
	6–9	55	2.5	3.3	
	10–14	42	1.5	2.4	
	15–18	49	2.0	3.3	
	19+	48	3.0	4.2	

[a]For multiple groups, the Kruskal-Wallis chi square statistic is reported. Paired tests report the z-score for the Mann-Whitney test.
*$p<.05$. **$p<.01$.

Correlates of Negative Religious Coping: Bi-Variate Associations

As can be seen from Table 3.3, the CHF patients had slightly higher levels of negative religious coping than the patients in the other two groups. However, this difference was not statistically significant. Age was the only demographic characteristic that was associated with negative religious coping, with younger patients reporting higher scores. There were also significant differences associated with worship attendance. Those who attended worship once a week or more reported the lowest negative religious coping scores. The highest scores were from those who rarely attended worship.

Correlates of Negative Religious Coping: Multi-Variate Associations

As can be seen from Table 3.4, in the multi-variate regression model, age had a significant inverse association with negative religious coping. Both measures of religion also had significant associations with negative religious coping, but in opposite directions. Compared to those who never attended services, those who attend at least once a week reported lower levels of negative religious coping. In contrast, higher levels of positive religious coping were associated with higher levels of negative religious coping, except for those with mid-range positive religious coping scores (10–14). In this adjusted model, the higher negative religious coping scores of the CHF patients, compared to the other two groups of patients, were statistically significant.

Table 3.4 **Demographic, Religious, and Diagnostic Predictors of Negative Religious Coping**[a] (*N* = 238)

Variable	Standardized Beta
Age	−0.289***
Gender	−0.091
Married	−0.012
Race	0.071
Education	−0.057
Worship attendance[b]	
Rarely	−0.024
Monthly	−0.053
Weekly or more	−0.251*
Positive Religious Coping Score[c]	
6–9	0.221*
10–14	0.148
15–18	0.241**
19+	0.280**
Diabetic patients	0.022
CHF patients	0.164*

[a] The regression equation employed the opposite of the inverse of negative religious coping score.
[b] The reference group was Never Attend.
[c] The reference group was Positive Religious Coping Score 0–5.
*$p<0.05$. **$p<0.01$. ***$p<0.001$.

Association between Negative Religious Coping and Mental Distress

As can be seen from Table 3.5, after adjustment for age and gender, negative religious coping was associated with higher levels of emotional distress and depressive symptoms in all three patient groups. In addition, it was associated with higher levels of anxiety and hostility in the CHF patients.

Table 3.5 **Negative Religious Coping and Emotional Distress**[a]

Measure (source)	Patient group		
	Diabetic	CHF	Oncology
Psychological distress (PAID)	.31*	—	—
Depressed mood (CMDI)	.35**	—	—
Emotional symptoms (LHFQ)	—	.30*	—
Depression (POMS)	—	.42***	.22*
Anxiety (POMS)	—	.32*	.16
Hostility (POMS)	—	.29*	.16
Emotional well-being (FACT-G)	—	—	-.23*

[a] The values are partial correlations, adjusted for age and gender. The opposite of the inverse of negative religious coping score was employed in this analysis.

Empty cell reflects the fact that different measures of mental distress were employed in each sample. *PAID* = Problem Areas in Diabetes Survey; *CMDI* = Chicago Multiple Depression Inventory; *LHFQ* = Minnesota Living with Heart Failure Questionnaire; *POMS* = Profile of Mood States; *FACT-G* = Functional Assessment of Cancer Therapy—General

*$p<.05$. **$p<.01$. ***$p<.001$.

DISCUSSION

Our results suggest that while the majority of patients in these three diagnostic groups report no religious struggle, as many as 15% may have moderate to high levels of negative religious coping. How does this compare to other clinical and community samples? The level of negative religious coping in these three patient groups was similar to that reported for a sample of 551 older medical patients (average score for seven negative religious coping items = 2.25 and 2.59 respectively) (Pargament, Smith, Koenig and Perez 1998). In 1998, the two negative religious coping items about feeling abandoned or punished by God were included in the General Social Survey (GSS). In this representative survey of 1,400 U.S. adults, 5% of the respondents reported they felt this way "quite a bit" or "a great deal" (Fetzer Institute/National Institute on Aging Working Group 1999). In contrast, 9% and 11% respectively of the patients in the present study gave similar responses for these two negative religious coping items, suggesting, as might be expected, a higher level of religious struggle in the clinical sample.

Correlates of Religious Struggle

CHF patients had higher levels of negative religious coping than patients with diabetes or cancer. There may be differences in the disease process or symptoms of CHF that place its sufferers at greater risk for religious struggle than those with other diseases. While both diabetes and CHF are chronic diseases, the progress of CHF frequently leaves little experience of relief. Common CHF symptoms, including difficulty concentrating due to a shortage of oxygen, shortness of breath, and heart palpitations, suggest a physical struggle to survive. Perhaps the course of the illness and/or its symptoms compromise the ability to resolve religious struggles associated with the illness. Although there is evidence that depression, anxiety, and hostility are associated with CHF (Rozanski, Blumenthal and Kaplan 1999), these variables do not account for all of the variance in negative religious coping in our sample.

The present study indicates that younger people are at greater risk than older people for experiencing religious struggles. This finding is consistent with the results from the GSS mentioned above, where the mean negative religious coping scores of those younger than 65 were higher than for those age 65 or older (Idler et al. 2003). Developing a serious illness, such as CHF or cancer, may cause greater religious struggle for younger people compared to older people. It is also possible that some forms of religious development or maturity come with age and protect older persons against religious struggles (Ingersoll-Dayton, Krause and Morgan 2002); alternatively, a cohort effect may exist, such that today's generation of young people are more likely to question or challenge their faith than were persons of previous generations. Among these three groups of patients there were no significant gender differences in negative religious coping. This is also consistent with the findings from the 1998 GSS (Idler et al. 2003).

Religious struggle had opposite associations with the two different dimensions of religion employed in the study. It was inversely associated with worship attendance, a measure of religious practice, but positively associated with a measure of another aspect of religious coping. Regarding the relationship with worship attendance, those who reported the most frequent attendance had lower levels of religious struggle. Unfortunately, the cross-sectional design of our study prevents us from determining whether painful, unresolved feelings associated with religious struggles contribute to low worship attendance, or whether those who attend services less frequently are more likely to experience such struggles. Further, in our study we were not able to test whether this association was confounded by patient's level of disability.

The results of the present study also suggest that the frequent use of positive religious coping does not indicate an absence of religious struggle. Positive religious coping is not the opposite of negative religious coping. Pargament and colleagues report small associations between the two sub-scales in both college students ($r=.17$, $p<.001$) and hospitalized patients ($r=.18$, $p<.001$) (Pargament, Smith, Koenig and Perez 1998). There was no association between brief measures of positive and negative religious coping in the GSS survey (Idler et al. 2003). It is possible that the relationship between the two measures may take at least two forms. For some, religion may be a source of comfort and strength, unburdened by guilt or doubt. In contrast, others may make frequent use of religion to cope with illness or other stressful events and this coping may have positive as well as negative elements. In the present study, evidence for this second pattern is seen in highest mean negative religious coping score among those with the highest level of positive religious coping.

Religious Struggle and Emotional Distress

Evidence from this and previous studies suggests that religious struggle cannot be reduced to negative affect or depression. The size of the partial correlations between negative religious coping and depressive symptoms in the three patient groups in this study (r from 0.22 to 0.42) suggests that religious struggle is associated with but cannot be reduced to depression. This is consistent with the finding that religious struggle was associated prospectively with poorer recovery in medical rehabilitation patients (Fitchett, Rybarczyk, DeMarco and Nicholas 1999) and increased mortality in elderly medical patients (Pargament, Koenig, Tarakeshwar and Hahn 2001), even after adjustment for emotional distress or depression.

Other investigators have reported an association between religious struggle and emotional distress (Taylor, Outlaw, Bernardo and Roy 1999; Fitchett, Rybarczyk, DeMarco and Nicholas 1999; Koenig, Pargament and Nielsen 1998; Trenholm, Trent and Compton 1998; Exline, Yali and Lobel 1999; Exline, Yali and Sanderson 2000; Mickley, Pargament, Brant and Hipp 1998). In a meta-analysis, which included eight studies that examined the association between negative religious coping and depressive symptoms, Smith and colleagues reported a weighted mean correlation between negative religious coping and depression of 0.136 (95% CI 0.06, 0.21) (Smith, McCullough and Poll 2003). The results of the present study are consistent with these findings and suggest that as many as 15% of medical patients may have levels of religious struggle that place them at risk for poor physical or mental health outcomes.

Limitations

A limitation of this study is that only one measure of religious struggle was used. Although the Brief RCOPE is frequently used to assess religious struggle, other measures exist,[2] and could aid in examining other forms that religious struggle may take. The items in the negative religious coping subscale of the Brief RCOPE assume a belief in God and the devil, as well as involvement in a religious congregation. Responses to these items appear to be a reasonable measure of religious struggle, but other measures are needed to assess other forms of spiritual or existential struggle with serious illness or life events.

In addition, the cross-sectional nature of our studies precluded an examination of several important issues associated with religious struggle. These include the causal relationship between religious struggle and emotional distress, as well as worship attendance. Patients who declined to participate in the studies often said they were feeling too ill to do so. If physical symptoms increase religious struggle, this sampling bias may have created an underestimation of the extent of religious struggle among these patients.

Further Research

Further research is needed to help us understand who is more likely to experience painful religious struggles, including differences that may be associated with different diagnoses. At present, very little is known about the course of religious struggle, but clinical experience and anecdotal evidence suggest that these struggles persist for some persons and resolve for others (Ingersoll-Dayton, Krause and Morgan 2002). Longitudinal research is needed to examine the causal relationship between religious struggle and emotional distress as well as religious activity. Additionally, further research is needed to enhance our understanding of the course of religious struggles, for whom they persist versus resolve, and what, if anything, helps people resolve their religious struggles. Further research is

2. For measures of alienation from God and difficulty forgiving God see: Exline, Yali, and Lobel, "When God Disappoints," 365–79; Exline, Yali, and Sanderson, "Guilt, Discord, and Alienation," 1481–96. For a Spiritual Injury Scale see: Berg, "The Use of the Computer," 11–25; Berg, Fonss, Reed, and VandeCreek, "The Impact of Religious Faith," 359–63.

also needed to determine if religious struggle is independent of other risk factors and to develop the best measures of this risk.

Clinical Implications

As physicians and other health professionals become more interested in the religious and spiritual dimension of their patients' lives (Maugans and Wadland 1991; McKee and Chappel 1992; Daalman and Frey 1998; Kristeller, Zumbrun and Schilling 1999), it becomes important to consider when to discuss religion or spirituality, and how such a discussion might best occur (Sloan et al. 2000). Barriers to physician discussions of spirituality include inadequate training and difficulty identifying the patients with whom such a discussion should be a priority (Ellis, Vinson and Ewigman 1999). Physicians have been encouraged to respond empathically in cases where patients' comments indicate troubling spiritual concerns (Lo et al. 2002). Being able to screen for religious struggle (Fitchett, 1999; Fitchett and Handzo 1998)—to efficiently assess and identify patients whose religious struggles may compromise their physical or mental health—may help physicians know when and how to discuss religion or spirituality with their patients. It may also guide them in knowing when and how to refer these patients for specialized spiritual care. Asking questions such as, "Is religion or faith important to you?" and, particularly if the answer is "No," following up with, "Has that always been the case?" is one approach to screening for religious struggle (Anandarajah and Hight 2001). Where patient's responses indicate possible religious struggle, clinicians should consider referral to a trained, professional chaplain or pastoral counselor (VandeCreek and Burton 2001).

ACKNOWLEDGEMENTS

We wish to acknowledge the following individuals for their important contributions to this work: Lucy Mullen, R.N., B.S., C.D.E. and Judy Carter, M.D. for their assistance with the diabetes study; David Rasmussen, M.Div. and Marc Silver, M.D. for their assistance with the CHF study; Judith Paice, Ph.D., R.N. and Trey Buchanan, Ph.D. for their assistance with the oncology study; Susan Shott, Ph.D. for her helpful statistical consultation; and Howard M. Kravitz, D.O., M.P.H., Susan A. Everson-Rose, Ph.D., M.P.H., and Carlos Mendes de Leon, Ph.D. for their helpful comments on an earlier version of the manuscript.

The diabetes study was supported in part by a grant from the History and Research Committee, North Central Region, Association for

Clinical Pastoral Education, Inc. The CHF study was supported by funds from Advocate Health Care, Oak Brook, Illinois. The cancer study was supported by a grant from the Coleman Foundation to the Robert H. Lurie Comprehensive Cancer Center of Northwestern University. This work was also supported in part by a Career Development Award from the NIA (K08AG20145) to George Fitchett.

REFERENCES

Albrecht, S. L. and Cornwall, M. 1989. "Life Events and Religious Change." *Review of Religious Research* 31:1, 23–38.

Anandarajah, G. and Hight, E. 2001. "Spirituality and Medical Practice: Using the HOPE Questions as a Practical Tool for Spiritual Assessment." *American Family Physician* 63:81–89.

Bennett, S. J., Baker, S. L. and Huster, G. A. 1998. "Quality of Life in Women with Heart Failure." *Health Care for Women International* 19:3, 217–29.

Berg, G. E. 1994. "The Use of the Computer as a Tool for Assessment and Research in Pastoral Care." *Journal of Health Care Chaplaincy* 6:1, 11–25.

Berg, G. E., Fonss, N., Reed, A. J. and VandeCreek, L. 1995. "The Impact of Religious Faith and Practice on Patients' Suffering from a Major Affective Disorder: A Cost Analysis." *Journal of Pastoral Care* 49:4, 359–63.

Bradshaw, A. and Fitchett, G. 2003. "'God, Why Did This Happen To Me?' Three Perspectives on Theodicy." *Journal of Pastoral Care and Counseling* 57:179–89.

Carpenter, J. S., Brockopp, D. Y. and Andrykowski, M. A. 1999. "Self-transformation as a Factor in the Self-esteem and Well-being of Breast Cancer Survivors. *Journal of Advanced Nursing* 29:1402–11.

Cella, D. F., Tulsky, D. S., Gray, G., Sarafian, B., Lloyd, S., Linn, E., Bonomi, A., Silberman, M., Yellen, S. B., Winicour, P., Brannon, J., Eckberg, K., Purl, S., Blendowski, C., Goodman, M., Barnicle, M., Stewart, I., McHale, M., Bonomi, P., Kaplan, E., Taylor, S., Thomas, C. and Harris, J. 1993. "The Functional Assessment of Cancer Therapy (FACT) Scale: Development and Validation of the General Measure." *Journal of Clinical Oncology* 11:3, 570–79.

Daalman, T. P. and Frey, B. 1998. "Prevalence and Practice of Physician Referral to Clergy and Pastoral Care Providers." *Archives of Family Medicine* 7:548–53.

Ellis, M. R., Vinson, D. C. and Ewigman, B. 1999. "Addressing Spiritual Concerns of Patients: Family Physicians' Attitudes and Practices." *Journal of Family Practice* 48:2, 105–9.

Ellison, C. G. and Taylor, R. J. 1996. "Turning to Prayer: Social and Situational Antecedents of Religious Coping among African Americans." *Review of Religious Research* 38:111–31.

Exline, J. J., Yali, A. M. and Lobel, M. 1999. "When God Disappoints: Difficulty Forgiving God and its Role in Negative Emotion." *Journal of Health Psychology* 4:3, 365–79.

Exline, J. J., Yali, A. M. and Sanderson, W. C. 2000. "Guilt, Discord, and Alienation: The Role of Religious Strain in Depression and Suicidality." *Journal of Clinical Psychology* 56:12, 1481–96.

Ferraro, K. F. and Kelley-Moore, J. A. 2000. "Religious Consolation among Men and Women: Do Health Problems Spur Seeking?" *Journal for the Scientific Study of Religion* 39:2, 220–34.

Fetzer Institute/National Institute on Aging Working Group. 1999. *Multidimensional Measurement of Religiousness/Spirituality for use in Health Research*. Kalamazoo, MI: The Fetzer Institute.

Fitchett, G. 1999. "Screening for Spiritual Risk." *Chaplaincy Today* 15:1, 2–12.

Fitchett, G. and Handzo, G. F. 1998. "Spiritual Assessment, Screening, and Intervention." In *Psycho-oncology*, edited by J. C. Holland, 790–808. New York: Oxford University Press.

Fitchett, G. and Roberts, P. A. 2003. "In the Garden with Andrea: Spiritual Assessment in End-of-Life Care." In *Walking Together: Physicians, Chaplains and Clergy Caring for the Sick*, edited by C. M. Puchalski, 23–31. Washington, DC: The George Washington Institute for Spirituality and Health. [Article 8 in this volume]

Fitchett, G., Rybarczyk, B. D., DeMarco, G. A. and Nicholas, J. J. 1999. "The Role of Religion in Medical Rehabilitation Outcomes: A Longitudinal Study." *Rehabilitation Psychology* 44:4, 333–53. [Article 1 in this volume]

Gorkin, L., Norvell, N. K., Rosen, R. C., Charles, E., Shumaker, S. A., McIntyre, K. M., Capone, R. J., Kostis, J., Niaura, R., Woods, P., Hosking, J., Garces, C., Handberg, E., Ahern, D. K. and Follick, M. J. 1993. "Assessment of Quality of Life as Observed from the Baseline Data of the Studies of Left Ventricular Dysfunction (SOLVD) Trial Quality-of-Life Substudy." *American Journal of Cardiology* 71:12, 1069–73.

Idler, E. L. 1987. "Religious Involvement and the Health of the Elderly: Some Hypotheses and an Initial Test." *Social Forces* 66:1, 226–38.

Idler, E. L. and Kasl, S. 1992. "Religion, Disability, Depression and the Timing of Death." *American Journal of Sociology* 97:4, 1052–79.

Idler, E. L., Musick, M. A., Ellison, C. G., George, L. K., Krause, N., Ory, M. G., Pargament, K. I., Powell, L. H., Underwood, L. G. and Williams, D. R. 2003. "Measuring Multiple Dimensions of Religion and Spirituality for Health Research." *Research on Aging* 25:327–65.

Ingersoll-Dayton, B., Krause, N. and Morgan, D. 2002. "Religious Trajectories and Transitions Over the Life Course." *International Journal of Aging and Human Development* 55:51–70.

Kaldjian, L. C., Jekel, J. F. and Friedland, G. 1998. "End-of-Life Decisions in HIV-positive Patients: The Role of Spiritual Beliefs." *AIDS* 12:103–7.

Koenig, H. G., Pargament, K. I. and Nielsen, J. 1998. "Religious Coping and Health Status in Medically Ill Hospitalized Older Adults." *Journal of Nervous and Mental Disease* 186:513–21.

Kristeller, J. L., Zumbrun, C. S. and Schilling, R. F. 1999. "'I Would if I Could': How Oncologists and Oncology Nurses Address Spiritual Distress in Cancer Patients." *Psycho-Oncology* 8:5, 451–58.

Lo, B., Ruston, D., Kates, L. W., Arnold, R. M., Cohen, C. B., Faber-Langendoen, K., Pantilat, S. Z., Puchalski, C. M., Quill, T. R., Rabow, M. W., Schreiber, S., Sulmasy, D. P. and Tulsky, J. A. 2002. "Discussing Religious and Spiritual Issues at the End of Life: A Practical Guide for Physicians." *Journal of the American Medical Association* 287:749–54.

Maugans, T. A. and Wadland, W. C. 1991. "Religion and Family Medicine: A Survey of Physicians and Patients." *Journal of Family Practice* 32:2, 210–13.

McKee, D. D. and Chappel, J. N. 1992. "Spirituality and Medical Practice. *Journal of Family Practice* 35:2, 201–8.

McNair, D. M., Lorr, M. and Droppleman, L. F. 1992. *EdITS Manual for the Profile of Mood States*. San Diego: Educational and Industrial Testing Service.

Mickley, J. R., Pargament, K. I., Brant, C. R. and Hipp, K. M. 1998. "God and the Search for Meaning among Hospice Caregivers." *The Hospice Journal* 13:1–17.

Murberg, T. A., Bru, E., Torbjorn, A. and Svebak, S. 1998. "Functional Status and Depression among Men and Women with Congestive Heart Failure." *International Journal of Psychiatry in Medicine* 28:3, 273–91.

Nyenhuis, D. L., Luchetta, T., Yamamoto, C., Terrien, A., Bernardin, L., Rao, S. M. and Garron, D. C. 1998. "The Development, Standardization, and Initial Validation of the Chicago Multiscale Depression Inventory." *Journal of Personality Assessment* 70:2, 386–401.

Oxman, T. E., Freeman, D. H. Jr. and Manheimer, E. D. 1995. "Lack of Social Participation or Religious Strength and Comfort as Risk Factors for Death after Cardiac Surgery in the Elderly." *Psychosomatic Medicine* 57:5–15.

Pargament, K. I. 1997. *The Psychology of Religion and Coping: Theory, Research, Practice*. New York: Guilford.

Pargament, K. I., Koenig, H. G., Tarakeshwar, N and Hahn, J. 2001. "Religious Struggle as a Predictor of Mortality among Medically Ill Elderly Patients: A Two-Year Longitudinal Study." *Archives of Internal Medicine* 161:15, 1881–85.

Pargament, K. I., Smith, B. W., Koenig, H. G. and Perez, L. 1998. "Patterns of Positive and Negative Religious Coping with Major Life Stressors." *Journal for the Scientific Study of Religion* 37:4, 710–24.

Polonsky, W. H., Anderson, B. J., Lohrer, P. A., Welch, G., Jacobson, A. M., Aponte, J. E. and Schwartz, C. E. 1995. "Assessment of Diabetes-related Distress." *Diabetes Care* 18:6, 754–60.

Rector, T. S., Frances, G. S. and Cohn, J. N. 1987. "Patients' Self-assessment of their Congestive Heart Failure, Part I: Patient Perceived Dysfunction and Its Poor Correlation with Maximal Exercise Tests." *Heart Failure* 3:192–96.

Rector, T. S., Kubo, S. H. and Cohn, J. N. 1987. "Patients' Assessment of their Congestive Heart Failure, Part II: Content, Reliability, and Validity of a New Measure, the Minnesota Living with Heart Failure Questionnaire." *Heart Failure* 3:198–209.

Rozanski, A., Blumenthal, J. A. and Kaplan, J. 1999. "Impact of Psychological Factors on the Pathogenesis of Cardiovascular Disease and Implications for Therapy." *Circulation* 99:2192–19.

Sloan, R. P., Bagiella, E., VandeCreek, L., Hover, M., Casalone, C., Hirsch, T. J., Hasan, J., Kreger, R. and Poulos, P. 2000. "Should Physicians Prescribe Religious Activity?" *New England Journal of Medicine* 342:25, 1913–16.

Smith, T. B., McCullough, M. E. and Poll, J. 2003. "Religiousness and Depression: Evidence for a Main Effect and the Moderating Influence of Stressful Life Events." *Psychological Bulletin* 129:614–36.

Strawbridge, W. J., Shema, S. J., Cohen, R. D., Roberts, R. E. and Kaplan, G. A. 1998. "Religiosity Buffers Effects of Some Stressors on Depression but Exacerbates Others." *Journal of Gerontology: Social Sciences* 53B, 3, S118–S126.

Taylor, E. J., Outlaw, F. H., Bernardo, T. R. and Roy, A. 1999. "Spiritual Conflicts Associated with Praying about Cancer." *Psycho-oncology* 8:386–94.

Trenholm, P., Trent, J. and Compton, W. C. 1998. "Negative Religious Conflict as a Predictor of Panic Disorder." *Journal of Clinical Psychology* 54:59–65.

VandeCreek, L. and Burton, L. 2001. "Professional Chaplaincy: Its Role and Importance in Healthcare." *Journal of Pastoral Care* 55:1, 81–97.

Welch, G. W., Jacobson, A. and Polonsky, W. 1997. "The Problem Areas in Diabetes Scale: An Evaluation of its Clinical Utility." *Diabetes Care* 20:5, 760–66.

ARTICLE 4

Re-examining the Contributions of Faith, Meaning, and Peace to Quality of Life

A Report from the American Cancer Society's Studies of Cancer Survivors–II (SCS–II)[1]

—Andrea L. Canada
Rosemead School of Psychology, Biola University, La Mirada, CA

—Patricia E. Murphy
Religion, Health, and Human Values, Rush University Medical Center, Chicago, IL

—George Fitchett
Religion, Health, and Human Values, Rush University Medical Center, Chicago, IL

—Kevin Stein
Behavioral Research Center, American Cancer Society, Atlanta, GA

WHEN WE WERE DEVELOPING *the Department's research program in the 1990s, Rush had a strong team of clinical psychologists/researchers in our*

1. A. L. Canada, P. E. Murphy, G. Fitchett, and K. Stein. 2016. "Re-examining the Contributions of Faith, Meaning, and Peace to Quality of Life: A Report from the American Cancer Society's Studies of Cancer Survivors–II (SCS–II)." *Annals of Behavioral Medicine* 50:1, 79–86. https://doi.org/10.1007/s12160-015-9735-y

cancer center. I was familiar with the developing research about the role of religion/spirituality in coping with cancer and approached them about possible collaboration. They were very supportive and became some of my first research colleagues and mentors. During that time, I assisted them in developing what has become a widely used measure of spiritual well-being, the FACIT—Sp. This paper shows how we used FACIT—Sp scores, along with other data from American Cancer Society's studies, to recommend a new understanding of how meaning, peace and faith contribute to cancer patients' quality of life. This is one of a series of papers we published based on the ACS SCS I and II data, and it made an important contribution to understanding the role of religion/spirituality in coping with cancer.

ABSTRACT

Background

Prior research on spirituality in cancer survivors has often failed to distinguish the specific contributions of faith, meaning, and peace, dimensions of spiritual wellbeing, to quality of life (QoL), and has misinterpreted mediation analyses with these indices.

Purpose

We hypothesized a model in which faith would have a significant indirect effect on survivors' functional QoL, mediated through meaning and/or peace.

Methods

Data were from the American Cancer Society's Study of Cancer Survivors-II ($N = 8405$). Mediation analyses were conducted with the Functional Assessment of Chronic Illness Therapy—Spiritual Well-being Scale (FACIT—Sp) predicting the mental component summary (i.e., mental functioning) as well as the physical component summary (i.e., physical functioning) of the SF-36.

Results

The indirect effect of faith through meaning on mental functioning, 0.4303 (95% CI, 0.3988, 0.4649), and the indirect effect of faith through meaning and peace on physical functioning, 0.1769 (95% CI, 0.1505, 0.2045), were significant.

Discussion

The study findings suggest that faith makes a significant contribution to cancer survivors' functional QoL. Should future longitudinal research replicate these findings, investigators may need to reconsider the role of faith in oncology QoL studies.

Key words: Cancer survivors; Faith; Meaning; Peace; Quality of life

INTRODUCTION

Improvements in cancer screening and treatment have led to the existence of nearly 14.5 million cancer survivors in the USA, and, as cancer treatment improves and the population ages, this number is expected to grow (American Cancer Society 2014). Most, but not all, cancer survivors report good health and good quality of life (QoL) (Stein, Syrjala and Andrykowski 2008). Estimates of the proportion of cancer survivors who experience problematic physical and/or emotional symptoms, however, vary. One review found reports of depression in 10 to 25% of cancer patients (Pirl 2004). Another review of long-term survivors established pooled rates of 20 to 30% of ongoing cancer-related physical and psychological problems (Foster et al. 2009). Whereas rates of psychosocial distress among survivors vary, one consistent finding is that nearly 80% of cancer survivors report that religion/spirituality (R/S) is important in coping with their cancer (Feher and Maly 1999; Silberfarb et al. 1991). For example, in a survey of 752 cancer survivors with diverse diagnoses, 77% reported using prayer to assist them in coping (Yates et al. 2005).

Evidence from studies of survivors of many types of cancer demonstrates that R/S is associated with better QoL. The largest such study (N = 1610) found that spiritual well-being, a dimension of R/S, was positively associated with overall QoL in models that adjusted for other dimensions of QoL and social desirability (Brady et al. 1999). There are similar findings for survivors of breast (Cotton et al. 1999), prostate (Krupski et al. 2006), ovarian (Canada et al. 2006), and advanced cancer (Daugherty et al. 2005). (Reviews of this literature are available; see: Mytko and Knight 1999; Sherman and Simonton 2007; Stefanek, McDonald and Hess 2005; Visser, Garssen and Vingerhoets 2010; Masters and Hooker 2013). However, with the exception of the study by Brady et al. (1999), many of these studies used small, homogeneous, unrepresentative samples, and there have been no studies of this association in large, diverse samples of long-term survivors.

An additional problem with the existing evidence is the way in which investigators have modeled and interpreted the effects of different dimensions of R/S. For example, a common finding reported in studies that simultaneously tested both factors in the two-factor model of the Functional Assessment of Chronic Illness Therapy—Spiritual Well-being Scale (FACIT—Sp) (Peterman et al. 2002) is that meaning/peace has a stronger association with QoL than faith (Brady et al. 1999; Visser, Garssen and Vingerhoets 2010). It is not uncommon for investigators (e.g., Yanez et al., 2009) to misinterpret this as evidence for "the general superiority" of meaning/peace over faith for the QoL and adjustment of cancer survivors (p. 736). An alternative possibility is a mediated relationship. That is, to paraphrase MacKinnon (2008), meaning and peace are intermediate in the theorized causal pathway between faith and QoL. Evidence for such a mediated relationship has been found by two investigators (Edmondson et al. 2008; Nelson et al. 2009). However, in these studies, proper consideration was not given to the indirect effects of faith on QoL. For example, Edmonson et al. (2008) described the association between faith and QoL as "fully accounted for" by the mediator meaning/peace (p. 165). This interpretation has led these and other investigators (e.g., Yanez et al. 2009) to conclude that it is primarily meaning that contributes to survivors' QoL and that faith is of little importance.

Contrary to prior interpretations of such findings, we propose that faith plays a more central role in survivors' QoL via indirect effects through meaning and peace. This hypothesis is informed by theoretical work on the role of R/S in finding meaning. For example, Park (2005) describes a model in which R/S plays a key role in shaping a person's larger, global framework of beliefs. When events, such as a cancer diagnosis or long-term symptoms occur, a person's global framework of beliefs (i.e., faith) plays an important role in ascribing significance (i.e., meaning) to the situation. Park et al. (2008) have also reported evidence among congestive heart failure patients that prior religiosity influences subsequent meaning. This theoretical model and related research support our view that meaning and peace are mediators of the way that faith influences cancer survivors' QoL.

Evidence from participants in the American Cancer Society's Studies of Cancer Survivors-II (SCS-II) indicates that R/S is a very important resource for helping survivors cope with their disease; 69% reported that R/S was helpful for coping with their cancer experience "very much" or "quite a bit," whereas fewer than 10% reported it was "not at all" helpful (Canada et al. 2013). Findings from this study also revealed that factors like medical status (e.g., number of comorbid conditions) were associated with lower levels of meaning and peace but had negligible associations with faith. This evidence suggests that faith may be a more dispositional dimension of R/S, influencing QoL by strengthening meaning and/or peace. In addition, two studies (Canada et al. 2008; Murphy et al. 2010) recently reported a new model for the FACIT—Sp, which separates the former meaning/peace factor into a cognitive factor (meaning, "I have a reason for living") and an affective one (peace, "I feel peaceful"). The third factor, reflecting the salience of faith ("I find strength in my faith"), did not warrant change.

Whereas existing evidence suggests that R/S makes positive contributions to cancer survivors' QoL, we believe there is a serious misunderstanding about how this occurs, that is, about the contribution of specific dimensions of spiritual well-being (meaning, peace, and faith) to QoL. Thus, the objective of this study was to clarify the relationship between these dimensions of spiritual well-being and cancer survivors' QoL. We propose a plausible model in which faith influences both meaning and peace and, through their mediation, is related to better functional QoL (Fig. 1). We test the following related hypotheses using data from the SCS-II:

> Hypothesis 1: Faith has an indirect effect ($a_1 \cdot b_1$) on mental functioning, an important aspect of QoL, measured by the SF-36 mental component summary, through the mediator meaning as well as a direct effect (c') on QoL. The sum of these comprises the total effect (c) of faith on mental functioning.
>
> Hypothesis 2: Faith has an indirect effect ($a_1 \cdot b_1$) on physical functioning, also an important aspect of QoL, measured by the SF-36 physical component summary, through the mediators meaning and peace as well as a direct effect (c') on QoL. The sum of these comprises the total effect (c) of faith on physical functioning.

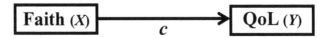

A. Model for Total Effects of Faith on QoL

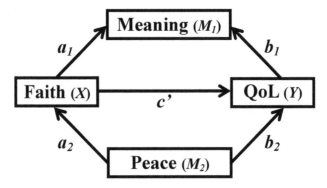

B. Model for Direct and Indirect Effects of Faith on QoL

Figure 4.1 Hypothesized Model for Mediation

$a_1 \cdot b_1$ indirect path from faith to QoL via meaning; $a_2 \cdot b_2$ indirect path from faith to QoL via peace; c total path from faith to QoL; c′, direct path from faith to QoL. Models control for age, race/ethnicity, gender, marital status, region of the USA, educational level, income level, language chosen for survey, diagnosis, time since diagnosis, and number of comorbid conditions; QoL quality of life.

METHODS

Participants

Data for this study are from the American Cancer Society's Studies of Cancer Survivors-II (SCS-II), a national, cross-sectional study of cancer survivors' QoL and psychosocial functioning (Smith et al. 2007; Stein et al. 2006). SCS-II participants were age 18 or older at the time of diagnosis; had stage I–IV cancer; were diagnosed either 2, 5, or 10 years prior to the time of sampling; and were able to read/write English or Spanish. The sample was stratified by cancer type (6 diagnoses), time since diagnosis, and race/ethnicity (minorities were oversampled to ensure adequate representation). Of the total of 36,647 cancer survivors who were eligible from cancer registries in 14 different states, this study used data from the 8405 participants with complete or imputed data and whose race/ethnicity was White, Black, or

Hispanic. A previous publication provides detailed information regarding the identification and selection of cases, physician notification/consent, recruitment, and data collection procedures by the American Cancer Society (Smith et al. 2007). Information about imputation and selection of cases in this study has also been previously described (Murphy et al. 2010).

Measures

Spiritual well-being was measured with the three factor model of the Functional Assessment of Chronic Illness Therapy—Spiritual Well-being scale (Peterman et al. 2002; Canada et al. 2008; Murphy et al. 2010). The three subscales, meaning, peace, and faith, each include four items with Likert scale responses from 0 (not at all) to 4 (very much). Examples of items representing each subscale are "I have a reason for living" (meaning), "I feel a sense of harmony within myself" (peace), and "I find strength in my faith or spiritual beliefs" (faith).

Functional QoL was measured with scales from the SF-36 (Ware, Kosinki and Keller 1994; Ware and Sherbourne 1992). The SF-36 is a multipurpose, short-form, self-report, health survey: the physical component summary is a composite measure consisting of items measuring physical functioning (i.e., ability to perform physical activities, including bathing and climbing stairs); the mental component summary is a composite measure consisting of items measuring mental functioning (i.e., ability to engage in social functioning, or lack of emotional problems' interference with functioning). This study used scores based on published norms (Ware, Kosinki and Keller, 1994). Higher scores on the component summaries indicate better functional QoL.

Demographic covariates included age, gender, race/ethnicity (White, Black, Hispanic), marital status, level of education, family income, language of the survey, and region of the country. Medical covariates included in the analyses were cancer type (breast, prostate, colorectal, bladder, uterine, melanoma), time since diagnosis (2, 5, 10 year), and sum of comorbid conditions (none, one, two, ≥three).

Analyses

Recent developments in mediation analysis point to problems with Baron and Kenny's (1986) widely used method. For mediation analysis in this report, we used the approach of MacKinnon and others (MacKinnon 2008; Ryu, West and Sousa 2009; Hayes 2013). Specifically, we used the PROCESS macro for SPSS v.2.13 (Hayes 2015) to conduct the statistical analyses of our hypothesized models and estimated effect sizes. The methods behind this procedure are described by Hayes (2013). The first step in PROCESS provides the associations of faith with the mediators meaning (path $a1$) and peace (path $a2$) when demographic and medical variables are controlled. (See Fig. 1 for hypothesized model.) The next step determines the b paths by determining the coefficients for meaning and/or for peace as predictors of the given QoL outcome when all variables in the model are controlled. The third step establishes the direct effect of faith (c' path) as a predictor of QoL controlling for the demographic and medical variables. The final step determines the indirect effects for each mediator, which are determined by the product of the a path with the associated b path. The total indirect effect is the sum of indirect effects for each mediator in the model. This information supports the testing of a plausible causal model such as Fig. 1B. Preacher and Hayes (2008) provide an argument for using bootstrap estimates for the 95% confidence intervals to avoid the problem of a non-normal distribution that is common for indirect effects (Fritz, Taylor and MacKinnon 2012). We chose to use 5000 bootstrap samples with data replacement. A confidence interval that includes zero represents non-significance.

RESULTS

The characteristics of the SCS-II sample can be seen in Table 4.1. A previous publication offers a comparison of those who completed the survey vs. non-responders (Smith et al. 2007). The authors found that the groups generally less likely to respond were the elderly, males, and non-Whites as well as those with certain medical characteristics (e.g., survivors of bladder cancer, cohorts at longer periods post-diagnosis). The mean age of participants was 63 years of age, and most survivors were married (71.6%). Nearly half were male (44.9%). Whereas the majority of the sample was White (81.2%), there were 914 Black and 664 Hispanic participants (10.9 and 7.9%, respectively). Approximately one in five of the Hispanic participants completed the survey in Spanish. The level of education and annual income reported by participants were widely distributed with 40% having a high school education or less and more than half making less than US$40,000/year. Three quarters of the sample included survivors of breast, prostate, or colorectal cancer. Consistent with the ACS SCS-II study design, 34.8% of participants were 2-year survivors, 35.7% 5-year survivors, and 29.4% 10-year survivors. Approximately 75% of the participants had one or more comorbid conditions.

Table 4.1 **Sample Demographic Characteristics** (*N* = 8405)

Characteristic	Values	
Age	Mean	62.7 (11.9)
	Range	23.7–100
Gender	Female	4632 (55.1 %)
	Male	3773 (44.9 %)
Race/ethnicity	White	6827 (81.2 %)
	Black	914 (10.9 %)
	Hispanic	664 (7.9 %)
Marital status	Married	6017 (71.6 %)
	Not married	2388 (28.4 %)
Education level	Less than HS	1042 (12.4 %)
	HS	2211 (26.3 %)
	Some college	2455 (29.2 %)
	College +	2697 (32.1 %)
Annual income	less than 20K	1408 (16.8 %)
	20–39K	3189 (37.9 %)
	40–74K	2350 (28.0 %)
	75K+	1458 (17.3 %)
Language	English	8266 (98.3 %)
	Spanish	139 (1.7 %)
Region	Northeast	1762 (21.0 %)
	South	497 (5.9 %)
	Midwest	2571 (30.6 %)
	West	3575 (42.5 %)
Diagnosis	Breast	2618 (31.1 %)
	Prostate	2056 (24.5 %)
	Colorectal	1782 (21.1 %)
	Bladder	535 (6.4 %)
	Uterine	684 (8.1 %)
	Melanoma	730 (8.7 %)
Time since diagnosis	2 years	2933 (34.9 %)
	5 years	2999 (35.7 %)
	10 years	2473 (29.4 %)

	None	2055 (24.4 %)
Comorbid conditions	One	2104 (25.0 %)
	Two	1790 (21.3 %)
	Three or more	2456 (29.2 %)

Descriptive statistics for the FACIT—Sp and SF-36 are provided in Table 4.2. Scores on the mental component summary and the physical component summary in the current study fell well within one standard deviation of the mean of the normative samples. The average FACIT—Sp Total Score for the present sample (37.35, SD=8.6) is similar to that reported by Peterman et al. (2002) (mean = 38.5, SD = 8.1); however, the current faith subscale score is somewhat lower ((Peterman et al. 2002) mean faith=13.3, SD=3.6). Table 4.3 reports the zero order correlations among the spiritual well-being and QoL measures.

Table 4.2 **Sample Spirituality and Quality of Life Characteristics**

Scale	Mean	SD	Possible range	Actual range
FACIT—Sp				
Meaning	13.66	2.8	0–16	0–16
Peace	11.98	3.4	0–16	0–16
Faith	11.70	4.3	0–16	0–16
Total	37.35	8.6	0–48	0–48
SF-36				
MCS	52.2	9.6	0–100	9.1–78.4
PCS	46.8	10.8	0–100	11.9–73.8

MCS mental component summary, *PCS* physical component summary

Table 4.3 **Correlations Among Measures of Spirituality and Quality of Life**

	Faith	Meaning	Peace	SF36-MCS	SF36-PCS
Faith	1				
Meaning	0.398***	1			
Peace	0.433***	0.688***	1		
SF36-MCS	0.233***	0.530***	0.644***	1	
SF36-PCS	0.053***	0.268***	0.246***	0.100***	1

SF36-MCS mental component summary, *SF36-PCS* physical component summary
***$p < 0.001$

A mediation analysis using only meaning as a mediator of the impact of faith on the mental component summary of the SF-36, to avoid inflation of results from similar items in the measurement of peace and mental functioning, included age, racial/ethnicity, gender, marital status, level of education, income level, years since diagnosis, number of comorbidities, type of cancer, region of the country, and language of the survey (English or Spanish) as covariates and accounted for 35% of the variance in the mental component summary. The total indirect effect of the mediation was 0.430 with a completely standardized indirect effect of faith through meaning on the mental component summary of 0.20. For a unit increase in faith, there was an indirect effect of an increase of 0.430 in the mental component summary (Table 4.4A). An analysis with 5000 bootstrap samples did not include 0 in any of the 95% confidence intervals, indicating the indirect effects were significant. The direct effect of faith on the mental component summary after mediation was 0.099; SE=0.022, t=4.440, p=0.000. This implies that there was also an increase of 0.099 in mental component summary for a unit increase in faith. The model for the effects of faith on mental functioning is depicted in Fig. 2.

Table 4.4 **Models of the Effect of Faith on QoL with Mediators of Meaning and Peace**

A. Unstandardized coefficients for the associations of meaning with faith for model predicting mental functioning

	Coefficients	SE	t	p
Total effect of faith on MCS	0.530	0.023	23.321	0.000
Effects of faith on MCS in mediated model				
Direct effect of faith on mediator	Coefficient	SE	t	p
Meaning	0.2704	0.0064	42.3143	0.000
Direct effect of faith with MCS	0.0993	0.0224	4.4400	0.000
Indirect effects of faith on MCS	Effect	Boot SE	Boot LLCI	Boot ULCI
Meaning	0.4303	0.0168	0.3988	0.4649

B. Unstandardized coefficients for the association of meaning and peace with faith for model predicting physical functioning

	Coefficients	SE	t	p
Total effect of faith on PCS	0.198	0.023	8.51	0.000
Effects of faith on PCS in mediated model				
Direct effect of faith on mediator	Coefficient	SE	t	p
Meaning	0.2704	0.0064	42.3143	0.000
Peace	0.3479	0.0076	45.7505	0.000
Direct effect of faith with PCS	0.0210	0.0261	0.8050	0.4209
Indirect effects of faith on PCS	Effect	Boot SE	Boot LLCI	Boot ULCI
Total	0.1769	0.0138	0.1505	0.2045
Meaning	0.0704	0.0141	0.0420	0.0979
Peace	0.1065	0.0155	0.0766	0.1370

Model for total effects controls for age, race/ethnicity, gender, marital status, region of the USA, educational level, income level, language chosen for survey, diagnosis, time since diagnosis, and number of comorbid conditions; reported results are unstandardized; mediated models also include mediator of meaning for MCS and mediators of meaning and peace for PCS

QoL quality of life, *MCS* mental component summary, *PCS* physical component summary, *LLCI* lower limit confidence interval, *ULCI* upper limit confidence interval

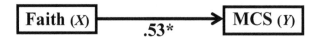

A. Model for Total Effects of Faith on Mental Functioning

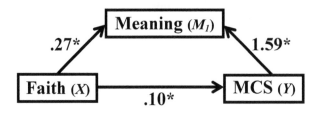

B. Model for Direct and Indirect Effects of Faith on Mental Functioning

Figure 4.2 The Effects of Faith on Mental Functioning

Models control for race/ethnicity, gender, marital status, region of the USA, educational level, income level, language chosen for survey, diagnosis, time since diagnosis, and number of comorbid conditions; reported results are unstandardized; MCS mental component summary. *p<0.001

The model testing meaning and peace as mediators of the association between faith and the physical component summary of the SF-36 and with the controls noted above, accounted for 36% of the variance in the physical component summary. The total indirect effect of the mediation was 0.177. None of the bootstrapped confidence intervals included 0, indicating that all the indirect effects were significant. For a unit increase in faith, there was an indirect effect of an increase of 0.177 in the physical component summary. The indirect effect through meaning was 0.070 and through peace was 0.107 (Table 4.4B). The completely standardized total indirect effect was 0.08. The direct effect of faith on the physical component summary after mediation was 0.021; SE=0.026, t=0.805, p=0.421. The model for the effects of faith on physical functioning is presented in Fig. 3.

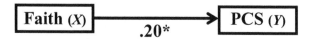

A. Model for Total Effects of Faith on Physical Functioning

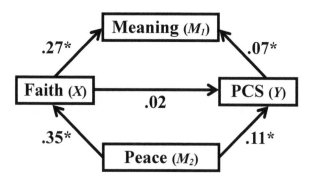

B. Model for Direct and Indirect Effects of Faith on Physical Functioning

Figure 4.3 The Effects of Faith on Physical Functioning

Models control for race/ethnicity, gender, marital status, region of the USA, educational level, income level, language chosen for survey, diagnosis, time since diagnosis, and number of comorbid conditions; reported results are unstandardized; PCS physical component summary. *p<0.001

DISCUSSION

The aim of this investigation was to test a model of the direct and indirect effects of faith on cancer survivors' QoL. The findings support our hypothesis that faith makes significant and meaningful contributions to cancer survivors' functional QoL, both directly and indirectly through meaning and peace. They also suggest that investigators (Yanez et al. 2009; Edmondson et al. 2008; Nelson et al. 2009) who imply that the role of faith in QoL is minimal or non-existent have misinterpreted their findings. Park and colleagues (2013) describe a meaning system derived from religion (i.e., faith) that is likely universal to the human experience. This religious meaning system serves as the source for many essential functions, including anxiety management, self-regulation, agency, control, and identity. In the face of stress, the importance of religion appears to only increase as it provides comfort, reduces uncertainty, addresses existential questions, and aids in the reinterpretation of negative events as opportunities for growth. The results described here are consistent with a religious meaning system and stand in contrast to the reports of other studies (Yanez et al. 2009; Edmondson et al. 2008) that have asserted it is primarily meaning, not faith, that accounts for the association between spiritual well-being and QoL in survivors of cancer. Our finding that faith has a larger effect on mental functioning than physical functioning is consistent with other reports (e.g., Koenig, 2012; Meisenhelder, & Chandler, 2002). In fact, Koenig (2012) states, "One would expect stronger relationships between R/S and mental health since R/S involvement consists of psychological, social, and behavioral aspects that are more 'proximally' related to mental health than to physical health" (p. 3).

Several limitations should be kept in mind as the findings from this study are considered. Religion and spirituality have many dimensions (Fetzer Institute/National Institute on Aging Working Group 1999), and we have only examined three general dimensions (meaning, peace, and faith) with one measure, the FACIT—Sp. Likewise, our QoL indices are limited to the two component summaries from the SF-36. In addition, data presented here are cross-sectional. The mediation models provided include implications about causality that should be tested in future longitudinal studies. Another limitation is related to the general observation that certain groups are less likely to respond to surveys. Systematic exclusion of those who are minorities, elderly, and/or more ill may lead to an overestimation of QoL. Although the extent to which this occurred in SCS-II sample is unclear, selection bias should be considered when interpreting QoL indicators from these data.

The findings reported here indicate a number of issues to be addressed in future research. A notable portion of the research in religion/spirituality and cancer has employed the FACIT—Sp (Bredle et al. 2011). In light of its widespread use, several concerns about the FACIT—Sp must be considered, including what it measures. Critics of the FACIT—Sp suggest the items simply measure emotional well-being or quality of life (Visser, Garssen and Vingerhoets 2010; Hall, Meador and Koenig 2008). This debate about the FACIT—Sp reflects the ongoing debate about definitions of religion and spirituality (e.g., Miller and Thoresen 2003; Oman 2013; Pargament et al. 2013; Zinnbauer, Pargament and Scott 1999; Zinnbauer and Pargament 2005). Investigators should become familiar with the literature about definitions and measurement of R/S before assuming that, because of its widespread use, the FACIT—Sp is the best measure for a given project. Future research will benefit from a move beyond broad measures of generic R/S or spiritual well-being, such as the FACIT—Sp, to examine the role of more specific dimensions of R/S in coping with cancer. Once this goal is accomplished, the models described here will need to be retested.

In the current study, faith made a direct contribution to cancer survivors' functional QoL as well as an indirect contribution mediated through meaning and peace. If these findings are replicated in longitudinal designs, investigators will need to reconsider the role of faith in studies of QoL with oncology populations.

ACKNOWLEDGEMENTS

The American Cancer Society (ACS) Study of Cancer Survivors-II (SCS-II) was funded as an intramural research project conducted by the ACS Behavioral Research Center (BRC). We wish to acknowledge the cooperation and efforts of the cancer registries from the states of Arizona, California (regions 2–6), Colorado, Delaware, Illinois, Iowa, Maine, Massachusetts, Michigan, Nebraska, New Jersey, Pennsylvania, Washington, and Wyoming. We also thank the staff of the hundreds of hospitals contributing cases to the participating cancer registries; their data made this research possible. Lastly, we salute the thousands of cancer survivors, their physicians, and their loved ones who contributed to the collection of these data. The authors assume full responsibility for analyses and interpretation of these data.

Authors' Statement of Conflict of Interest and Adherence to Ethical Standards

Authors Canada, Murphy, Fitchett, and Stein declare that they have no conflict of interest. All procedures performed in studies involving human participants were in accordance with the ethical standards of the institutional and/or national research committee and with the 1964 Helsinki declaration and its later amendments or comparable ethical standards.

Informed consent

Informed consent was obtained from all individual participants included in the study.

REFERENCES

American Cancer Society. 2014. *Cancer Treatment and Survivorship Facts, & Figures 2013–2014.* Atlanta: American Cancer Society.

Baron, R. M. and Kenny, D. A. 1986. "The Moderator-Mediator Variable Distinction in Social Psychological Research: Conceptual, Strategic, and Statistical Considerations." *Journal of Personality and Social Psychology* 51:6, 1173–82.

Brady, M. J., Peterman, A. H., Fitchett, G., Mo, M., Cella, D. 1999. "A Case for Including Spirituality in Quality of Life Measurement in Oncology." *Psycho-Oncology* 8:5, 417–28.

Bredle, J. M., Salsman, J. M., Debb, S. M., Arnold, B. J. and Cella D. 2011. "Spiritual Well-being as a Component of Health-related Quality of Life: The Functional Assessment of Chronic Illness Therapy—Spiritual Well-Being Scale (FACIT—Sp)." *Religion* 2:1, 77–94.

Canada, A. L., Fitchett, G., Murphy, P. E., Stein, K., Portier, K., Crammer, C. and Peterman, A. H. 2013. "Racial/Ethnic Differences in Spiritual Well-being among Cancer Survivors." *Journal of Behavioral Medicine* 36:5, 441–53.

Canada, A. L., Murphy, P. E., Fitchett, G., Peterman, A. H. and Schover, L. R. 2008. "A 3-Factor Model for the FACIT—Sp." *Psycho-Oncology* 17:9, 908–916.

Canada, A. L., Parker, P. A., de Moor, J. S., Basen-Engquist, K., Ramondetta, L. M., Cohen, L. 2006. "Active Coping Mediates the Association between Religion/Spirituality and Quality of Life in Ovarian Cancer." *Gynecologic Oncology* 101:1, 102–7.

Cotton, S. P., Levine, E. G., Fitzpatrick, C. M., Dold, K. H., Targ, E. 1999. "Exploring the Relationship among Spiritual Well-being, Quality of Life, and Psychological Adjustment in Women with Breast Cancer." *Psycho-Oncology* 8:5, 429–38.

Daugherty, C. K., Fitchett, G., Murphy, P. E., Peterman, A. H., Banik, D. M., Hlubocky, F. and Tartaro, J. 2005. "Trusting God and Medicine: Spirituality in Advanced Cancer Patients Volunteering for Clinical Trials of Experimental Agents." *Psycho-Oncology* 14:2, 135–46.

Edmondson, D., Park, C. L., Blank, T. O., Fenster, J. R. and Mills, M. A. 2008. "Deconstructing Spiritual Well-being: Existential Well-being and HRQOL in Cancer Survivors." *Psycho-Oncology* 17:2, 161–69.

Feher, S. and Maly, R. C. 1999. "Coping with Breast Cancer in Later Life: The Role of Religious Faith." *Psycho-Oncology* 8:5, 408–16.

Fetzer Institute/National Institute on Aging Working Group. 1999. *Multidimensional Measurement of Religiousness/Spirituality for Use in Health Research.* Kalamazoo, MI: The Fetzer Institute. Accessed August 17, 2020, https://fetzer.org/sites/default/files/images/resources/attachment/%5Bcurrent-date%3Atiny%5D/Multidimensional_Measurement_of_Religousness_Spirituality.pdf

Foster, C., Wright, D., Hill, H., Hopkinson, J., and Roffe, L. 2009. "Psychosocial Implications of Living 5 Years or More Following a Cancer Diagnosis: A Systematic Review of the Research Evidence." *European Journal of Cancer Care (England)* 18:3, 223–47.

Fritz, M. S., Taylor, A. B. and MacKinnon, D. P. 2012. "Explanation of Two Anomalous Results in Statistical Mediation Analysis." *Multivariate Behavioral Research* 47:1, 61–87.

Hall, D. E., Meador, K. G. and Koenig, H. G. 2008. "Measuring Religiousness in Health Research: Review and Critique." *Journal of Religion and Health* 47:2, 134–63.

Hayes, A. F. 2013. *Introduction to Mediation, Moderation, and Conditional Process Analysis: A Regression-Based Approach.* New York: Guilford.

Hayes, A. F. 2015. *The PROCESS macro for SPSS and SAS*. Columbus, OH: The Ohio State University. Accessed August 17, 2020, http://www.processmacro.org/

Koenig, H. G. 2012. "Religion, Spirituality, and Health: The Research and Clinical Implications." *International Scholarly Research Network Psychiatry* 1–33.

Krupski, T. L., Kwan, L., Fink, A., Sonn, G. A., Maliski, S., Litwin, M. S. 2006. "Spirituality Influences Health Related Quality of Life in Men with Prostate Cancer." *Psycho-Oncology* 15:2, 121–31.

MacKinnon, D. P. 2008. *Introduction to Statistical Mediation Analysis*. New York: Lawrence Erlbaum Associates.

Masters, K. S. and Hooker, S. A. 2013. "Religiousness/Spirituality, Cardiovascular Disease, and Cancer: Cultural Integration for Health Research and Intervention." *Journal of Consulting and Clinical Psychology* 81:2, 206–16.

Meisenhelder, J. B. and Chandler, E. N. 2002. "Spirituality and Health Outcomes in the Elderly." *Journal of Religion and Health* 41:3, 243–52.

Miller, W. R. and Thoresen, C. E. 2003. "Spirituality, Religion, and Health: An Emerging Research Field." *American Psychologist* 58:1, 24–35.

Murphy, P. E., Canada, A. L., Fitchett, G., Stein, K., Portier, K., Crammer, C. and Peterman, A. H. 2010. "An Examination of the Three Factor Model and Structural Invariance across Racial/Ethnic Groups for the FACIT—Sp: A Report from the American Cancer Society's Study of Cancer Survivors-II (SCS-II)." *Psycho-Oncology* 19:3, 264–72.

Mytko, J. J. and Knight, S. J. 1999. "Body, Mind and Spirit: Towards the Integration of Religiosity and Spirituality in Cancer Quality of Life Research." *Psycho-Oncology* 8:5, 439–50.

Nelson, C., Jacobson, C. M., Weinberger, M. I., Bhaskaran, V., Rosenfeld, B., Breitbart, W. and Roth, A. 2009. "The Role of Spirituality in the Relationship between Religiosity and Depression in Prostate Cancer Patients." *Annals of Behavioral Medicine* 38:2, 105–14.

Oman, D. 2013. "Defining Religion and Spirituality." In *Handbook of the Psychology of Religion and Spirituality*, 2nd ed., edited by R. F. Paloutzian and C. L. Park, 23–47. New York: Guilford.

Pargament, K. I., Mahoney, A., Exline, J. J., Jones, J. W. and Shafranske, E. P. 2013. "Envisioning an Integrative Paradigm for the Psychology of Religion and Spirituality." In *APA Handbook of Psychology, Religion, and Spirituality (Vol 1): Context, Theory, and Research*, edited by K. I., Pargament, J. J. Exline and J. W. Jones, 3–19. New York: American Psychological Association.

Park, C. L. 2005. "Religion and Meaning." In *Handbook of the Psychology of Religion and Spirituality*, edited by R. F. Paloutzian and C. L. Park, 295–314. New York: Guilford.

Park, C. L., Edmondson, D. and Hale-Smith, A. 2013. "Why Religion? Meaning as Motivation. In *APA Handbook of Psychology, Religion, and Spirituality (Vol 1): Context, Theory, and Research*, edited by K. I. Pargament, J. J. Exline and J. W. Jones, 157–71. New York: American Psychological Association.

Park, C. L., Malone, M. R., Suresh, D. P., Bliss, D. and Rosen, R. I. 2008. "Coping, Meaning in Life, and Quality of Life in Congestive Heart Failure Patients." *Quality of Life Research* 17:1, 21–26.

Peterman, A. H., Fitchett, G., Brady, M. J., Hernandez, L. and Cella, D. 2002. "Measuring Spiritual Well-being in People with Cancer: The Functional Assessment of Chronic

Illness Therapy-Spiritual Wellbeing scale (FACIT—Sp)." *Annals of Behavioral Medicine* 24:1, 49–58.

Pirl, W. F. 2004. "Evidence Report on the Occurrence, Assessment, and Treatment of Depression in Cancer Patients." *Journal of the National Cancer Institute Monographs* 32:32–39.

Preacher, K. J. and Hayes, A. F. 2008. "Asymptotic and Resampling Strategies for Assessing and Comparing Indirect Effects in Multiple Mediator Models." *Behavior Research Methods* 40:3, 879–91.

Ryu, E., West, S. G. and Sousa, K. H. 2009. "Mediation and Moderation: Testing Relationships between Symptom Status, Functional Health, and Quality of Life in HIV Patients." *Multivariate Behavioral Research* 44:2, 213–32.

Sherman A. C. and Simonton S. 2007. "Faith and Health: Psychological Perspectives." In *Spirit, Science, and Health: How the Spiritual Mind Fuels Physical Wellness*, edited by T. G. Plante, and C. E. Thoresen, 157–75. Westport, CT, US: Praeger/Greenwood.

Silberfarb, P. M., Anderson, K. M., Rundle, A. C., Holland, J., Cooper, M. R. and McIntyre, O. R. 1991. "Mood and Clinical Status in Patients with Multiple Myeloma." *Journal of Clinical Oncology* 9:12, 2219–24.

Smith, T., Stein, K. D., Mehta, C. C.,Kaw, C., Kepner, J. L., Buskirk, T., Stafford, J. and Baker, F. 2007. "The Rationale, Design, and Implementation of the American Cancer Society's Studies of Cancer Survivors." *Cancer* 109:1, 1–12.

Stefanek, M., McDonald, P. G. and Hess, S. A. 2005. "Religion, Spirituality, and Cancer: Current Status and Methodological Challenges." *Psycho-Oncology* 14:6, 450–63.

Stein, K. D., Smith, T., Kim, Y., Mehta, C. C. B., Stafford, J., Spillers, R. L. and Baker, F. 2006. "The American Cancer Society's Studies of Cancer Survivors: The Largest, Most Diverse Investigation of Long-term Cancer Survivors So Far." *American Journal of Nursing* 106:(3 Suppl) 83–85.

Stein, K. D., Syrjala, K. L. and Andrykowski, M. A. 2008. "Physical and Psychological Long-term and Late Effects of Cancer." *Cancer* 112:(Suppl), 2577–92.

Visser, A., Garssen, B. and Vingerhoets, A. 2010. "Spirituality and Well-being in Cancer Patients: A Review." *Psycho-Oncology* 19:6, 565–72.

Ware, J. E., Kosinki, M. and Keller, S. 1994. *SF-36 Physical and Mental Health Summary Scales: A User's Manual*. Boston: The Health Institute, New England Medical Center.

Ware, J. E. and Sherbourne, C. D. 1992. "The MOS 36-item Short-form Health Survey (SF-36). I. Conceptual Framework and Item Selection." *Medical Care* 30:6, 473–83.

Yanez, B., Edmondson, D., Stanton, A. L., Park, C. L., Kwan, L., Ganz, P. A. and Blank, T. O. 2009. "Facets of Spirituality as Predictors of Adjustment to Cancer: Relative Contributions of Having Faith and Finding Meaning." *Journal of Consulting and Clinical Psychology* 77:4, 730–41.

Yates, J. S., Mustian, K. M., Morrow, G. R., Gillies, L. J., Padmanaban, D., Atkins, J. N. Issell, B., Kirshner, J. J. and Colman, L. K. 2005. "Prevalence of Complementary and Alternative Medicine Use in Cancer Patients during Treatment." *Support Care Cancer* 13:10, 806–11.

Zinnbauer, B. J. and Pargament, K. I. 2005. "Religiousness and Spirituality." In *Handbook of the Psychology of Religion and Spirituality*, edited by R. F. Paloutzian and C. L. Park, 21–42. New York: Guilford.

Zinnbauer, B. J., Pargament, K. I. and Scott, A. B. 1999. "The Emerging Meanings of Religiousness and Spirituality: Problems and Prospects." *Journal of Personality* 67:6, 889–919.

ARTICLE 5

CPE and Spiritual Growth[1]

—GEORGE FITCHETT

AT THE TIME I wrote this essay I was very interested in theories of faith development. In part, my interest was professional, helping me understand the faith journeys of my CPE students. A conversation with a CPE colleague had help me realize that, in contrast to most theological education at the time, where classmates came from the same faith tradition, the multi-faith nature of CPE made it unique in the professional formation of many students. But in part, my interest in faith development was personal, as I was trying to understand my own journey from Calvinism to Quakerism. As a result, this paper is the most personal in this collection. Clinical pastoral education (CPE) has played a very central role in my personal and professional development and working as a CPE Educator was a very gratifying part of my career.

INTRODUCTION

When CPE goes well it is a profound, life changing experience. A recent student summarized her experience of a basic quarter saying:

> I have had a wonderful time at Rush. I cannot remember a time
> in my life when I have been challenged by my work and at the

1. G. Fitchett. 1998–1999. "CPE and Spiritual Growth." *Journal of Supervision and Training in Ministry* 19:130–46. Reprinted in *Expanding the Circle: Essays in Honor of Joan Hemenway*, edited by C. F. Garlid, A. A. Zollfrank and G. Fitchett, 213–34. Decatur, GA: Journal of Pastoral Care Publications, Inc. 2009.

same time, so fulfilled by it. At the end of each day I have people and conversations that have added dimension to my life.[2]

Another student in that training group wrote:

> CPE offered me a more powerful way inside myself. The depth and completeness astounded me. To see myself reflected in my colleagues and patients, to find myself starkly revealed against the hospital background was more intense than expected, more wonderful and awe-ful than expected, and more catalytic to change than expected.

At the end of their year of training, several residents from a recent training group also commented on the significant changes that had taken place for them. One man wrote:

> "Never underestimate the energy of this chaplain." I take that as the starting point of this evaluation of myself and my experience this unit. I have had a taste of the switch from analog to digital and from copper wiring to fiber optics in my inner connectedness. The psychic, spiritual, and physical energy boost that has taken place over the past two units has been very exciting for me.

A woman in the group wrote:

> The past quartet has been so filled. I can't believe it. I don't know how to hold everything up. I was surprised about my own pastoral care. I have found a way to reflect on visits which helps me much more than verbatims. I need to include the scene, the smells, the feelings. I found a new awareness of different levels of interaction. It has also given me more ground to reflect on how God happens in these encounters. I was so surprised when George brought in a candle [and lit it] after I read one of these stories to him in supervision. I think I had not recognized at that time that I have found my own way of being a pastor, in what I am doing and also in how I am writing about it, allowing readers to enter the experience.

Another woman in the group wrote:

> I wish I had the right words. Words that would convey the wholeness of the last twelve months. My feelings are mixed. The sadness and pain of letting go. Gratitude. Affection. Joy. Hope. Fear. Longing. I feel I have made progress. This experience has

2. All students' quotes are used with their permission.

been transformative. I can see myself becoming the pastor I'd hoped to be, comfortable with my own authority, certain of my love and concern for others, and hopeful that redemption will arise out of suffering. I have grown to trust my pastoral skills and instincts.

Our standards say that our work is about assisting students with growth in personal and professional identity, knowledge, and skills, but growth or changes in those areas, as important as they may be, would not evoke words such as these about the impact of the CPE experience on the students' lives. I believe that one reason why CPE has a reputation for being a profound, life-transforming experience, one reason why the experience of CPE leads students to write comments such as those above, is that CPE, at its best, is an experience of spiritual growth; it is an experience that touches and transforms our soul.

In this paper I will begin by sharing a personal story which CPE helped me to see was an important formative spiritual experience. I will place that experience in the context of a theory of spiritual development and identify three features of CPE that I believe contribute to its potential to facilitate spiritual growth. I will then illustrate and expand on this theory with stories from several CPE students. I will conclude with a discussion of the implications of this for CPE supervision.

BAPTISM IN THE FLUSHING REFORMED CHURCH

I was raised in the Reformed Church in America, a moderate to conservative denomination of Dutch-descended Calvinists. Fifteen years ago I left the Reformed Church and joined the Religious Society of Friends, the Quakers. Recovering memories of the baptism liturgy in the Flushing Reformed Church, the church in which I was raised, helped me understand why I felt the need to leave the Reformed Church and find a new spiritual home.

Excepting the annual Christmas pageant, there was nothing about worship in the Reformed tradition, in the imposing sanctuary of the Protestant Reformed Dutch Church of Flushing, New York, which made it appealing to the spirituality of a child. It was worse than unappealing. It was torture. A friend tells a story that gives a good illustration of the particular manner in which this torture was carried out. He recalls the first time as a child he attended a performance of the oratorio *The Messiah*. As the choir repeated the verse, "All we like sheep have gone astray," over and over, my friend recalls a great despair gripped his soul. He knew the oratorio was based on the Bible. He knew the Bible was a huge book with many verses. He put two and two together and realized that if each verse were repeated as many times as this verse was, he would be sitting there for the rest of his life.

Long choral works with many verses repeated over and over and over again were some of the sacred acts that were performed in the sanctuary of the Reformed Church of Flushing. Long sermons and prayers that lasted forever were also a feature of the worship as I remembered it. As a child, sitting through these services effectively began the lesson that faith was composed of self-discipline, of repression of the natural tendency to wiggle, talk, gaze about, or otherwise behave like a child. It set the stage for understanding God and what you did in God's house. It was like being at the home of a distant relative. You wore uncomfortable clothes and behaved unnaturally and were scolded for being yourself.

The arrival of Spring brought some hope for a break in this annual liturgical calendar of torturous self-control. In the Spring, proud families brought their newborn infants to the church to be baptized. The whole tone of those Sundays seemed different. The windows seemed to let in more light. The members of the congregation seemed to let slight smiles break the solemnity of their expressions.

On those Sundays I eagerly awaited the time when the pastor would come down from the pulpit and stand with the family around the baptismal font. In large part, the excitement of these times stemmed from an uncertainty about how the infant would take to this encounter with God's grace, and how the family and pastor would take to the infant's reaction. The times when the babes slept peacefully through the whole event spoke to us of the soothing, maternal aspects of God, but offered little relief from the agonizing liturgical year.

The best times were when the infants cried. It was even better if the infant was quiet right up until the moment when the minister gently sprinkled the water of blessing on the forehead and then the baby let out with anguished wailing. What excitement there was in watching the scene that followed. The pastor would sputter as he tried to find the closing prayer and recite it over the noise of the screaming child. Embarrassment would be written all over the faces of the infant's parents, undone that their precious one should be so misbehaved in God's house. Anxious grandparents would reach for the babe, offending the parents and ensuring an increase in their anxiety and thus in the child's anxious crying.

As soon as the Amen was out of the minister's mouth, the offending infant and embarrassed parents would be ushered out the side door. The elders and pastor would quickly restore order and proceed with the rest of the service. But the return to the weekly liturgy did not dampen my joy in knowing that a new recruit had made their protest against our common liturgical oppression known in no uncertain terms.

As I grew older and began to hear and understand the words which were spoken in the baptism liturgy, my hope that our side might eventually win diminished sharply. It was clear from the liturgy that the church took this business of self-discipline seriously. The very first words of the baptism liturgy effectively set the mood. Whatever smiles might be found on the faces of the congregation, as they resonated with the pride and joy of the new parents, were quickly wiped away as the minister began reading. Whatever lightness and light had been brought into the sanctuary by the infant was soon darkened by the church's teaching. The liturgy begins with the following words:

> The principal parts of the doctrine of holy Baptism are . . .
> *First.* That we, with our children, are conceived and born in sin, and therefore are children of wrath, insomuch that we cannot enter into the kingdom of God, except we are born again. This the dipping in or sprinkling with water teaches us, whereby the impurity of our souls is signified, and we are admonished to loathe and humble ourselves before God, and seek for purification and salvation without ourselves. (Board of Publication RCA. 1873, 23)

I had seen the joy and delight which the infants had brought to the faces of their parents and to the congregation around me. But the liturgy contradicted what I thought I knew from experience. Nothing could be more pure than an infant brought into the church to be baptized, but the church declared it was otherwise. "We are admonished to loathe and humble ourselves before God, and seek for our purification and salvation without ourselves." In our Reformed tradition, nothing was left to our faulty imagination. Lest the family or congregation lose sight of what this smiling infant was really like, the very first words of the liturgy were there to remind us.

These first words of the baptism liturgy became symbolic of what was for me destructive in the Reformed tradition. They were words that directed me to loathe myself and seek to understand myself "without" myself. I later realized, in part through CPE, in part through therapy, for me to be saved I had to begin to free myself from the faith which these words proclaimed. I had to leave the sanctuary of the Flushing Reformed Church to see if the sacred, as I was coming to know it from my experience, could be found dwelling in another place.

SPIRITUAL GROWTH AND CPE

There are many theories of spiritual growth or faith development available to help us interpret our own spiritual stories and our students' (see for example, Ivy, 1997). One of the ones I like the best was described by John Westerhoff. (1976, especially Chapter Four, 79–103). Westerhoff sees the pilgrimage of faith proceeding through four styles. The first style is *experienced faith*. It is the non-verbal experience of the trustworthiness of existence formed in infancy and childhood by our interactions with primary caregivers. The second style is *affiliative faith*. It refers to the beliefs and practices we develop through participation in the religious life of our family. The third style is *searching faith*. It is a time of questioning the faith of our family. It is a time of experimenting with alternative beliefs and practices, and hopefully a time of renewed connection with our own experiences of the holy. The fourth style is *owned faith*. It is a time when, through the process of searching, we have formed a faith where our beliefs are rooted in our experiences and our rituals and practices give expression to those beliefs and experiences.

The importance of community in the first two styles is obvious. "Good enough" parenting provides a positive foundation for experienced faith. Abusive or neglectful parenting plants seeds of despair or chaos. In the stage of affiliative faith, the family and/or primary faith community communicate foundational beliefs and morals, and introduce the rituals which teach and reinforce them.

The role of community for the second two styles is no less crucial, but generally more problematic. For most people, the style of searching faith is experienced as a time of un-faith. Key figures from the period of affiliative faith usually disapprove of the questions and behavior that constitute searching faith. Our exemplars in the affiliative period were rarely people whose stories of searching faith, if they had one, were told. Sustaining the search in this period is a demanding process. Some searchers foreclose its uncertainty with a new affiliation. Others adopt the identity of non-believer and assume the search is ended. A community which values and tolerates people in the midst of searching faith is rare.

Such communities, when they are found, are often the communities that also welcome people with owned faith. They find themselves enriched, not threatened, by the diversity of beliefs and practices of a group of people with owned faith.

My experience of CPE was one of being part of a community of people in the process of searching and owned faith. Consequently, my experience of CPE had a significant impact on my spiritual growth. The CPE experience, and especially the relationships with peers and supervisors, provided me with an important antidote to Calvinist self-negation. By suggesting that experience and process could be trustworthy, CPE also exposed me to a radically new theology of inspiration.

As I reflect on my CPE experience and the experiences of my students, three features of the CPE experience seem to play an important role in facilitating the kind of spiritual growth Westerhoff describes: questions, answers, and community. First, CPE is a time of encounter with major questions about life, death, self, and ministry. Second, in CPE the answers to these questions are not simple or clear and the sources of authority for answering them are complex. Third, when CPE is at its best, as students experience these questions and search for the answers, they are supported in gracious and caring relationships with peers and supervisors.[3] Let me tell the stories of several students to illustrate the different ways CPE influences the spiritual growth of students at these different points in their faith development. As most students come to us during the affiliative or searching phases of their faith development, the stories and discussion focus on those two phases.

BAPTISM IN THE ROYAL CHILDREN'S HOSPITAL[4]

David Dawes, chaplain and supervisor in training, has written the following:

> Gilbert was anxious, anxious to do the right thing by the program, by me and by the church. The following dialogue named a conflict right from the start. This conversation occurred during our first supervisory conference after Gilbert had an opportunity to explore the hospital and the wards he was to provide ministry to.

G.1 So do I start on call this week?

3. Parker J. Palmer (*The Courage to Teach*) offers rich observations about the importance of these elements of teaching and learning. Regarding questions see his discussion of subject-centered education (p. 115ff). Regarding answers see his discussion of the teacher within (p. 29ff), and education and the disconnected life (p. 35ff). Regarding community see his discussion of knowing in community (p. 89ff).

4. The following account was written by David Dawes, chaplain and supervisor in training at the Royal Children's Hospital, Melbourne, Australia. I am grateful to David, and to his student, Gilbert, for their permission to use this material. In this and all following discussions of specific students, I have employed pseudonyms to protect their confidentiality.

D.1 I was thinking maybe next week after you have had some time to get used to the hospital and become familiar with it and the issues of pastoral care to sick kids.

G.2 Yeah. What are the main things that the on call chaplain gets called to?

D.2 We primarily get called to crisis events such as death, immanent death, distressed families who have just received poor prognosis and we get called to baptize sick or dying children. And occasionally we are asked to baptize children who are already dead.

G.3 You wouldn't do that. You'd offer them a blessing.

D.3 Ah, no. I am prepared to baptize. I have baptized a small number of kids who have been brought into Emergency already dead. Any child who appears to have died from Sudden Infant Death is automatically brought into here.

G.4 Yeah, but the child is dead, baptism is for the living.

D.4 The parents are living and are going through the worst time of their lives. I don't want to add to their horror by adhering to a strict interpretation. I've baptized children who are alive only because of the machines they are on and as soon as they are extubated they are no longer alive.

G.5 So it is a pastoral response, meeting the needs of the parents?

D.5 Yeah, but it is also a theological response because God is not offended by my action. Well, I don't think he is.

G.6 You've given me something to think about.

This was one part of a discussion that had a profound impact on Gilbert causing him to have a few sleepless nights wrestling with the issue. It was revisited in each of the next three supervisory conferences.

Gilbert wrote in his journal:

> My preparation for ministry has involved a theological understanding of Baptism of the living. In fact in the UCA [Uniting Church of Australia] Baptism of the dead is considered an inappropriate practice. For me it was a simple straightforward stance which afforded no great difficulty.
>
> There is a sense in which our "alienation" from God is *past* [Gilbert's emphasis] because of what Christ has done for us. But I have to say that Christ has done for us something for which our Baptism changes nothing (i.e.) God's love for us in Jesus Christ

> is undeserved, free and for all and is not dependent on *Baptism*.
> Paul's word in Romans 8 "nothing can separate us from God's
> love . . . not even death." And yet, the pleading heart of Mum
> and Dad for their child (dead) is a confronting pastoral issue.

In supervision, my response to Gilbert was to affirm that it is his decision
and that I would support either decision for either decision was appropriate.
I told Gilbert in our third supervisory session, before he went on call, that in
the event of him being called and requested to baptize a child who had died
I was able to be called. Gilbert continued to wrestle with the theological and
pastoral issues raised by either decision.

Several weeks later, in the early hours of the morning, Gilbert had the
opportunity to confront, in the practice of ministry, the conflict that until
now had been academic. Gilbert was called to the Neonatal Unit where
a family, whose six week old daughter was on the cusp between life and
death, requested that she be baptized. Gilbert spent a long time with Rebecca's parents and was prepared to wait until the mother Sarah's sister and
husband arrived before baptizing Rebecca. Gilbert said in our supervisory
session later in the day,

G.7 Once I had decided for myself that Rebecca did not have to be alive
for me to be able to baptize her, the pressure just slipped away. I was
able to be present with the family with no need to rush.

D.7 So you decided that for you to baptize Rebecca she did not have to
be alive?

G.8 Yes and I felt my need to rush just fall away and I was able to sit and
be with Sarah and Alan without putting any further pressure on them.

D.8 It sounds like your decision was freeing?

G.9 Yes it was.

D.9 Were you worried about the church?

G.10 No. I was more concerned about being there for this couple.

D.10 Congratulations, it feels like a celebration.

G.11 Yes. Yes it is and it has been a long and painful journey. But when I
was there with Sarah and Alan all I could think about was being there
for them, caring for them.

Gilbert was now able to be present to the family and able to meet their needs
for he was able to let go of his anxiety of doing the right thing by the church
and was able to be pastorally present to the family. He was able to claim

his responsibility to provide ministry to this family as he best thought fit. Gilbert later wrote of this baptism in his Final Evaluation.

> Sitting with the parents, watching the struggle of staff to save their daughter and hearing their story of pain during the past year, especially the last six weeks since the pre-mature birth of their child [*sic*]. I was asked to baptize the baby and did so. Before doing this though I spoke to the parents about alerting other members of the family they may want to be present. For the first time in my life I faced the issue of pastoral ministry and where it diverged from book learning. In deciding to baptize I decided I would do this, in the context of this particular pastoral situation, even if the baby died before other family members could arrive. By arriving at this decision, I took away the division that threatened to be a barrier to my being present to the family.

* * * * * *

Gilbert's Experience of Questions, Answers, and Community

In Gilbert's story we see all three spiritually formative features of CPE at work. First, pediatric hospital ministry raises profound questions for Gilbert, questions about baptism, sacraments, and Christology; questions he may never encounter in the classroom, and perhaps not in the parish. Is it permissible to baptize a dead child? Is baptism necessary for us to be saved? How do you balance the importance of correct ritual and doctrine with the pastoral needs of anxious parents? These were abstract questions that confronted Gilbert as he began CPE. The questions caused Gilbert some sleepless nights and he raises them again in the next three supervisory conferences. The questions became a pressing issue requiring him to make some important choices when he was called to be with Rebecca and her family.

Second, CPE does not offer any simple answers for the questions Gilbert encounters. "You wouldn't baptize a dead child, would you?" Gilbert asks his supervisor? "Yes," David says, "I would." "Well, you'd really only do it to comfort the family, right?" Gilbert asks. "Well, yes," David answers. "But I don't think God is offended by my action," he adds. David's responses to Gilbert's questions give Gilbert "something to think about." Where can he go for the answers? He considers doctrine and scripture, but the answers there aren't clear. His supervisor shares his position, but doesn't insist that

Gilbert agree with it. His CPE experience forces Gilbert to face the complexity of this question and the absence of clear, simple answers to it.[5]

But CPE also provides Gilbert with a supportive community as he wrestles with this issue. In this story, that support is evident in David's relationship with Gilbert. David gives Gilbert time to become familiar with the hospital before he asks him to be on-call. David listens as Gilbert wrestles with the baptism question, wrestles with it for several weeks. David assures Gilbert, "that it is his decision and that [he] would support either decision for either decision was appropriate," and that he could be called if there was a request for baptism that Gilbert wished to refer. Finally, after Gilbert's ministry with Rebecca's family and decision to be present with the family, David senses the importance of the moment and affirms Gilbert's decision, "Congratulations, it feels like a celebration." I would propose that, in part, it was David's gracious, supportive relationship with Gilbert that allowed Gilbert to enter into the questions raised by the baptism issue and not defend against them. And that this relationship also allowed Gilbert to respond compassionately and graciously rather than rigidly to the needs of this distressed family.

From the limited material we have about Gilbert, it isn't clear to me where he is on his spiritual pilgrimage. My guess is that he was primarily working out of an affiliative faith. His CPE experience and specifically his wrestling with the issue of baptism may have challenged that faith a little, but probably not enough to push him into an extended time of searching faith. In terms of spiritual growth, the primary result of Gilbert's experience in CPE, at least as we know it, was to help him move toward a more compassionate balance between law and grace, between obedience to the formal teachings of his church and the pastoral needs of those to whom he ministered.

FINDING GRACE, VOICE AND LIBERATION

In contrast to students like Gilbert, for whom CPE is a time of moderate spiritual growth, there are other students, and they are obviously the students with whom I identify most strongly, for whom CPE is a time of intense spiritual struggle and search for an owned faith. Let me illustrate this with the words of several women who have been in our training program.

---

5. Gilbert is not alone in wrestling with the complexity of this issue. It was explored by his supervisor, David Dawes ("A Response to Baptismal Demands," 147–60). For an alternative view see Smith, "Pastoral and Ritual Response," 25–35. Also see Anderson, and Foley, *Mighty Stories,* especially 128–34.

Jean wrote:

> One of the biggest areas of growth that has been clarified for me this quarter is regarding my need for definition, for direction, for right answers, for success. I want to know what my assignment is, how to do it, and then to do it well. I have known this about myself, but it became problematic this quarter. I have been able to talk about the strengths of that way of being, but it has caused a lot of distress this quarter. As my verbatims clearly showed, I was continually feeling that I wasn't doing the pastoral care work right and I had difficulty just being with people even though that is what I most want to be able to do for myself and have others do for me.
>
> A theme that also seemed to come out of supervision and verbatims is what a heavy burden these expectations become. So, I would like to find some ways to lighten the load, to be responsible, but not to get drug [sic] down by these expectations that are coming from my past and from myself.

Earlier in this evaluation, Jean addresses a key theological issue that seems to be linked to her sense of heavy burden. "In my basic quarter of CPE, grace became an important theological theme for me as I struggled with some of the issues I currently struggle with—wanting to do things right and follow the plan or the rules. I have not been too aware of grace this quarter, which has probably made those frustrating times even more difficult."

Another student, Grace, wrote:

> Once again [this quarter] I was told I was being hard on myself—a response that surprised me because I didn't see it. The conversation has left me pondering once again the meaning of self-acceptance. JoAnn (one of my supervisory colleagues) pushed me to accept what I keep trying to change—To accept myself in this way seems to be "settling for what is" with an unwillingness to change.
>
> I have been trying so hard to "get rid of" what I don't like about myself that accepting those characteristics I am ashamed of or thinking about God's accepting me as I am now instead of as I hope to be someday just hasn't ever occurred to me. I really have spent my life trying to "be" better hoping that someday I would "be" good enough. To move out of this mode feels somewhat like putting down my armor—to quit fighting—myself. Even in the writing of this I can feel my heart softening—what would it mean to quit fighting, to relax, to just be who I am and to say—thank you. It would be grace.

Grace has struggled with this issue a lot. In her evaluation of the previous quarter she acknowledged the spiritual dimension of the struggle even more explicitly.

> I am beginning to realize that much of what I am learning cannot be forced. It is a process of learning to trust myself and the spirit of the divine within. It feels very risky, very new. I want to go where the spirit leads, yet I am afraid and find it hard to let go as much as I say I want to do so.

One of the keys to the process of liberation Jean and Grace are describing is being able to name the bondage they are experiencing. To do that, a student must find her voice. That was also an important goal for Cathy.

> I have already mentioned the issue of "voice." Just last week, George helped me to see that this included the voice of pain and sadness as well as the voice of strength. It was important for me to be able to "give voice" to my feelings of heaviness and weariness and to share them in the group instead of stoically holding them myself. I have also learned how essential it is to speak with my voice rather than attempting to assume the voice of someone else, and to be aware of when and how I can be tempted to give my voice away. Having a voice also relates for me to coming out of hiding, being willing to be visible, to acknowledge the light.

Reflecting on her year of CPE, Linda is even more explicit about what it has meant to find the voice to name her experience.

> What would it mean to be known? That's the question which has echoed through my mind and through my experience of these last four quarters. I began the year with a commitment—to you and to me. A commitment to speak the truth. But I had missed a step. To speak the truth, I would first have to know the truth. I would have to believe it. You have heard me talk about how difficult and painful the year has been in many ways. The pain comes from knowing the truth about myself. There are many things about myself, my talents and abilities, which I appreciate, many ways in which I love myself for who I am and who I am becoming. In general, I like being me. I like who I am. But there are other ways I have refused to know myself, other parts of who I have been or who I am that I have not admitted to myself until recently. I have had to know myself differently than I allowed before. Today, I know myself as the child of alcoholic parents, as once anorexic, as sexually traumatized, as a victim of my mother's depression. It may sound strange, but I have lived

most of my life not facing these realities and all that they imply. The stories I have shared with you hurt. Sometimes I can barely utter the words. I've heard them come out of my mouth before, but now, with you, they sound different. They fill my head and I know they are my words. They are me, who I have been, who I am, who I fear. Eating disorder—alcoholism—starvation—depression—abuse. Words that are mine in one way or another. Words I have come to know. But even now, knowing brings a certain liberation. I am beginning to imagine letting go of the past in a deeper, more complete way. I know better who I have been and because of it, who I am capable of becoming. I am not fully liberated. One theme we have heard in evaluations so far is that one is never fully liberated from the burdens acquired in childhood. I still feel very close to the past, to the old hurts, but not confined to them. I can imagine freedom now, even where I have not yet achieved it.

For these women, finding a voice lets them tell their story, lets them name their reality, lets them know themselves and be known to others. This time of searching is a time when old images and ideas are collapsing. Grace, a former doctoral student in theology, finds an important parallel process occurring for her.

I have struggled significantly with my faith and continue to grapple with images of God that are not helpful. I know what it means to "have the rug pulled out from under me," to have all that I had put together in my head pulled apart. This has helped me to be with others who find the world, as they have known it, falling part. I know the importance of "finding one's own way" and am grateful for those who have accompanied me. As a chaplain I try to do the same, accompany the other with respect for their process, their wisdom.

For some students, the images and methods of their affiliative faith block the path forward into searching faith and must be torn down. Sophia tells about her struggle to write her final theology of pastoral care.

I am sitting at the desk, unable to get my thoughts together. This is supposed to be my big thing. The result of one year of searching for my passion and my voice. The search for my truth, for what I believe in. It should all come together and make breathtaking sense. And I panic because I will never be able to do that. In my mind, "Theology" becomes again a systematic answer. I thought I was over that. But the very idea of theology implies so much of the tradition I studied, of the God I grew up with. The word God carries associations and values that I can't get out of my mind, lest out of my feelings. God is linked with fear, power, feeling never good enough, focusing on my shortcomings. As much as I try, God keeps showing up as a male figure—Like a weed it grows back, saying, "You ain't gonna get rid of me!" The Weed-God, He-God, the system of the father's father's. I try to cut it back, because it is not good for me. But it keeps growing.

When she abandons the systematic method of the father's father's and takes up her own method something different happens.

Because I can't write, I take refuge in the watercolors. Maybe they can help me out of my frozen state. The next day, the colors dry by now, I glance over to the picture, and what I see is incredible. I can feel my heart beating. I am so surprised and in awe: there she is, a woman imprisoned, naked, her hands tied in the back, trying to get free.

Theology Go to Hell! You are the step family, the enemy that strips off my clothes, ties me down and locks me in a cell. I am not doing this again to me. Not this time. I don't want to do theology. I don't want the Weed-God, He-God.

I want to thrive.

The truth is in me. I just have to take time for her. She comes in dreams, in paintings. She comes in pieces. She does not have to be consistent. She makes me alive. Her names are: beauty, creativity, I am who I am.

The quotations from these students tell the story of what it is like to be in a time of searching faith. For these women, the three spiritually formative features of CPE, questions, answers, and community, were important aspects of their search. Unlike Gilbert, these women did not need CPE to put them in touch with profound questions about life, self, faith, or ministry. They were experiencing the pain of their questions, the bondage of old ideas and images of themselves, of ministry, of God. For them, CPE was a place where they found a voice that enabled them to name their pain and bondage, a voice that enabled them to raise questions about the suffering they experienced, the burdensome expectations to be perfect, the struggle for self-acceptance, the pain of hiding and then naming the truth of one's life.

The community these women found in CPE played an essential role in their time of searching faith. It helped them find their voice and name their experience. It sustained them in their lament, in their pain and questions. It encouraged them when they were hesitant or resistant to naming their bondage. It celebrated with them when the searching led to liberation and new life. While the quotations I have shared here do not capture the key role of the peer group for each of these women, it, as well as competent and compassionate individual supervision, was an essential element in their experience.

For each of these women, CPE was also a place that recognized there are many right answers to life's deepest questions. It was a place that recognized that theology could be written or painted. It was a place that affirmed that the best answers to the questions with which they wrestled were the answers that were in harmony with the truth of their experience, answers that affirmed the presence of the divine spirit within them. "The truth is in me," Sophia wrote. "I just have to take time for her."

For some students, like Gilbert, CPE is a time of modest spiritual growth. For other students, such as Jean, Grace, Cathy, Linda, and Sophia, CPE is a time of intense spiritual searching. CPE's attitude toward questions, answers and community makes it an ideal context to support students who are in that phase of their spiritual growth. My goal in CPE however, is not to keep students in an endless process of searching faith. My hope is that by providing students like Grace, Linda, and Sophia with a community that understands and supports their time of searching faith, it will develop into something like the owned faith Linda described. "This experience has been transformative. I can see myself becoming the pastor I'd hoped to be, comfortable with my own authority, certain of my love and concern for others, and hopeful that redemption will arise out of suffering." Like many of our students whose time of searching faith in CPE is followed by owned faith, since completing CPE, Linda and Sophia have returned to their respective faith groups and are in the process of becoming ordained.

IMPLICATIONS FOR SUPERVISION

So what? What are the implications of these ideas for our work as supervisors? Let me answer that by referring to the three key spiritual features of CPE.

Regarding the role of questions, for students in a time of affiliative faith, such as Gilbert, the confrontation with issues of life and death and ministry often raises significant questions. It is important to trust such students to select, from among the many questions arising from this experience, the one or ones that they are ready to address. As in other matters, pressing these students to address some other question or issue of obvious importance to us is only likely to create defensiveness and not facilitate learning.

Students who are in a time of searching faith are likely to bring significant questions with them. CPE need only be a place that welcomes their engagement of these questions. Some students who come to CPE may be in the process of a transition from affiliative to searching faith. Asking deep questions about their affiliative faith may feel strange and uncomfortable to them. It may feel like un-faith, like betrayal. It takes little more than helping them name their questions as an essential component of the process of growth in faith to help them move into the searching process.

Regarding answers, CPE's central gift, for me and for so many students, is captured in the well-worn phrase, "trust the process." I've come to believe that the best theology is sung, and regarding answers, I love the hymn, "Lead on O Cloud of Yahweh. The journey is our home." Regarding answers, I feel some affinity with Roy Bradley's emphasis on "keeping the mystery present" to our students.[6] Our best gift to our students is like David's gift to Gilbert, clarity about our own perspectives, and support and encouragement to help our students find the answers that have the authority of their experience.

Regarding community, I feel affinity with Bradley's emphasis on "redemptive relationships." I would also emphasize that part of what has made CPE redemptive for me and for many of our students has been its ability to be welcoming and inclusive of many different people: women and men, lay and ordained, gay and straight. Community is what makes CPE a place where spiritual growth can take place. Our programs, our peer groups, our supervisory relationships must be places where students feel welcomed, respected and safe. When these things are present, the rest of the process almost takes care of itself.

But unfortunately, we cannot take respect and safety in relationships in CPE for granted. As I was writing it, I shared some of my ideas for this paper with a good friend and respected teacher of pastoral care. I told him I was going to make a case for CPE as a place of spiritual formation because in CPE anxious students experienced gracious relationships with peers and supervisors that enabled them to grow in awareness of God's gracious love for them. "That wasn't my experience in CPE," he reminded me. And I remembered his story about how, years ago, as an eager but anxious and awkward young seminarian, his CPE supervisor and peers criticized and humiliated him week after week. Fortunately, I believe we have outgrown the worst of our confrontive and "boundary-less" days in CPE. But if CPE

---

6. Roy Bradley, senior CPE supervisor in Australia, has defined pastoral care as "The art of keeping the mystery of God present to humanity through redemptive relationships" (Bradley, "What Are We Doing in Supervision?" 18).

is to be a place for spiritual exploration and growth, we must ensure it is a place where students feel respected and safe.

CONCLUSION

What a gift it is to be a CPE supervisor and to be with students on their spiritual journeys. I can't imagine doing any other work. Here is what Grace said at the end of a quarter last year:

> How different life is becoming! There are hints that I am on my way to that more gracious, grace-filled space. Choosing to come to Rush was the first big step in that process. I feel some shifts happening in my family relationships, some new spaces opening up within me. I am more aware that my anger is often a means of defense/protection. I am learning about my need/right to create boundaries for myself. I am becoming aware of my tendency to take things personally which aren't personal. I am also discovering some areas that are particularly "charged" for me, places that have me hooked. The learning has been difficult but worthwhile. My imagination is being stretched—because there are new moments where I can just be in the midst of what is and say with genuine gratitude—Thank you!

But my favorite image of a student's spiritual growth, of her owned spirituality, comes from Sophia, who after wrestling with the Weed-God, He-God writes:

> I am making myself a dress. I have been wearing a lot of grays and blues, hiding myself. I was wearing what I thought I was supposed to wear. To fit in. If I am in the image of God, I want to be worthy of her. I want beautiful fabrics and warm and strong colors. I want to shine. I want to honor the body I am given, the talents that I have, the things I don't like about myself. It is hard to believe that she is ok with all of that, but she somehow *is* in all of that. Of course, impatient as I am, I wanted the dress to be finished within two days. But after two sewing machines failed, it is still in pieces, in the making. And that is actually as well. That's the place where I am at.
>
> I am bringing her alive, and I think she is quite excited that she appears!
>
> *There will come a day, when all dry bones will be alive again. The hearts will beat. And all will wear red golden clothes. They will enjoy each other's beauty.*

As I supervise, I think of the work I do as supporting my student's spiritual growth, as enjoying their unfolding spiritual beauty. In this paper I have tried to describe the kinds of spiritual growth that I have seen and how I think CPE facilitates that growth.

REFERENCES

Anderson, H. and Foley, E. 1998. *Mighty Stories, Dangerous Rituals,* San Francisco, Jossey Bass.

Board of Publication RCA. 1873. *The Liturgy of the Reformed Church in America.* New York: The Board of Publication of the Reformed Church in America (p. 23).

Bradley, R. 1997. "What Are We Doing in Supervision?" In *Clinical Pastoral Education Beyond 2000.* Proceedings of a conference at Austin and Repatriation Medical Centre, Heidelberg, Victoria, Australia, August 28.

Dawes, D. 1997. "A Response to Baptismal Demands and Requests." *Ministry, Society and Theology* 11:2, 147–60.

Ivy, S. S. 1997. "Spiritual Assessment as a Tool for the Pastoral Supervisor." *Journal of Supervision and Training in Ministry* 18:32–45.

Palmer, P. J. 1998. *The Courage to Teach.* San Francisco: Jossey-Bass.

Smith, T. M. 1998–99. "Pastoral and Ritual Response to Perinatal Death: A Narrative of a Departmental Policy Change." *Journal of Supervision and Training in Ministry* 19:25–35.

Westerhoff, J. H. III. 1976. *Will Our Children Have Faith?* New York: Seabury.

ARTICLE 6

Making Our Case(s)[1]

—GEORGE FITCHETT

Department of Religion, Health, and Human Values, Rush University Medical Center, Chicago, IL

THE IMPETUS FOR THIS paper came from re-reading two published reports of randomized clinical trials (RCTs) of chaplain care. A key feature of an RCT is a good description of the intervention that is being investigated. I thought such descriptions were lacking in these reports. I had assumed that chaplain case study literature would provide descriptions of chaplain care (interventions). However, I was surprised to find that chaplains' case studies didn't exist. My response was to reach out to colleagues to see who might be interested in writing case studies about their chaplaincy care. Since 2009, collaboration with many colleagues has led to over 30 published chaplain case studies, mainly published in three books,‡ and a special issue of the journal Health and Social Care Chaplaincy (2017). More cases are anticipated from colleagues in the Netherlands, who have taken a particularly strong interest in this research.

‡ G. Fitchett and S. Nolan, eds. 2015. *Spiritual Care in Practice: Case Studies in Healthcare Chaplaincy*. London: Jessica Kingsley.

G. Fitchett and S. Nolan, eds. 2018. *Case Studies in Spiritual Care: Healthcare Chaplaincy Assessments, Interventions and Outcomes*. London: Jessica Kingsley.

M. J. Wirpsa and K. Pugliese, eds. 2020. *Chaplains as Partners in Medical Decision-Making: Case Studies in Healthcare Chaplaincy*. London: Jessica Kingsley.

1. G. Fitchett. 2011. "Making Our Case(s)." *Journal of Health Care Chaplaincy* 17:1–2, 3–18. https://doi.org/10.1080/08854726.2011.559829

ABSTRACT

Health care chaplaincy needs to develop a body of published case studies. Chaplains need these case studies to provide a foundation for further research about the efficacy of chaplains' spiritual care. Case studies can also play an important role in training new chaplains and in continuing education for experienced chaplains, not to mention educating health care colleagues and the public about the work of health care chaplains. Guidelines for writing case studies are described, herein, as is a project in which three experienced oncology chaplains worked together to write case studies about their work. Steps that chaplains, and professional chaplain organizations, can take to further the writing and publishing of case studies are described.

Key words: Cancer; Case study; Chaplain; Research

WHY CHAPLAIN CASE STUDIES?

There is a growing consensus about the importance of research for the future of health care chaplaincy (Bay and Ivy 2006; Flannelly et al. 2003; Gleason 2004; Koenig 2008; O'Connor et al. 2001; VandeCreek 2002; Weaver, Flannelly and Liu 2008). Two reasons for chaplains' increased involvement with research have been described. The first and most important reason is well-stated by O'Connor and Meakes (1998): "Evidence from research needs to inform our pastoral care. To remove the evidence from pastoral care can create a ministry that is ineffective or possibly even harmful" (p. 367). The second reason is that in order to tell our story effectively to our health care colleagues, in order to build the case that we are productive members of the health care team, we have to provide evidence for the beneficial effects of the care we provide (Bay and Ivy 2006; Koenig 2008; Weaver et al. 2008).

This commitment to transforming health care chaplaincy into a research-informed profession is reflected in The Standards of Practice for Professional Chaplains in Acute Care, recently affirmed by the Association for Professional Chaplains (Association of Professional Chaplains 2009). Specifically, Standard 12 states: "The chaplain practices evidence-based care including ongoing evaluation of new practices and, when appropriate, contributes to or conducts research." The Interpretation that accompanies Standard 12 describes different levels of chaplains' involvement in research. At the basic level, it suggests that all chaplains "should be sufficiently familiar with existing evidence to present it to their health care

colleagues from other disciplines, read and reflect on new research's potential to change their practice and be willing and able to integrate that
which is better for patients, families, or staff." It also describes the possibility of more extensive involvement in research. "In some cases, where the
chaplain has sufficient skills and support, this will also mean participating
in, or creating, research efforts to improve chaplaincy care." Chaplains in
the United Kingdom (UK) and Australia are also actively involved in developing an evidence-based approach to health care chaplaincy (for the
UK, see Folland 2006; Mowat 2008; Speck 2005; for Australia, see Spiritual
Health Australia, https://spiritualhealth.org.au/about).

When the subject of research is raised, many chaplains naturally think
of complicated studies such as randomized clinical trials (RCTs). The work
of William Iler or Paul Bay and their colleagues (Iler, Obershain and Camac
2001; Bay et al. 2008) demonstrates that chaplains can organize successful
RCTs of their spiritual care. However, I want to argue that RCTs are not the
kind of research that chaplains need at this point in our history. Before we
can do good clinical trials about our spiritual care we need good case studies
describing our work. Trying to make our case with case studies may initially
seem like a bad idea. As many chaplains know, in evidence-based care there
is a hierarchy of evidence. In this hierarchy case studies are ranked as the
weakest form of evidence (APA Presidential Task Force on Evidence-based
Practice 2006; Hundley 1999. See Flyvbjerg (2006) for a vigorous argument against the view of case studies as an inferior research method.) RCTs
and systematic analyses of data from multiple RCTs (meta-analyses) are
the strongest form of evidence. But, good RCTs and other more complex
types of research require a foundation of theory, practice, and preliminary
research. Case studies play a critical role in developing the foundation from
which more advanced studies can be developed.

The research studies that provide evidence for the effectiveness of any
health care intervention are actually the result of a process of prior research.
One model describes three stages in this process (Rounsaville, Carroll and
Onken 2001). Stage 1 focuses on developing the basic elements of the intervention and measures of its effects. This stage has two parts. The first, Stage
1A, includes developing a detailed description of the intervention, often
called a protocol or manual, demonstrating with a few cases that the intervention is feasible and acceptable, and selecting and testing measures of the
effects of the intervention. The second part, Stage 1B consists of pilot testing
the intervention with a small number of cases. In Stage 1B investigators
focus on whether there is any evidence the intervention has the intended
effects, on whether there are any negative effects associated with the intervention, and on maximizing consistency in the delivery of the intervention.

It is only after this work has been successfully completed that investigators move to Stage 2, in which the efficacy of the intervention is tested in the familiar RCT. If there is evidence the intervention has the intended effects in the ideal world of the RCT, then investigators move to Stage 3, in which further research examines whether the intervention is effective in the real world of clinical practice.

The argument I wish to make is that before chaplains can do Stage 2 RCTs about their spiritual care, we need to build the Stage 1A and 1B foundations. Weaver and colleagues (2008) make a similar point, "Studying processes must necessarily precede studying outcomes" (p. 12). This is where case studies come in. We need good case studies to provide detailed information about three things that are part of Stage 1A research: 1) descriptions of the patient (or family) to whom we provided care; 2) descriptions of the spiritual care that was provided; and 3) descriptions of the changes that occurred as a result of that spiritual care.

Once we have several case studies about a specific type of spiritual care, we need to link the spiritual care described in them with theories about our work (see Canada 2011). When we have a sufficient body of theoretically-illuminated case material then we will be in a position to begin Stage 1A, to develop a detailed spiritual care intervention protocol, select appropriate outcomes measures (again, see Canada 2011), and test the intervention with a few cases. After making revisions based on the Stage 1A experience we can consider a Stage 1B trial to see if similar spiritual interventions, provided to patients with similar conditions, have the measurable effects on the outcomes that we have specified. It is only if this preliminary trial yields evidence for an effect from the chaplain's visit that it is time to consider a Stage 2 randomized trial in which the effects of the chaplain's care are compared to no care or some other intervention. However, what I want to emphasize here are not the details of the later stages of this process. It is the important role of case studies in the first stage.

I also want to underscore that this new emphasis on research does not mean that all chaplains should become investigators. That is not what is recommended in the new Standards of Practice for Professional Chaplains. Designing and conducting the Stage 1A and 1B studies that lead to Stage 2 RCTs is a job for teams of experienced investigators. These teams should include chaplains with training in research. As the Interpretation for Standard 12 states, "In some cases, where the chaplain has sufficient skills and support, this will also mean participating in, or creating, research efforts to improve chaplaincy care." But in contrast, when it comes to writing case studies about our work, many chaplains should be able to make a contribution. The research process I have described will be best served if we can build on case studies written by skilled and experienced chaplains, not case studies written by students or candidates for certification, the least experienced members of our profession.

In addition to their important role in developing research about chaplains' spiritual care, there are at least two other reasons why chaplains should be writing and publishing case studies. It would improve the training of new chaplains and the continuing education of experienced chaplains if we had a body of published case material that we could read and critique. Right now new chaplains mostly learn from cases written by the least experienced members of our profession, the cases they and their peers share in their clinical pastoral education programs. In addition, published case studies would provide colleagues in other health professions with a better understanding of what chaplains do, especially if some of the cases are published in journals that our colleagues are regularly reading.

FINDING OUR CASE STUDIES

If what I have just said has whet your appetite for reading chaplains' case studies you may be disappointed to discover there are essentially none to be found in print. There are case vignettes, but I have yet to find an extended case study that provides detailed information about the three topics (who was the patient, what was the intervention, what changed) I described previously. This is ironic in light of the early history of our field. Anton Boisen, who was a founder of clinical pastoral education (CPE) and a pioneer in modern mental health chaplaincy, had an intense interest in case studies (Asquith 1980, 2005). Boisen is best remembered for *Out of the Depths* (1960), his case study about his own experience with mental illness, but throughout his career he was writing case studies and examining patterns in these cases as a way to better understand the relationship between religion and mental illness. Students in his CPE programs spent their time reading and discussing the cases he wrote (Boisen 1971/1936. Boisen's cases can also be viewed at a website created by Boisen scholar Jesús Rodríguez Sánchez at the Interamerican University of Puerto Rico. See http://web.metro.inter.edu/facultad/esthumanisticos/anton_boisen.asp).

It may be helpful to briefly mention three examples of case material that chaplains have published. In their article "An image of contemporary hospital chaplaincy," Gibbons and Miller (1989) tell the story of a chaplain's work with a couple whose child is born with suspected trisomy-13 and dies the next day. They use the case to briefly identify eleven features of the work of hospital chaplains including chaplains' integration into hospital protocols and teams, chaplains' training that enables them to relate effectively to people in the midst of painful crises, and chaplains' ability to recognize and address complex ethical issues.

In what may have been the first paper to use the term "evidence-based pastoral care," O'Connor and Meakes (1998) describe the case of Mary, a 40-year-old woman with cerebral palsy, who lives in a chronic care hospital. After the onset of seizure activity, Mary was no longer able to use her electric wheelchair. This left her feeling depressed, not able to attend church as she had in the past, and wondering why God would not help her. This brief case description (one paragraph) is followed by a review of research that would be relevant to providing spiritual care for Mary, including research about spirituality and disability. As the authors note, there is actually very little research that is directly relevant to this case. After the literature review, the authors describe the spiritual care that was provided to Mary, and the changes that occurred as a result of that care. While brief, these descriptions include a remarkable level of specificity about the counseling interventions that took place.

The final example is a case study published by Julie Berger (2001). The case is a woman in her forties, newly diagnosed with breast cancer. Chaplain Berger uses the case to illustrate Art Lucas' model for spiritual assessment, *The Discipline for Pastoral Care Giving* (2001). She describes her initial assessment, care plan, and goals ("desired contributing out-comes") both after the initial encounter with the patient and at critical points in the journey with the patient. Of the published cases I have seen, Chaplain Berger's case comes the closest to providing the information I believe must be included in our case studies. The focus on the chaplain's contribution to specific outcomes is one of the strengths of Lucas' model and Chaplain Berger's case. However, there are many details about the patient's background, the care provided by the chaplain, and the conclusion of the case that are not presented.

I have also published some case studies. There are three chapter-length cases in my book, *Assessing Spiritual Needs* (1993/2002). Another case, "Linda Krauss and the Lap of God," was published as an article (Fitchett 1995), and a fifth case, "In the Garden with Andrea," written with Patricia Roberts, was published in an article (Fitchett and Roberts 2003 [Article 8 in this volume]) and reprinted in a chapter I co-authored (Massey, Fitchett and Roberts 2004). Each of these cases was written to illustrate the 7x7 model for spiritual assessment. As such, they give detailed information about the patients in the cases, especially my spiritual assessment of them, but they do not include detailed information about the spiritual care provided in each case, nor the outcomes of the cases.

My search for case studies about chaplains' spiritual care has been far from exhaustive. I would be very glad to learn of any other case studies of chaplains' spiritual care that have been published in articles or books, from the United States or other national contexts.

BACKGROUND FOR THE ONCOLOGY CHAPLAIN CASE STUDY PROJECT

When I became convinced of the importance of case studies for research about chaplains' spiritual care, and when I realized there were essentially no published cases by chaplains about their spiritual care, I decided to try to change that. I began by trying to recruit a small group of chaplains who would work together to present and publish case studies about their spiritual care. Consistent with my research objectives, it was important for the case studies to be about spiritual care with similar patients. Because I knew colleagues in several cancer centers I decided to begin with spiritual care for adult cancer patients. In March 2009, I sent an e-mail message to a number of colleagues seeking names of "experienced colleagues (at least 3 years since board certification), who work in the area of oncology, who would be willing to prepare and share a case study." As you can see, my criteria for selecting participants for the project were that they were Board Certified Chaplains who were currently working in adult oncology. Since one of my aims was to publish the cases studies, it was a plus for the participating chaplains to have good writing skills, for example having any prior publications.

Case Study Project: The Participants

Within a few weeks I had found three chaplains who were willing to be part of the project: Rhonda Cooper at Johns Hopkins in Baltimore, Stephen King at the Seattle Cancer Care Alliance, and Richard (Dick) Maddox at the M.D. Anderson Cancer Center in Houston. The medical centers where these chaplains work are all part of the National Comprehensive Cancer Network, a group of 21 of the nation's leading cancer treatment and research centers. For this article I asked each of them to provide some background about themselves to help me introduce them to you.

Rhonda S. Cooper began hospital chaplaincy work in 1998, after serving congregations for 15 years in Tennessee and Virginia as a United Methodist pastor. She enrolled in CPE as a resident at North Carolina Baptist Medical Center (in Winston-Salem) as a "mid-career" opportunity to re-tool her kills and deepen her understanding of group dynamics. The deep sense of meaning and challenge that she experienced persuaded her that ministry in the hospital setting could be fulfilling. The empathy and support she received from her CPE supervisors became a model for her interactions with patients, family members, and staff.

Rhonda assumed her role as Oncology Chaplain at the Sidney Kimmel Comprehensive Cancer Center at Johns Hopkins in 2005, a few months after her own father died of lung cancer. She works closely with the oncology social workers as a member of the Patient and Family Services Department as well as the Department of Pastoral Care. She serves the adult inpatient units, including critical care, surgery, and bone marrow transplant, and outpatient units, clinics, and treatment areas housed in the Cancer Center. Rhonda became an APC Board Certified Chaplain during her work on this project. In light of her experience in cancer chaplaincy and being in process with her application for Board Certification, I felt she met the criteria for participation in the project.

Stephen King has been working in chaplaincy for 30 years, primarily in academic health care settings. The past 18 years his work has focused on oncology. He has been at the Seattle Cancer Care Alliance for the last 11 years. During this time, he has served primarily as manager but has also had clinical responsibilities in both inpatient and outpatient contexts. He is ordained in the Christian Church (Disciples of Christ) and is a Board Certified Chaplain (APC). He recently co-chaired the APC Quality Commission Task Force that drafted The Standards of Practice for Professional Chaplains in Acute Care.

Dick T. Maddox is the staff chaplain for the Children's Cancer Hospital at the University of Texas M.D. Anderson Cancer Center (UTMDACC/MDACC). He also serves as chaplain for the head and neck cancer surgical unit for UTMDACC. In his seven-year tenure at MDACC, he has served on its Institutional Review Board (current member), Clinical Ethics Committee, and numerous department and division committees and task forces. Dick is a Board Certified Chaplain (APC) and is ordained in the Christian Church (Disciples of Christ). He served local congregations for 15 years before making a career change to chaplaincy. Before entering ministry, Dick had a career in environmental engineering.

Case Study Project: Our Process

Our team met monthly by conference call. Our first meeting, in April 2009, was used to get acquainted and discuss the goals for the project. Our early meetings addressed the question of what should be in a good case study (see the following section) and the ethical issues related to asking a patient for permission to publish or present a case study about them. In July 2009 we discussed our first case, an initial draft of Rhonda's work with a patient she called Doris. In the next few months we discussed case studies written by Stephen and Dick. We continued to look for and discuss books and articles about case studies.

Soon after we began, we had to turn our attention to planning for the workshop at the APC 2010 meeting. Because of our aims, and the limited time for the workshop, we chose to focus on one case study; Rhonda's report of her work with Doris was selected (see Cooper 2011). Our approach also included two responses to the case. The first response was from a chaplain colleague (see King 2011). For us, the chaplain's response to the case was designed to model how chaplains can use case studies to discuss and debate the strengths and weaknesses of the spiritual care described in the case. The second response was designed to show how to build the link between case studies and research. Specifically, we wanted to provide a theoretical framework for the spiritual care provided in the case and to describe ways that the changes observed in the case could be measured (see Canada 2011). Because none of us had the expertise to provide this response, and as a way to model interdisciplinary collaboration in this research process, we invited Andrea Canada, a health psychologist, who specializes in cancer care to provide this response. Andrea is an Assistant Professor in the Department of Behavioral Sciences at Rush University Medical Center. She has a long-standing interest in the role of religion and spirituality in coping with cancer and has collaborated with me and my colleague Patricia Murphy in several research and writing projects (Canada et al. 2008; Fitchett and Canada 2010; Murphy, Fitchett and Canada 2008).

After a year of conference calls, the APC workshop in April 2010 provided the first opportunity for our team to meet in person. The workshop went well and received positive reviews from the participants, including the following: "Great case study, reflection and responses. Thank you!" "Very well done. Gives a good example of how to do case study research." "We need to add more of this!"

Since the workshop we have continued our monthly calls. Now, our goals include getting all of the case studies published. As I have noted, in some of the team's initial conversations we discussed requesting permission from the patients to use material about them in the case studies the chaplains were writing. Actually we spent a lot of time on this issue and learned a lot about it. Dick gave a brief summary of what we learned at the APC workshop. However, because we realized how important and complex this topic was we decided that it needed to be presented in an article of its own by someone with expertise in the area of ethics. I approached Dave McCurdy to help with this and thankfully he agreed (see McCurdy and Fitchett 2011). Dave is a Board Certified Chaplain (APC) and a certified supervisor (ACPE). He is presently Senior Ethics Consultant and Director of Organizational Ethics for Advocate Health Care in Park Ridge, Illinois. He was formerly a staff member and director of publications at the Park Ridge Center for the Study of Health, Faith, and Ethics.

Case Study Project: Impact on the Participants

Over the past 15 months, all of us who have participated in this project have learned a great deal. We have tried to share some of what we have learned in the essays in this issue of the *Journal of Health Care Chaplaincy* [17, 1–2]. The project has given me the opportunity to get to know and work with three talented and committed oncology chaplains. It has also confirmed my belief in the importance of case studies for our profession. I want to close this description of the project by sharing what the team members wrote about the impact of the project on their work as chaplains.

Rhonda: "As a result of the project, I have gained deeper appreciation for the privacy concerns of the patient, family or staff who are subjects of case studies. Initially I was resistant to asking for authorization from the subject of my study and I did not approach her until our relationship was well established. In writing the case and being in dialogue with colleagues also engaged in spiritual care of oncology patients, I found myself being more aware of the needs-interventions-outcome relationship so that I am more intentional in my approach. I have also come to appreciate the value of peer review and consultation."

Stephen: "First, participation in the project highlighted the importance both within chaplaincy and to non-chaplain health care providers of chaplains articulating clearly the needs, interventions, and outcomes. The writing of my own case study also enhanced my focus upon desired negotiated outcomes with the patient/family. Second, participation in the project led to a departmental change whereby every chaplain now annually presents a case study to the department. Although time consuming, the chaplains want to continue this practice as a wonderful learning opportunity through writing the case, receiving feedback from other chaplains, and learning about the chaplaincy care provided by others. In both the case study project and the departmental project, the group relationship building via the case discussions was a highlight."

Dick: "I find myself much more attentive to the construct and implementation of spiritual care assessments, and more disciplined about considering and characterizing spiritual care interventions before applying them and evaluating them afterwards. And I have become far more concerned with how I might be able to measure outcomes and relate them to interventions."

WHAT DOES A GOOD CASE STUDY LOOK LIKE?

One of the things that I hope will result from this project is that more chaplains will be convinced of the importance of case studies for our profession and will begin to write, publish, and discuss case studies about their spiritual care. As you begin to do that, one of the first issues you will face is what you should include. What does a good case study look like? As we began this project our team faced the same question. As I have already indicated, we did not find anything in the chaplaincy literature to help us.

Next, we looked at the literature in related fields. A number of things we found there went into the description of a good case study that appears in the following. For example, earlier I mentioned that good case studies provide detailed information about three things: 1) descriptions of the patient (throughout this also refers, where appropriate, to the patient's family) to whom care was provided; 2) descriptions of the spiritual care that was provided; and 3) descriptions of the changes that occurred as a result of that spiritual care. I took these three things from a research method known as practice-based evidence (Horn and Gassaway 2007; 2010). I think they are especially important for case studies that are written to help provide the foundation for research that tests the effects of chaplains' spiritual care.

My earlier interest in self-psychology made me familiar with the important role of detailed case studies in psychoanalytic psychology (e.g., Goldberg 1978; Kohut 1979). I assumed there might be a similar case study literature in psychology that could be helpful to chaplains. Some searching in that field led me Ronald B. Miller's book, *Facing Human Suffering: Psychology and Psychotherapy as Moral Engagement* (2004), the most important resource for writing about case studies that I have found thus far. Miller's interest is larger than just case studies. His book presents his critique of how psychology and the training of psychotherapists have gotten away from the moral issues that he feels are at the heart of human suffering. In presenting his case for clinicians' need to develop clinical knowledge, he argues for the important role of case studies in developing clinical knowledge. Miller and his students have developed a searchable archive of psychotherapy case studies and his book includes appendices with several lists of psychotherapy case studies. My description of a good case study below has been shaped by my appreciation for Miller's work.

A good case study has the following characteristics:

1. It makes a point or tells an important story.

    In his discussion of psychotherapy case studies, Miller (2004) describes writing case studies in order to make an argument for the effectiveness of a particular therapeutic approach in a specific case or group of cases. Similarly, chaplains might think of case studies as a way to describe the beneficial effects of their spiritual care with patients or families. There might also be value in writing case studies about the harmful effects for patients whose spiritual needs go unmet because chaplains were not available to them. The introduction is the place to tell the reader why you have written this case.

2. It makes our case with cases.

    To elaborate on the previous point, one of the reasons that chaplains should write case studies is to help colleagues in other professions understand what chaplains do and understand why what we do is important. When this is the point of a case study, chaplains should consider specifically addressing two questions: 1) in what ways does this case demonstrate that the chaplain's care caused a change for the patient that would not have occurred if the care had not been provided; and, 2) are there any ways in which the care provided by the chaplain was different from, or could not have been provided by, a local clergy person or clergy volunteer, or by a professional from another discipline, such as a social worker or psychologist.

3. It begins with background.

    The case study should include detailed information about the patient, the chaplain, and the institutional context in which they meet. The information about the patient should include thorough demographic, medical, psychosocial, and religious characteristics. Providing this thorough background information will help the reader of the case study understand to what other cases one can generalize the spiritual care that was described in the case study. It will also provide the reader of the case study with sufficient information to critically evaluate the chaplain's assessment and spiritual care, (see McCurdy and Fitchett 2011, for a discussion of the important issue of how to include detailed information about the case while also protecting the confidentiality of the subject of the case study). It is also important to include information about the chaplain(s) who provided the care and who wrote the case study. This should begin with basic demographic information and include information about religious affiliation and professional training. Beyond such basic information, a good case study will also provide information about the chaplain's awareness of his/her feelings about the patient in the case study and their role in that relationship.

4. It describes the chaplain-patient relationship.
   The heart of the case study is the story of the chaplain-patient relationship. Key information here includes a description of the spiritual care provided by the chaplain. We also want to know about any changes in the patient that occurred during or after the relationship with the chaplain, including changes that might be attributed to the care provided by the chaplain. If nothing changed that is also important to know. The general rule is the more detail the better. Chaplains like verbatims and this might be a place to include verbatim reports of selected portions of the chaplain-patient conversation. Narrative summaries of the relationship will be needed to communicate what occurred in longer chaplain-patient relationships. In many cases our spiritual care is provided in the context of consultation with, and care provided by, other members of the health care team. Important information about the care team's work should be included in the case study.

5. It includes a spiritual assessment.
   Including a spiritual assessment will help the reader know the chaplain's interpretation of the case, including the observations that influenced the chaplain's care plan. The spiritual assessment may have deepened or changed over time and that should be noted. Of course, I am partial to the 7x7 model for spiritual assessment (Fitchett 1993/2002), but other helpful models for spiritual assessment have been published, including the work of Pruyser (1976) and Lucas (2001).

6. It ends with a summary.
   The case study should end with a summary. This is the place to remind readers of the point(s) that you were trying to make with your case. When the case was written to describe the impact of the chaplain's spiritual care this is the place to review the patient's spiritual needs, the spiritual care that was provided, and the effects of the spiritual care on those needs. Here may be the place, if appropriate to the case study, to articulate in what ways, if any, the care that was provided was uniquely spiritual care provided by a professional chaplain.

7. It could include discussions of theory or measurement.

Improving chaplains' spiritual care, and strengthening the case for it, will require informed descriptions of the theories that support chaplains' interventions or care, and careful attention to measuring the changes that come about as a result of that care. Some chaplains will write case studies to illustrate a theory of spiritual care or to illustrate the kinds of changes that come about as a result of spiritual care. In the introduction the chaplain can indicate if any of these are the aims of the case study. Such case studies would also include an extended discussion of the theory or measurement issue after the case has been presented.

NEXT STEPS: MAKING OUR CASE(S)

As I described earlier, the work of the oncology chaplain case study team is nearing completion and will end when all three cases have been published. To help promote chaplain case studies I plan to recruit a new team, with a different clinical specialty, and help those chaplains present and publish their cases. However, for our profession to realize the full benefit of this focus on case studies, many chaplains need to get involved. Let me conclude this essay by sharing some suggestions for how our profession can encourage case studies and use case studies to improve our care and make our case.

I begin with several things we can do within our profession to further the use of case studies. First, we can make case studies a common part of training for chaplains. Writing case studies is encouraged in some CPE residency programs, but it would help build a familiarity with case studies and their importance if reading, writing, and critiquing them were a well-integrated element of the curriculum in the second half of all residency programs. Publishing the best CPE case study outlines and curricula that integrate case study work will help this to happen. Second, we should make a case study one of the required pieces of clinical work for Board Certified Chaplains. Third, we should amend the continuing education requirements for chaplains to make writing, presenting, and publishing case studies an area of emphasis. Fourth, we should encourage workshops about case studies at state, regional, and national chaplaincy conferences. These could include beginning workshops about how to write case studies, as well as more advanced workshops where experienced chaplains discuss the strengths and weaknesses of one or more case studies. Finally, we should encourage the publication of case studies in chaplaincy journals. To advance our field it is especially important for some of those case studies to be accompanied by the kind of critical responses that are included with the case study published in this issue of this journal.

Beyond what we do within our profession, it is important for chaplains to share their cases with health care colleagues in other professions, at their meetings and in their journals. The importance of this was underscored by the comment of a chaplain who was a participant in a study about chaplains and quality improvement. "[A colleague] and I did a presentation to a palliative care conference . . . And what we did was [role play] a verbatim . . . We brought down the house because it was like they never . . . experienced a chaplain's visit before" (Lyndes et al. 2008, 74).

The majority of our health care colleagues have little or no education to help them gain a meaningful appreciation for what we contribute to the care of patients and their families. This is not going to change quickly so chaplains must be persistent and creative in looking for ways to tell the story of who we are and what we do. Case studies presented at the professional meetings of other health professions and published in the journals of those professions can be a very effective way to help our colleagues develop a better understanding of what we do.

SUMMARY

Case studies were central to what Anton Boisen, a founder of modern chaplaincy and clinical pastoral education, was about as a chaplain, pastoral educator, and researcher. They play a central role in developing the foundations for research about the effects of chaplains' spiritual care. They can also be an effective way to help colleagues in other health care professions develop a better understanding of the chaplains' contribution to care for patients and families. Health care chaplaincy is in the process of becoming a research-informed profession. Every chaplain can play an important role in that process, not by conducting RCTs or other quantitative research, but by writing case studies about the work they do every day.

ACKNOWLEDGEMENT

I am grateful for the feedback on earlier versions of this manuscript from members of the oncology chaplain case study project, Rhonda Cooper, Stephen King, Dick Maddox, Andrea Canada, and Dave McCurdy.

REFERENCES

APA Presidential Task Force on Evidence-based Practice. 2006. "Evidence-based Practice in Psychology." *American Psychologist* 61:4, 271–85. doi: 10.1037/0003–066X.61.4.271.

Association of Professional Chaplains. 2009. *Standards of practice for professional chaplains in acute care.* [Editors: the 2009 version has been superseded by subsequent versions. The latest version, titled *Standards of Practice for Professional Chaplains*, was accessed August 17, 2020, https://www.professionalchaplains.org/content.asp?pl=198&sl=198&contentid=200]

Asquith, G.H., Jr. 1980. "The Case Study Method of Anton T. Boisen." *Journal of Pastoral Care* 34:2, 84–94. Reprinted 1992 in *Vision from a Little Known Country: A Boisen Reader*, edited by G. H. Asquith, Jr. Decatur, GA: Journal of Pastoral Care Publications.

Asquith, G. H., Jr. 2005. "Case Study Method." In *Dictionary of Pastoral Care and Counseling* (Expanded edition), edited by R. Hunter. Nashville, TN: Abingdon.

Bay, P. S., Beckman, D., Trippi, J., Gunderman, R. and Terry, C. 2008. "The Effect of Pastoral Care Services on Anxiety, Depression, Hope, Religious Coping, and Religious Problem Solving Styles: A Randomized Controlled Study." *Journal of Religion and Health* 47:57–69. doi: 10.1007/s10943-007-9131-4.

Bay, P. S. and Ivy, S. S. 2006. "Chaplaincy Research: A Case Study." *Journal of Pastoral Care and Counseling* 60:4, 343–52.

Berger, J. A. 2001. "A Case Study: Linda." *Journal of Health Care Chaplaincy* 10:2, 35–43. Co-published as *The Discipline for Pastoral Care Giving*, edited by L. VandeCreek and A. M. Lucas, 35–43. Binghamton, NY: Haworth Pastoral. doi: 10.1300/J080v10n02_02.

Boisen, A. T. 1971/1936. *The Exploration of the Inner World: A Study of Mental Disorder and Religious Experience*. Philadelphia: University Pennsylvania Press.

Boisen, A. T. 1960. *Out of the Depths: An Autobiographical Study of Mental Disorder and Religious Experience*. New York: Harper, & Brothers.

Canada, A. L. 2011. "A Psychologist's Response to the Case Study: Application of Theory and Measurement." *Journal of Health Care Chaplaincy* 17:1–2, 46–54. doi: 10.1080/08854726.2011.559854.

Canada, A. L., Murphy, P. E., Fitchett, G., Peterman, A. H. and Schover, L. R. 2008. "A 3-Factor Model for the FACIT—Sp." *Psycho-Oncology* 17:9, 908–16. doi: 10.1002/pon.1307.

Cooper, R. S. 2011. "A Case Study of a Chaplain's Spiritual Care for a Patient with Advanced Metastatic Breast Cancer." *Journal of Health Care Chaplaincy* 17:1–2, 19–37. doi: 10.1080/08854726.2011.559832.

Fitchett, G. 1993/2002. *Assessing Spiritual Needs: A Guide for Caregivers* (Original edition: Minneapolis: Augsburg, 1993). Reprint edition, Lima, OH: Academic Renewal, 2002.

Fitchett, G. 1995. "Linda Krauss and the Lap of God: A Spiritual Assessment Case Study." *Second Opinion* 20:4, 41–49.

Fitchett, G. and Canada, A. L. 2010. "The Role of Religion/Spirituality in Coping with Cancer: Evidence, Assessment, and Intervention." In *Psycho-Oncology*, 2nd ed., edited by J. C. Holland, W.S. Breitbart, P. B. Jacobson, M. S. Lederberg, M. J. Loscalzo and R. McCorkle, 440–46. New York: Oxford University Press.

Fitchett, G. and Roberts, P. A. 2003. "In the Garden with Andrea: Spiritual Assessment in End-of-Life Care." In *Walking Together: Physicians, Chaplains and Clergy Caring for the Sick*, edited by C. M. Puchalski, 23–31. Washington, DC: The George Washington Institute for Spirituality and Health. [Article 8 in this volume]

Flannelly, K. J., Liu, C., Oppenheimer, J. E., Weaver, A. J. and Larson, D. B. 2003. "An Evaluation of the Quantity and Quality of Empirical Research in Three Pastoral Care and Counseling Journals, 1990–99: Has Anything Changed?" *Journal of Pastoral Care and Counseling* 57:167–78.

Flyvbjerg, B. 2006. "Five Misunderstandings about Case-Study Research." *Qualitative Inquiry*, 12, 2, 219–45. doi: 10.1177/1077800405284363.

Folland, M. 2006. "Opportunity and Conflict: Evidence-based Practice and the Modernization of Healthcare Chaplaincy." *Contact* 149:12–20.

Gleason, J. J. 2004. "Pastoral Research: Past, Present, and Future." *Journal of Pastoral Care and Counseling* 58:295–306.

Gibbons, J. L. and Miller, S. L. 1989. "An Image of Contemporary Hospital Chaplaincy." *Journal of Pastoral Care* 43:4, 355–61.

Goldberg, A. ed. 1978. *The Psychology of the Self: A Casebook (written with the collaboration of Heinz Kohut)*. New York: International Universities Press.

Horn, S. D. and Gassaway, J. 2007. "Practice-based Evidence Study Design for Comparative Effectiveness Research." *Medical Care* 45(10 Suppl 2): S50–S57. doi: 10.1097/MLR.0b013e318070c07b.

Horn, S. D. and Gassaway, J. 2010. "Practice-based Evidence: Incorporating Clinical Heterogeneity and Patient-reported Outcomes for Comparative Effectiveness Research." *Medical Care* 48(6 Suppl): S17–S22. doi: 10.1097/MLR.0b013e3181d57473.

Hundley, V. 1999. "Evidence Based Practice: What Is It? And Why Does It Matter? *Scottish Journal of Healthcare Chaplaincy* 2:1, 11–14.

Iler, W. L., Obershain, D. and Camac, M. 2001. "The Impact of Daily Visits from Chaplains on Patients with Chronic Obstructive Pulmonary Disease (COPD): A Pilot Study." *Chaplaincy Today* 17:1, 5–11.

King, S. D. W. 2011. "Touched by an Angel: A Chaplain's Response to the Case Study's Key Interventions, Styles, and Themes/Outcomes." *Journal of Health Care Chaplaincy* 17:1–2, 38–45. doi: 10.1080/08854726.2011.559841.

Koenig, H. G. 2008. "Why Research Is Important for Chaplains." *Journal of Health Care Chaplaincy* 14:2, 83–90. doi: 10.1080/08854720802129026.

Kohut, H. 1979. "The Two Analyses of Mr. Z." *The International Journal of Psychoanalysis* 60:1, 3–27.

Lucas, A. M. 2001. "Introduction to the Discipline for Pastoral Care Giving." In *The Discipline for Pastoral Care Giving*, edited by L. VandeCreek and A. M. Lucas, 1–33. Binghamton, NY: Haworth.

Lyndes, K. A., Fitchett, G., Thomason, C. L., Berlinger, N. and Jacobs, M. R. 2008. "Chaplains and Quality Improvement: Can We Make Our Case by Improving Our Care?" *Journal of Health Care Chaplaincy* 15:2, 65–79. doi: 10.1080=08854720903113416.

Massey, K., Fitchett, G. and Roberts, P. A. 2004. "Assessment and Diagnosis in Spiritual Care." In *Spiritual Care in Nursing Practice*, edited by K. L. Mauk and N. K. Schmidt, 209–42. Philadelphia: Lippincott, Williams, and Wilkins.

McCurdy, D. B. and Fitchett, G. 2011. "Ethical Issues in Case Study Publication: 'Making Our Case(s)' Ethically." *Journal of Health Care Chaplaincy* 17:1–2, 55–74. doi: 10.1080/08854726.2011.559855.

Miller, R. B. 2004. *Facing Human Suffering: Psychology and Psychotherapy as Moral Engagement.* Washington, DC: American Psychological Association.

Mowat, H. 2008. *The Potential for Efficacy of Healthcare Chaplaincy and Spiritual Care Provision in the NHS (UK): A Scoping Review of Recent Research.* Aberdeen, Scotland: Mowat Research Ltd.

Murphy, P. E., Fitchett, G. and Canada, A. L. 2008. "Adult Spirituality for Persons with Chronic Illness." In *Spiritual Dimensions of Nursing Practice*, edited by V. B. Carson and H. G. Koenig, 193–235. West Conshohocken, PA: Templeton Foundation.

O'Connor, T. S., Koning, F., Meakes, E., McLarnon-Sinclair, K., Davis, K., and Loy, V. 2001. "Quantity and Rigor of Qualitative Research in Four Pastoral Counselling Journals." *Journal of Pastoral Care* 55:271–80.

O'Connor, T. S., and Meakes, E. 1998. "Hope in the Midst of Challenge: Evidence-based Pastoral Care." *Journal of Pastoral Care* 52:4, 359–67.

Pruyser, P. W. 1976. *The Minister as Diagnostician.* Philadelphia: Westminster.

Rounsaville, B. J., Carroll, K. M. and Onken, L. S. 2001. "A Stage Model of Behavioral Therapies Research: Getting Started and Moving on from Stage I." *Clinical Psychology: Science and Practice* 8:2, 133–42. doi: 10.1093/clipsy.8.2.133.

Speck, P. 2005. "A Standard for Research in Healthcare Chaplaincy." *The Journal for Health Care Chaplaincy* 6:26–40.

VandeCreek, L. ed. 2002. *Professional Chaplaincy and Clinical Pastoral Education Should Become More Scientific: Yes and No.* Binghamton, NY: Haworth.

Weaver, A. J., Flannelly, K. J. and Liu, C. 2008. "Chaplaincy Research: Its Value, Its Quality, and Its Future." *Journal of Health Care Chaplaincy* 14:1, 3–19. doi: 10.1080/08854720802053796.

ARTICLE 7

Health Care Chaplaincy as a Research-Informed Profession [1]

—George Fitchett

Ph.D., BCC, ACPE Supervisor

—Daniel Grossoehme

D.Min., BCC

THIS CHAPTER REFLECTS THE *broad consensus emerging in the U.S. support-*
ing a research-informed or evidence-based approach to chaplaincy. The Asso-
ciation of Professional Chaplains had previously issued Standards of Practice
for Professional Chaplaincy *(2009) and included a standard about evidence-*
based practice. In the chapter, we gave a rationale for this research-informed
approach and described one approach to developing the research needed to
support it. We emphasized that this doesn't mean all chaplains need to become
researchers; but it does require all chaplains be research literate. We also wrote
that this approach requires the development of a group of academic research
chaplains, whose main task is to lead spiritual care research. A few years af-
ter the chapter was published, Wendy Cadge, a sociologist of religion from
Brandeis University, with a strong interest in chaplaincy, and I, along with oth-
ers, received the $4.5 million grant from the John Templeton Foundation that

1. G. Fitchett and D. Grossoehme. 2012. "Health Care Chaplaincy as a Research-Informed Profession." In *Professional Spiritual and Pastoral Care: A Practical Clergy and Chaplain's Handbook*, edited by S. Roberts, 387–406. Woodstock, VY: SkyLight Paths.

helped launch Transforming Chaplaincy (www.transformchaplaincy.org).
Among other things, this grant supported research education for 17 chaplains,
a number of whom are now working as academic research chaplains. There is
much work to be done, but over the past 20 years we have made remarkable
progress in developing an evidence-based approach to healthcare chaplaincy.

There is a growing consensus that health care chaplaincy should become a
research-informed profession. We begin this chapter with a brief description of theological foundations for this position. We continue by describing
some of the existing research about chaplaincy and next steps for chaplaincy
research. We end the chapter with a description of three levels of chaplain
involvement in research.

A RESEARCH-INFORMED PROFESSION: VISION AND RATIONALE

Professional chaplains should be "research-literate"—clinicians whose
practice of chaplaincy is informed (and open to change) by the available
evidence. This doesn't mean every chaplain should begin carrying out research projects. All chaplains need to be consumers of research to continu-
ously refine their clinical practice, while a minority design and collaborate
in research studies. Pastoral counselors Thomas O'Connor and Elizabeth
Meakes state that to do otherwise may lead to care "that is ineffective or
possibly even harmful" (O'Connor and Meakes 1998, 367). In most contemporary health care settings, chaplains are a limited resource and should not
waste their time with ineffective clinical practices.

The Association of Professional Chaplains (APC), the largest multi-
faith association of professional chaplains in the United States, recently
developed *Standards of Practice for Professional Chaplains in Acute Care
Settings*, which reflects this growing consensus for research-informed
chaplaincy. Standard 12 reads, "The chaplain practices evidence-based
care including ongoing evaluation of new practices and, when appropriate,
contributes to or conducts research" (Association of Professional Chaplains
2009). Chaplaincy within the United Kingdom has made similar steps,
culminating in *A Standard for Research in Health Care Chaplaincy* (Speck
2005). Contemporary health care in the United States and the United Kingdom (at least) has moved to evidence-based practices, and chaplaincy needs
to make the same transition.

Chaplains traditionally enjoy significant discretion over how their
time is managed. The current health care climate, in which chaplains are a

limited resource, means they must decide how to ration their time. This is not simply a time-management issue, but a theological issue of stewardship: what is the best use of the gift of time the chaplain has to offer? Research in chaplaincy is theologically grounded.

Theology and science have a long relationship, ranging from well integrated to antagonistic. Theologian Ian Barbour (1990) outlines four ways in which science and religion relate to one another. The first way is conflict. In this light, rationality and logic are prized above faith—or equally, the infallibility of scripture is prized above data. Both sides claim to be the sole means of arriving at knowledge and truth, and it is necessary to choose between them. The second way is independence. Without disparaging the other, science and religion move along different paths, exerting no influence upon the other field. Each field uses a different language to pursue answers to different questions, "how?" and "why?" respectively. Dialogue is the third way by which science and religion may relate to each other. The means of gaining knowledge by science and religion are distinct but have points of contact. Experiences of physical reality are a means of encountering the holy, which is done most fully through scriptures. Finally, Barbour describes the fourth way, integration. The essential point is a "coherent vision of reality can still allow for the distinctiveness of different types of experience" (Barbour 1990, 30). Chaplains making use of research do not abdicate their faith and trust in the holy, but instead seek knowledge wherever and however it may be found.

Faith-based acquisition of knowledge also has roots in the three monotheistic, Abrahamic faith traditions. Judaism has the tenet of *tikkun olam* (to repair the world). Efforts to repair the world are *mitzvot* (acts of human kindness rooted in commandments). Just as we may repair the world by prescribing an antibiotic to treat a bacterial infection, research studies leading to improved care repair the world. Repairing the world is not a choice but an obligation of faith. *Tikkun olam* was the motivation for engaging in research (instead of or in addition to clinical care of the sick) in a discussion among contemporary Jewish health service researchers and clinicians.[2] Among Christians, research follows from the theology of creation. Creation was given into the hands of humanity to care for; stewardship, including time, is a Christian responsibility. Research literacy can help chaplains be good stewards of their time. Christians are called to participate in the healing of brokenness by participating in the ongoing creation of the world according to God's plan by discovering and implementing new means of healing the

2. E. Lipstein, personal communication, October 29, 2010; M. Seid, personal communication, October 29, 2010.

world's brokenness. Islam has a long tradition of science (Barbour 1990). Narratives of the Prophet Muhammad's words and actions (known as *hadith*) speak directly to the relationship between science and faithfulness in Islam. Surgeon and scholar M. Bucaille records the *hadith*, "Seek for science, even in China," and "The seeking of knowledge is obligatory for every Muslim" (Bucaille 1979). It is not simply that knowledge acquisition is important, but it must be coupled with making it available to the wider community: "Acquire knowledge and impart it to the people." Adherents of each of the three monotheistic Abrahamic faith traditions stand firmly rooted in their own faith community when they make use of the knowledge gained by others through research and when they seek to gain knowledge themselves and make what they learn available to others.

RESEARCH ABOUT HEALTH CARE CHAPLAINCY: WHAT DO WE KNOW

While chaplains have a long way to go to become a research-informed profession, there already is a sizable body of research about what we do. Unfortunately, that research is scattered in many publications, making it difficult to get a good perspective on it. An important exception is a thorough, critical review of research about chaplaincy in the United Kingdom (Mowat 2008). This survey organized the existing U.K. research into eight categories (see Figure 7.1). Scottish social scientist Harriet Mowat found many articles with opinions about chaplaincy (65 percent of the U.K. articles), some research about what chaplains do, and no research about the effects of the spiritual care provided by chaplains. "The research literature . . . as it stands does not directly or substantially address the issue of efficacy in health care chaplaincy" (Mowat 2008, 7).

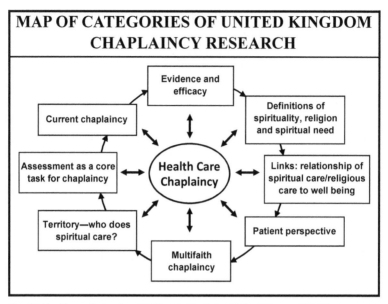

Reprinted with permission from H. Mowat, *The Potential for Efficacy of Healthcare Chaplaincy and Spiritual Care Provision in the NHS (UK): A Scoping Review of Recent Research* (Aberdeen, Scotland: Mowat Research Ltd., January 2008), 70.

Figure 7.1

While we do not have a comparable review, our assessment of the U.S. chaplaincy literature is similar to what Mowat reported for the U.K, with a few notable exceptions. We have many articles with opinions about chaplaincy, a modest and interesting body of research about what chaplains do, a few studies of the effects of chaplains' spiritual care, and two frequently quoted studies that on closer look do not provide evidence about the spiritual care chaplains provide.

Research about what chaplains do includes studies of the number and types of chaplain visits (Handzo et al. 2008; Handzo, Flannelly and Kudler 2008; Montonye and Calderone 2010) and studies of who makes referrals to chaplains (Galek, Flannelly, Koenig and Fogg 2007), including patient self-referrals (Chapman and Grossoehme 2002; Fitchett, Meyer and Burton 2000). There also is research about chaplains' different roles and health care colleagues' perceptions of them (Flannelly et al. 2006). An interesting study asked 535 discharged Mayo Clinic patients to rate different reasons they might want to see a chaplain (Piderman et al. 2008). Eighty-four percent of the patients indicated the chaplain's visits were important or very important because they were reminders "of God's care and presence"; 76 percent said having the chaplain visit at "times of particular anxiety or uncertainty" was important or very important.

Research about patient/family or staff satisfaction with chaplains is one type of research about the effects of chaplains' care. Larry VandeCreek and colleagues (VandeCreek and Lyons 1997; VandeCreek 2004) have done important work in this area, developing an instrument to measure patient/family satisfaction with chaplains and reporting their results. Other studies of patient/family satisfaction with chaplains' care have also been reported (Gibbons, Thomas, Vandecreek and Jessen 1973; Flannelly et al. 2009). A large national study of 1,102 physicians found that 90 percent had worked with chaplains, and among them, 90 percent were satisfied or very satisfied with that experience. (Fitchett, Rasinski, Cadge and Curlin 2009).

Some research reports the impact of care provided by chaplains in the context of a multidisciplinary intervention. Chaplains at the Mayo Clinic led four sessions in a multidisciplinary quality of life intervention for radiation oncology patients (Piderman and Johnson 2009). Compared to those in the control group, quality of life improved for the participants in the intervention. Another study of oncology patients near the end of their lives found that those who reported spiritual care from a chaplain or the medical team had better quality of life (Balboni et al. 2007).

Two randomized studies of the effects of chaplains' care have been reported in peer-reviewed journals. In one study, led by Chaplain William Iler, fifty patients with chronic obstructive pulmonary disease (COPD) were randomized to a daily chaplain visit or to usual care, which in this hospital was no chaplain visit (Iler, Obenshain and Camac 2001). Compared to those who did not receive chaplain visits, patients who did receive visits had a greater decrease in anxiety, shorter length of stay (average 9.0 versus 5.6 days, $p<0.05$), and higher ratings of satisfaction.

In the second study, led by Chaplain Paul Bay, 170 patients who received coronary artery bypass graft (CABG) surgery were randomized to receive chaplain visits or not (Bay et al. 2008). Outcomes were assessed one month and six month's post-surgery. There were no differences between the two groups for changes in depression or anxiety. At six-month follow-up, the patients who received chaplain visits had higher scores on positive religious coping and lower scores on negative religious coping.

Why did the COPD study find beneficial effects on anxiety for the chaplains' visits when the CABG study found no such effects for either anxiety or depression? One possible explanation is the difference in baseline levels of anxiety, which were generally low for the CABG patients but moderately high for the COPD patients. The important point here is that it may be difficult to find measurable benefits of chaplains' care among patients who are in minimal distress or coping well. It is very challenging to organize and conduct clinical trials, but they yield very convincing evidence. The chaplains who conducted these studies have made a major contribution by demonstrating that they can be done.

A study of orthopedic patients (Florell 1973) is one of two frequently cited studies that we would argue do not provide evidence of the beneficial effects of chaplains' care. This study examined whether it would lower their anxiety to provide patients with information about what to expect leading up to and after their surgery. The patients were assigned to receive one of three types of care: (a) a supportive preoperative visit, (b) a supportive visit with information about what to expect, and (c) neither support nor information. The support and information interventions were provided by chaplains, but the first concern with this study is that the chaplains were not there to provide spiritual care.

The second concern is that results are reported for 150 patients, but only 60 of them were randomly assigned to the support or support plus information groups. The overall results include 90 other patients who were not randomly assigned. The study reports that all the patients were relatively similar on background factors such as age, previous hospitalizations, and anxiety, and thus it could be assumed that any differences in the outcomes were due to the differences in the interventions they received. The key fact that is overlooked here is that random assignment matches groups on all background factors, including those that were not assessed. Thus, for this study we have no assurance that the results were not confounded by a difference between the groups in an unmeasured factor. This study is widely cited as providing evidence that chaplains' visits reduced patients' length of stay, need for pain medication, and calls for the nurse. Because of the issues we have described we do not believe this study provides evidence for these beneficial effects of chaplains' care.

The main claim in the second investigation is that "studies of the effect of chaplains' interventions in orthopedic, cardiac bypass surgery, CCU, and other relatively homogeneous groups, have already shown statistically significant savings of from 19.6 to 29.9 percent per case" (McSherry, Cuilla and Burton 1992, 36). The Florell orthopedic patient study described above is one of the references for this claim (Florell 1973). Another is a study that reports, "Patients who rated themselves as moderately to highly religious left the hospital 19.5% earlier than those rating themselves uninterested or little interested in religion" (McSherry 1987). This statement confuses the beneficial effects of patients' religiousness, for which there is good evidence (Brady et al. 1999; Chida, Steptoe and Powell 2009), with the effects of chaplains' care, for which no evidence is given. For understandable reasons, including their uncritical presentation in the well-respected *Handbook of Religion and Health* (Koenig, McCullough and Larson 2001, 420–21),

chaplains have taken these claims at face value. However, if we are to have credibility as research-informed professionals, we cannot perpetuate claims about our effectiveness that are not well supported by the evidence.

RESEARCH ABOUT HEALTH CARE CHAPLAINCY: NEXT STEPS

Several helpful discussions about next steps for chaplaincy research have been published (Mowat 2008; Weaver, Flannelly and Liu 2008). The following five-step outline is based on a description by pediatrician and researcher Chris Feudtner and colleagues (Feudtner, Haney and Dimmers 2003). The first step is to understand the religious and spiritual needs and resources of patients and families. Just as effective spiritual care is built on a sound spiritual assessment, research about chaplains' spiritual care should be built on knowledge about patients' and families' spiritual needs and resources. We have a head start here because a number of studies of patients' spiritual needs and resources have been published, in fact many more than can be cited in this brief overview. For example, each of us has published some work in this area (Fitchett, Burton and Sivan 1997; Fitchett et al. 2004; Grossoehme, Cotron and Leonard 2007; Grossoehme and Gerbetz 2004). Illustrative studies by colleagues in other professions include investigations about cancer patients (Alcorn et al. 2010), older adults in long-term care (Daaleman, Williams, Hamilton and Zimmerman 2008), and parents of children who died in the intensive care unit (Meert, Thurston and Briller 2005).

However, many of these existing studies are based on small, unrepresentative samples, so further investigation is important. In addition, few studies have followed patients or their families over time to describe the trajectory of religious/spiritual coping with illness. Examining these trajectories may disclose points of vulnerability where chaplains' spiritual care may be especially important. This initial step in the chaplain research process is a place where good case studies can play an important role in building a base of knowledge. This is also a place to remember the lesson from the randomized trials with the COPD and CABG patients and focus on patients with high levels of distress and/or spiritual struggle. Perhaps most important, we need critical reviews of this existing research to bring into focus what has been well established based on high-quality research and where additional research is needed.

The next step is to synthesize this descriptive research into theories about the role of religion and spirituality in coping with illness. Again, it makes sense to build on existing theoretical models such as the excellent work of psychologist Kenneth Pargament on religious coping (Pargament 1997, 2007). This theory has informed the research one of us (DG) has conducted about the role of religion in the lives of parents of children newly diagnosed with cystic fibrosis. Based on interviews with fifteen parents, this team developed a theoretical model of the role of religion in coping with this difficult event (see Figure 7.2) (Grossoehme et al. 2010). Along with two colleagues, the other of us (GF) used Pargament's work to develop a theory of religious coping with chronic illness, and we then used that theory to review the evidence about religious coping with mental illness and with cancer (Murphy, Fitchett and Canada 2008).

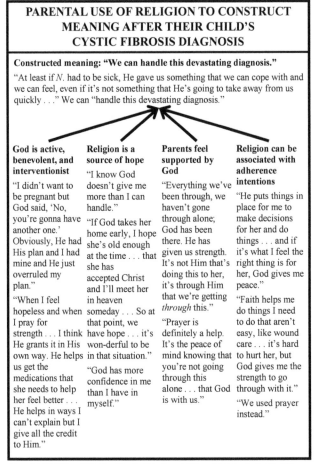

PARENTAL USE OF RELIGION TO CONSTRUCT MEANING AFTER THEIR CHILD'S CYSTIC FIBROSIS DIAGNOSIS

Constructed meaning: "We can handle this devastating diagnosis."

"At least if *N.* had to be sick, He gave us something that we can cope with and we can feel, even if it's not something that He's going to take away from us quickly . . ." We can "handle this devastating diagnosis."

God is active, benevolent, and interventionist

"I didn't want to be pregnant but God said, 'No, you're gonna have another one.' Obviously, He had His plan and I had mine and He just overruled my plan."

"When I feel hopeless and when I pray for strength . . . I think He grants it in His own way. He helps us get the medications that she needs to help her feel better . . . He helps in ways I can't explain but I give all the credit to Him."

Religion is a source of hope

"I know God doesn't give me more than I can handle."

"If God takes her home early, I hope she's old enough at the time . . . that she has accepted Christ and I'll meet her in heaven someday . . . So at that point, we have hope . . . it's won-derful to be in that situation."

"God has more confidence in me than I have in myself."

Parents feel supported by God

"Everything we've been through, we haven't gone through alone; God has been there. He has given us strength. It's not Him that's doing this to her, it's through Him that we're getting *through* this."

"Prayer is definitely a help. It's the peace of mind knowing that you're not going through this alone . . . that God is with us."

Religion can be associated with adherence intentions

"He puts things in place for me to make decisions for her and do things . . . and if it's what I feel the right thing is for her, God gives me peace."

"Faith helps me do things I need to do that aren't easy, like wound care . . . it's hard to hurt her, but God gives me the strength to go through with it."

"We used prayer instead."

Figure 7.2

The third step in a program of research for health care chaplaincy is to test the theories we use or develop. For example, one of us (GF) used Pargament's model to describe positive and negative religious coping among patients with diabetes, congestive heart failure, and cancer (Fitchett et al. 2004). Many other investigators, including Pargament and his colleagues, have also conducted studies of patients' religious coping (Pargament, Koenig, Tarakeshwar and Hahn 2004; Tarakeshwar et al. 2006). The team that interviewed the parents of children with cystic fibrosis also used these interviews to test which elements of Pargament's model of religious coping were most salient for these parents (Grossoehme et al. 2010).

A critical fourth step in chaplaincy research is to develop or select measures of key outcomes associated with effective spiritual care. Since Florell's (1973) work, chaplains have been interested in the impact of their care on patients' length of stay, and Iler and his colleagues (2001) found that daily chaplain visits did shorten COPD patients' length of stay. But for many groups of patients there is small variation and little excess in length of stay, and chaplains' care will have little influence on this outcome. In contrast, anxiety is a common and distressing symptom for COPD and other patients. Chaplains' care could reduce anxiety through reinforcing reassuring religious beliefs, repeating familiar religious rituals, and empathic listening. All these things made anxiety a smart choice of outcome for the COPD study. Chaplains' care may also have beneficial effects on patients' quality of life (Balboni et al. 2007).

What about the choice of negative religious coping for the CABG study? A growing body of research points to the harmful effects, for many groups of patients, of negative religious coping (also known as religious struggle), which includes feeling abandoned or punished by God or feeling angry with God. These harmful effects include poorer quality of life, greater depression, greater functional limitations, and possibly increased risk of death (Fitchett et al. 2004; Pargament, Koenig, Tarakeshwar and Hahn 2001; Sherman et al. 2009). This evidence supports the choice of negative religious coping as an important outcome for the CABG study. Selecting good outcomes for studies about chaplains' care requires a good understanding of important outcomes for the patients being studied. Developing new, reliable outcome measures should generally not be attempted unless colleagues with measurement expertise are available to collaborate.

Before we can implement the fifth and final step in chaplaincy research, testing the effects of chaplains' care, we need to develop a sound theoretical understanding of how what we do affects our patients. Iler's intervention with the COPD patients was a daily visit with them (Iler, Obenshain and Camac 2001). Beyond that, we do not know much about what occurred in those visits or why Iler thought they would have an impact on the patients' anxiety. But as we noted above, there are several ways in which we might specify the beneficial impact of a chaplain's visit for an anxious patient.

In contrast, Bay's ministry with the CABG patients (Bay and Ivy 2006) included structured visits that were based on an earlier model of spiritual care with CABG patients developed by Chaplains Robert Yim and Larry VandeCreek (Yim and VandeCreek 1996). Key themes in the Yim-Vande-Creek model included grief, hope, and meaning. The extent to which the Yim and VandeCreek model was grounded in research about the emotional or spiritual issues faced by CABG patients is not clear, and this weakness may have affected the results of this study.

Case studies can be a helpful approach for developing descriptions and theories about the elements of chaplains' care that make it effective (Fitchett 2011). It is striking and sad to realize that there are almost no published case studies about chaplains' care that include the kind of detail about what happened in the chaplain-patient relationship that is needed to build future research. Presenting case studies at our conferences and publishing them in our journals will provide an essential base for research about the effects of our care.

Conducting further research about the effects of chaplains' interventions is the fifth and final step in building a body of research about chaplaincy. The studies by Iler and Bay and their colleagues (Iler, Obenshain and Camac 2001; Bay and Ivy 2006) provide evidence that we can do this kind of research. We can learn from the strengths and the limitations of their studies, as well as the work by Florell (1973). The level of patient distress is important to keep in mind when planning studies of chaplains' care. As noted earlier, one of the reasons the CABG study may have found no effects of the chaplains' visits on patients' anxiety and depression was the overall low levels of anxiety and depression in the study participants. Repeating that study, but limiting it to patients with moderate or high levels of anxiety or depression, or to patients who showed evidence of religious struggle, might produce very different results.

A RESEARCH-INFORMED PROFESSION: HOW WE GET THERE

In the opening section, we described how chaplains in the United States and United Kingdom have been called to adopt evidence-based practices. Both have encouraged a tiered approach to research. The U.S. standard contains three levels of expertise, ranging from the research informed to major studies. We describe how chaplains might live into the fullness of this standard's spirit.

Research-Informed Chaplains: Basic Level

The distinguishing features of chaplains at this level is that they read and discuss research articles in professional journals, consider the practice implications, and use published material to educate administrators and others about chaplaincy's role, value, and impact. Research literacy implies a familiarity with current writings. There are two excellent journals in our own discipline, the *Journal of Pastoral Care and Counseling* and the *Journal of Health Care Chaplaincy, Health and Social Care Chaplaincy*? and individuals and departments may strongly consider subscriptions. However, other disciplines have extensive literature about religion and health that they publish in their journals. Accessing those articles can be arranged in some cases through the medical library in a health care institution. A "table of contents" service may be available, in which journals' tables of contents are photocopied and sent to you. Many publishers have an electronic subscription option on their journal's web page, providing e-mails with the table of contents of each new issue.

Not everything written is meaningful or of equal worth. To determine what is meaningful to you, don't read articles straight through. Read the abstract first. If the abstract suggests this article may be helpful, skip to the references. Are relatively current works cited, or only older, well-known reference works? Is there a balance of viewpoints, or is one person cited multiple times? The narrower (or newer) the topic, the fewer works there may be to cite. Next, look at the methods section, which should be clear enough that you could repeat the study if you had the same resources. Keep in mind how the data was collected. Data is easy to collect in a laboratory setting. How does the study strike the balance between what is practical and feasible (laboratory) and what will be meaningful ("real world"). All authors want to think they have written an "important work." However, authors need to make sure they do not overstate the importance of their results. Does the results section make explicit linkages between their findings and the study's hypotheses? To what extent do the authors generalize their findings? Are the findings "meaningful" or merely "significant"? Achieving statistical significance, in which two things are found to be different from one another, is much easier than showing that this difference matters. Why change your practice unless you can potentially make a meaningful difference? In the discussion, the questions are "So what?" and "Who cares?" Authors should discuss their findings in light of the material cited in the introduction. Where does this fit in terms of what was already known or believed? If you believe the study has implications for how you practice chaplaincy, how might you integrate the findings into your practice?

Some chaplains may process such questions individually. Others find it helpful to reflect with a group of peers. Electronic chaplains' discussion lists are forums where reflections might be posted with an invitation to discuss an article's implications. This is particularly helpful for chaplains in one-person departments. Multi-staff departments or settings where there are multiple institutions in the same geographic area might have a "journal club" meeting regularly (perhaps quarterly) to discuss an article during a staff meeting or at an off-site location such as a coffee house. A good source for interesting articles is the "Article-of-the-Month" feature on the ACPE Research Network website.[3]

The other avenue for discussion about research called for by the APC *Standards of Practice* is with health care administrators. Many administrators seek to be financially responsible with the limited assets they manage and won't reallocate assets unless someone presents evidence that a different allocation will change outcomes for patients, families, or staff. The "White Paper" summarizes a number of research studies that may be useful (VandeCreek and Burton 2001). Most chaplains have narratives about times when their care made a difference to a patient or a loved one. Stories rarely change attitudes toward spiritual care. For some, that is because stories cannot be quantified. For others, stories represent a different language. Christian. scriptures tell how the apostle Paul began his defense by speaking to the people of Athens in language they already understood (Acts 17). In contemporary health care, the language is evidence-based practice. Chaplains need to be able to speak that language to be understood and professionally valued by our peers.

Research-Informed Chaplains: Intermediate and Advanced Levels

What can one chaplain do? The answer may be more than you think. Case studies provided by individual chaplains make an important contribution to our new knowledge. In some settings, individual chaplains may be able to carry out studies with a small or moderate number of participants. Iler's study of patient outcomes following regular chaplain visits is an example of just how much one chaplain working with just a few others can contribute

3. See Resources at the end of this chapter for the ACPE Research Network website and other helpful research resources.

(Iler, Obenshain and Camac 2001). Some chaplains may already be devoting effort to research without realizing it, through participation in quality improvement projects. Although these two areas have differences, there is significant overlap with implications for our discussion. Research is usually considered to be the pursuit of new knowledge and involves testing hypotheses. Quality improvement applies knowledge and/or demonstrates changes of outcome due to evidence-based process changes. Quality improvement studies may be within the reach of many chaplains, especially those in larger institutions or health care systems.

Because most research questions are too complex and multidimensional for a single person, collaboration is essential to good research. In general, collaboration with investigators from other disciplines will provide expertise that is essential to the successful completion of chaplains' research. Chaplains can also collaborate on others' research studies. Just as we offer a unique perspective to care at the bedside, we can offer a theological perspective to a study.

Chaplaincy departments with multiple staff, health care systems with large chaplaincy departments, and chaplaincy departments situated in academic health care settings are likely to play a key role in the future of chaplaincy research. These departments typically have the resources, including time and finances, to devote to research efforts, as well as the research "culture" in which chaplains' efforts may flourish. It may be possible in these settings to develop "academic research chaplains" whose main task is to design and carry out studies, mentor chaplains in other settings, and build collaborations between chaplains and health care researchers. These chaplains will hold faculty appointments in the medical schools with which their institution is affiliated. The resources necessary to carry out good research may exist outside of the chaplains' department, typically coming from large, private foundations and the National Institutes of Health.

Just as large chaplaincy departments will likely play a key role in the future of chaplaincy research, professional chaplaincy organizations have a significant role in the development of research-informed professional chaplains by providing educational opportunities for their membership. The inclusion of research among the *Standards of Practice* for professional chaplains is a laudable and needed step, but it represents a step on the journey and not the destination. Opportunities for developing research literacy and even research skills can be effectively provided by such organizations in the context of national and regional meetings and workshops and increasingly through online media such as webinars. Initial steps have already been taken in this direction and need to be ongoing (Murphy and Fitchett 2010).

FINAL WORDS

As chaplains embrace the goal of becoming a research-informed profession, it is helpful to remember the work of Anton Boisen. Boisen is widely remembered as one of the founders of clinical pastoral education (CPE), but he should also be remembered as someone who practiced an evidence-based approach to pastoral care (Asquith 1992). Much of Boisen's research involved collecting and categorizing case studies of the psychiatric patients with whom he worked. One aim of his research was to identify patients whose psychiatric symptoms represented a religious crisis and to provide appropriate pastoral care for them (Boisen 1971/1936). Contemporary chaplains have embraced Boisen's view of patients as "living human documents." We encourage chaplains to also embrace Boisen as a model for research informed chaplaincy.

REFERENCES

Alcorn, S. R., Balboni, M. J., Prigerson, H. G., Reynolds, A., Phelps, A. C., Wright, A. A., Block, S. D., Peteet, J. R., Kachnic, L. A. and Balboni, T. A. 2010. "'If God Wanted Me Yesterday, I Wouldn't Be Here Today': Religious and Spiritual Themes in Patients' Experiences of Advanced Cancer. *Journal of Palliative Medicine* 13:5, 581–88.

Asquith, G. H. Jr. ed. 1992. *Vision from a Little Known Country: A Boisen Reader.* Decatur, GA: Journal of Pastoral Care Publications.

Association of Professional Chaplains. 2009. *Standards of Practice for Professional Chaplains in Acute Care.* [Editors: the 2009 version has been superseded by subsequent versions. The latest version, titled *Standards of Practice for Professional Chaplains*, was accessed August 17, 2020, https://www.professionalchaplains.org/content.asp?pl=198&sl=198&contentid=200]

Balboni, T. A., Vanderwerker, L. C., Block, S. D., Paulk, M. E., Lathan, C. S. Peteet, J. R. and Prigerson, H. G. 2007. "Religiousness and Spiritual Support among Advanced Cancer Patients and Associations with End-of-Life Treatment Preferences and Quality of Li"fe. *Journal of Clinical Oncology* 25:5, 555–60.

Barbour, I. 1990. *Religion in an Age of Science.* San Francisco: Harper, & Row.

Bay, P. S., Beckman, D., Trippi, J., Gunderman, R. and Terry, C. 2008. "The Effect of Pastoral Care Services on Anxiety, Depression, Hope, Religious Coping, and Religious Problem Solving Styles: A Randomized Controlled Study." *Journal of Religion and Health* 47:1, 57–69.

Bay, P. and Ivy, S. S. 2006. "Chaplaincy Research: A Case Study." *Journal of Pastoral Care and Counseling* 60:4, 343–52.

Boisen, A. T. 1971/1936. *Exploration of the Inner World: A Study of Mental Disorder and Religious Experience.* Philadelphia: University of Pennsylvania Press.

Brady, M. J., Peterman, A. H., Fitchett, G., Mo, M. and Cella, D. 1999. "A Case for Including Spirituality in Quality of Life Measurement in Oncology." *Psychooncology* 8:5, 417–28.

Bucaille, M. 1979. *The Bible, the Qur'an and Science.* Indianapolis: North American Trust Publications.

Chapman, T. R. and Grossoehme, D. H. 2002. "Adolescent Patient and Nurse Referrals for Pastoral Care: A Comparison of Psychiatric vs. Medical-Surgical Populations." *Journal of Child and Adolescent Psychiatric Nursing* 15:3, 118–23.

Chida, Y., Steptoe, A. and Powell, L. H. 2009. "Religiosity/Spirituality and Mortality: A Systematic Quantitative Review." *Psychotherapy and Psychosomatics* 78:2, 81–90.

Daaleman, T. P., Williams, C. S., Hamilton, V. L. and Zimmerman, S. 2008. "Spiritual Care at the End of Life in Long-term Care." *Medical Care* 46:1, 85–91.

Feudtner, C., Haney, J. and Dimmers M. A. 2003. "Spiritual Care Needs of Hospitalized Children and their Families: A National Survey of Pastoral Care Providers' Perceptions." *Pediatrics* 111:1, e67–e72.

Fitchett, G. 2011. "Making Our Case(s)." *Journal of Health Care Chaplaincy* 17:1, 3–18. [Article 6 in this volume]

Fitchett, G., Burton, L. A. and Sivan, A. B. 1997. "The Religious Needs and Resources of Psychiatric In-patients." *Journal of Nervous and Mental Disease* 185:5, 320–26.

Fitchett, G., Meyer, P. and Burton, L. A. 2000. "Spiritual Care in the Hospital: Who Requests It? Who Needs It?" *Journal of Pastoral Care* 54:2, 173–86. [Article 2 in this volume]

Fitchett, G., Murphy, P. E., Kim, J., Gibbons, J.L., Cameron, J. R., and Davis, J. A. 2004. "Religious Struggle: Prevalence, Correlates and Mental Health Risks in Diabetic, Congestive Heart Failure, and Oncology Patients." *International Journal of Psychiatry in Medicine* 34:179–96. [Article 3 in this volume]

Fitchett, G., Rasinski, K., Cadge, W. and Curlin, F. A. 2009. "Physicians' Experience and Satisfaction with Chaplains: A National Survey." *Archives of Internal Medicine* 169:19, 1808–10.

Flannelly, K. J., Handzo, G. F., Galek, K., Weaver, A. J. and Overvold, J. A. 2006. "A National Survey of Hospital Directors' Views about the Importance of Various Chaplain Roles: Differences among Disciplines and Types of Hospitals." *Journal of Pastoral Care and Counseling* 60:3, 213–25.

Flannelly, K. J., Oettinger, M., Galek, K., Braun-Storck, A. and Kreger, R. 2009. "The Correlates of Chaplains' Effectiveness in Meeting the Spiritual/Religious and Emotional Needs of Patients." *Journal of Pastoral Care and Counseling* 63:1–2, 9.1–15.

Florell, J. L. 1973. "Crisis Intervention in Orthopedic Surgery: Empirical Evidence of the Effectiveness of a Chaplain Working with Surgery Patients." *Bulletin of the American Protestant Hospital Association* 37:2, 29–36. Reprinted 2010 in *Spiritual Needs and Pastoral Services: Readings in Research*, edited by L. VandeCreek, 23–32. Decatur, GA: Journal of Pastoral Care Publications.

Galek, K., Flannelly, K. J., Koenig, H. G. and Fogg, S. L. 2007. "Referrals to Chaplains: The Role of Religion and Spirituality in Healthcare Settings." *Mental Health, Religion, & Culture* 10:4, 363–77.

Gibbons, J.L., Thomas, J., Vandecreek, L. and Jessen, A. K. 1973. "The Value of Hospital Chaplains: Patient Perspectives." *Journal of Pastoral Care* 45:2, 117–25.

Grossoehme, D. H., Cotron, S. and Leonard, A. 2007. "Spiritual and Religious Experiences of Adolescent Psychiatric Inpatients versus Healthy Peers." *Journal of Pastoral Care and Counseling* 61:3, 197–204.

Grossoehme, D. H. and Gerbetz, L. 2004. "Adolescent Perceptions of Meaningfulness of Inpatient Psychiatric Hospitalization." *Clinical Child Psychology and Psychiatry* 9:4, 589–96.

Grossoehme, D. H., Ragsdale, J., Cotton, S., Wooldridge, J. L., Grimes, L. and Seid, M. 2010. "Parents' Religious Coping Styles in the First Year after their Child's Cystic Fibrosis Diagnosis." *Journal of Health Care Chaplaincy* 16:3–4, 109–22.

Grossoehme, D. H., Ragsdale, J., Wooldridge, J. L., Cotton, S. and Seid, M. 2010. "We Can Handle This: Parents' Use of Religion in the First Year Following their Child's Diagnosis with Cystic Fibrosis." *Journal of Health Care Chaplaincy* 16:3–4, 95–108.

Handzo, G. F., Flannelly, K. J., Kudler, T., Fogg, S. L., Harding, S. R., Hasan, Y. H., Ross, A. M. and Taylor, B. E. 2008. "What Do Chaplains Really Do? II. Interventions in the New York Chaplaincy Study." *Journal of Health Care Chaplaincy* 14:1, 39–56.

Handzo, G. F., Flannelly, K. J., Murphy, K. M., Bauman, J. P., Oettinger, M., Goodell, E., Hasan, Y. H., Barrie, D. P. and Jacobs, M. R. 2008. "What Do Chaplains Really Do? I. Visitation in the New York Chaplaincy Study." *Journal of Health Care Chaplaincy* 14:1, 20–38.

Iler, W. L., Obenshain, D. and Camac, M. 2001. "The Impact of Daily Visits from Chaplains on Patients with Chronic Obstructive Pulmonary Disease (COPD): A Pilot Study." *Chaplaincy Today* 17:1, 5–11.

Koenig, H. G., McCullough, M. E. and Larson, D. B. 2001. *Handbook of Religion and Health*. New York: Oxford University Press.

McSherry, E. 1987. "Spiritual Resources in Older Hospitalized Men." *Social Compass* 34:4, 519.

McSherry, E., Cuilla, M. and Burton, L. A. 1992. "Continuous Quality Improvement for Chaplaincy." In *Chaplaincy Services in Contemporary Health Care*, edited by L. A. Burton, 33–42. Schaumburg, IL: College of Chaplains.

Meert, K. L., Thurston, C. S. and Briller, S. H. 2005. "The Spiritual Needs of Parents at the Time of their Child's Death in the Pediatric Intensive Care Unit and during Bereavement: A Qualitative Study." *Pediatric Critical Care Medicine* 6:4, 420–27.

Mowat, H. 2008. *The Potential for Efficacy of Healthcare Chaplaincy and Spiritual Care Provision in the NHS (UK): A Scoping Review of Recent Research*. Aberdeen, Scotland: Mowat Research Ltd.

Montonye, M. and Calderone, S. 2010. "Pastoral Interventions and the Influence of Self-reporting: A Preliminary Analysis." *Journal of Health Care Chaplaincy* 16:1–2, 65–73.

Murphy, P. E. and Fitchett, G. 2010. "Introducing Chaplains to Research: 'This could help me.'" *Journal of Health Care Chaplaincy* 16:3, 79–94.

Murphy, P. E., Fitchett, G. and Canada, A. L. 2008. "Adult Spirituality for Persons with Chronic Illness." In *Spiritual Dimensions of Nursing Practice*, rev. ed., edited by V. B. Carson and H. G. Koenig, 193–235. West Conshohocken, PA: Templeton Foundation.

O'Connor, T. S. and Meakes, E. 1998. "Hope in the Midst of Challenge: Evidence-based Pastoral Care." *Journal of Pastoral Care* 52:4, 359–67.

Pargament, K. I. 1997. *The Psychology of Religion and Coping: Theory, Research, Practice*. New York: Guilford.

Pargament, K. I. 2007. *Spiritually Integrated Psychotherapy: Understanding and Addressing the Sacred*. New York: Guilford.

Pargament, K. I., Koenig, H. G., Tarakeshwar, N and Hahn, J. 2001. "Religious Struggle as a Predictor of Mortality among Medically Ill Elderly Patients: A Two-Year Longitudinal Study." *Archives of Internal Medicine* 161:15, 1881–85.

Pargament, K. I., Koenig, H. G., Tarakeshwar, N and Hahn, J. 2004. "Religious Coping Methods as Predictors of Psychological, Physical and Spiritual Outcomes among Medically Ill Elderly Patients: A Two-Year Longitudinal Study." *Journal of Health Psychology* 9:6, 713–30.

Piderman, K. M. and Johnson, M. E. 2009. "Hospital Chaplains' Involvement in a Randomized Controlled Multidisciplinary Trial: Implications for Spiritual Care and Research." *Journal of Pastoral Care and Counseling* 63:3–4, 8.1–6.

Piderman, K. M., Marek, D. V., Jenkins, S. M., Johnson, M. E., Buryska, J. F. and Mueller, P.S. 2008. "Patients' Expectations of Hospital Chaplains." *Mayo Clinic Proceedings* 83:1, 58–65.

Sherman, A. C., Plante, T. G., Simonton, S., Latif, U. and Anaissie, E. J. 2009. "Prospective Study of Religious Coping among Patients Undergoing Autologous Stem Cell Transplantation," *Journal of Behavioral Medicine* 32:1, 118–28.

Speck, P. 2005. "A Standard for Research in Healthcare Chaplaincy." *The Journal for Health Care Chaplaincy* 6:26–40.

Tarakeshwar, N., Vanderwerker, L. C., Paulk, E., Pearce, M. J., Kasl, S. V. and Prigerson, H. G. 2006. "Religious Coping is Associated with Quality of Life of Patients with Advanced Cancer." *Journal of Palliative Medicine* 9:3, 646–57.

VandeCreek, L. 2004. "How Satisfied are Patients with the Ministry of Chaplains?" *Journal of Pastoral Care and Counseling* 58:4, 335–42.

VandeCreek, L. and Lyons, M. A. 1997. *Ministry of Hospital Chaplains: Patient Satisfaction.* Binghamton, NY: Haworth Pastoral.

Weaver, A. J., Flannelly, K. J. and Liu, C. 2008. "Chaplaincy Research: Its Value, Its Quality, and Its Future." *Journal of Health Care Chaplaincy* 14:1, 3–19.

VandeCreek, L. and Burton, L. 2001. "Professional Chaplaincy: Its Role and Importance in Healthcare." *Journal of Pastoral Care* 55:1, 81–97. Accessed August 17, 2020, www.professionalchaplains.org/content.asp?contentid=162

Yim, R. J. R. and VandeCreek, L. 1996. "Unbinding Grief and Life's Losses for Thriving Recovery after Open Heart Surgery." *The Caregiver Journal* 12:2, 8–11.

RESOURCES

Measures of Religion

Fetzer Institute/National Institute on Aging Working Group. 1999. *Multidimensional Measurement of Religiousness/Spirituality for Use in Health Research.* Kalamazoo, MI: Fetzer Institute. Accessed August 17, 2020, https://fetzer.org/resources/multidimensional-measurement-religiousnessspirituality-use-health-research

Abstracts

Pastoral Research Abstracts, edited by Noel Brown (oreresource@rocket-mail.com). For many years, Noel Brown has provided informative abstracts of important research in each issue of the *Journal of Pastoral Care and Counseling* and APC's *Chaplaincy Today*.

Journals

Journal of Health Care Chaplaincy.
https://www.tandfonline.com/toc/whcc20/current (Subscription with membership in Association of Professional Chaplains)

Journal of Pastoral Care and Counseling
www.jpcp.org (Subscription with membership in ACPE and other groups.)

Journal of Religion and Health
www.springer.com/public+health/journal/10943

Journal for the Scientific Study of Religion
https://onlinelibrary.wiley.com/journal/14685906 (Subscription with membership in Society for the Scientific Study of Religion.)

Websites

ACPE Research Network: www.acperesearch.net. The existence of this website and its excellent resources is not widely known or appreciated, but it should be. It is sponsored by the Research Network in ACPE, but it is open to everyone. It includes more than eight years of the "Article-of-the-Month" feature in which a research article relevant to the work of chaplains and chaplaincy educators is reviewed. In addition to a brief summary of the article, the reviews include helpful suggestions for using the article in CPE programs and regularly updated lists of research by the same authors or on related topics. Frequently there are links to free downloads of the articles. We all owe a big debt of gratitude to Chaplain John Ehman, who is the network convener and author of almost all of these excellent reviews.

George Washington Institute for Spirituality and Health, Christina Puchalski, MD, executive director: www.gwish.org

Pastoral Care Department, University of Pennsylvania Heath System: www.uphs.upenn.edu/pastoral/resed/index.html, Spirituality and Health Bibliographies. Check here for free copies of an annual annotated bibliography of research, begun in 1999, about issues of interest to chaplains. Another excellent resource from John Ehman.

ARTICLE 8

In the Garden with Andrea

Spiritual Assessment in End-of-Life Care[1]

—GEORGE FITCHETT

D. Min

—PATRICIA ROBERTS

D. Min

BEFORE I BECAME INVOLVED *in research about religion and health and spiritual care I was very involved with others in developing the 7 by 7 model for spiritual assessment. The initial response to the model was positive and in 1993 I published* Assessing Spiritual Needs *(Augsburg), which described the model and illustrated it with three case studies. Over time the book, and its 2002 reprint (Academic Renewal), became a frequently used text in academic and clinical education programs around the world. It was always a challenge to find a case study that could be used to illustrate this new approach to spiritual assessment in a 60 or 90-minute workshop. One day, Patty Roberts, then a resident in our clinical pastoral education program, shared a verbatim of her work with a woman with advanced breast cancer. It seemed like an excellent case for teaching spiritual assessment. My most recent work on spiritual*

---

1. G. Fitchett and P. A. Roberts. 2003. "In the Garden with Andrea: Spiritual Assessment in End of Life Care." In *Walking Together: Physicians, Chaplains and Clergy Caring for the Sick*, edited by C. M. Puchalski, 23–31. Washington, DC: The George Washington Institute for Spirituality and Health.

assessment takes a rather different approach than the 7 by 7 model, focusing on a quantified assessment of unmet spiritual concerns among patients receiving palliative care (see Article 10).

In recent years we have seen a welcome increase of interest in integrating religion and spirituality into holistic clinical care. This is especially evident in palliative care and among caregivers who focus on providing care at the end-of-life. An explicit, intentional, comprehensive approach to spiritual assessment can aid in integrating religion and spirituality in end-of-life care. Our discussion of spiritual assessment in this chapter will have four parts. First, we will describe spiritual assessment, why it is important, and how to implement it in clinical care. Second, we will share the case of Andrea, a woman with metastasized breast cancer who feels that the battle is being lost. Third, we will describe the "7-by-7" model for spiritual assessment by using it to create a spiritual assessment for Andrea. Finally, we will describe a plan for spiritual care with Andrea based on our spiritual assessment.

AN INTRODUCTION TO SPIRITUAL ASSESSMENT

Spiritual assessment is the process of discerning the religious and spiritual needs and resources of the person for whom we provide spiritual care. Spiritual assessment is important because it improves our ability to be accountable for our spiritual care. What are the goals of our care with a particular person? How do we know if the care we are providing is the care the person needs? What can help us guard against projecting our needs and assumptions onto the person we are caring for? In order to answer these important questions we require a way to describe the spiritual care we think a person needs. We can then provide that care and see if it has the effect we expected.

Spiritual assessment gives us a way to state the goals of our spiritual care as we enter into a new patient relationship. It gives us a way we can talk with the patient, or other person with whom we are working, to see if they share our understanding of their spiritual needs and agree with the kind of spiritual care we are suggesting. Spiritual assessment also gives us a better way to talk with staff colleagues about our understanding of a patient's needs and our goals for our spiritual care with them.

We make distinctions among spiritual screening, spiritual history-taking, and spiritual assessment. Spiritual screening or triage is a quick determination of whether a person is experiencing a serious spiritual crisis. Spiritual screening can help identify which patients may benefit from a more in-depth spiritual assessment. Spiritual history-taking is the process of interviewing a patient, asking him or her questions about his or her religious and spiritual life, in order to come to a better understanding of his or her religious and spiritual needs and resources.

Spiritual assessment refers to a more extensive process of listening to a patient's story as it unfolds in a professional relationship and summarizing the religious and spiritual needs and resources that emerge in that process. As such, unlike spiritual history-taking, spiritual assessment is based on listening to the patient's story as he or she needs to tell it, and not on an interview with predetermined questions. Many spiritual care providers feel that spiritual history-taking is inconsistent with the pastoral role and prefer the more open ended process of spiritual assessment.

Several brief instruments that may be useful in spiritual screening have recently been developed, but more work is needed to develop effective, reliable instruments for spiritual screening.[2] Several models for spiritual history-taking have been developed by physicians and chaplains. Models for spiritual history-taking developed by physicians include the work of Kuhn (1988), Maugans (1996), and Puchalski (1999). Gary Berg has developed a computer program for spiritual assessment. The Spiritual Injury Scale that is part of this program may also be used in spiritual screening (Berg 1994, 1999; see also Berg's website at www.spiritualassessment.com).

Resources for spiritual assessment have been available since the publication of Pruyser's (1976) *Minister as Diagnostician*. Many models for spiritual assessment, including the "7-by-7" model presented below, were intended to be used with people from many different religious traditions. Other models, such as Shulevitz and Springer's (1994) model for assessment of Jewish patients, were designed for use with people from one specific faith tradition. A helpful resource for exploration of different models for spiritual assessment is *Spiritual Assessment in Pastoral Care* (Fitchett 1993a), an annotated bibliography of twenty-seven published models. A chapter by Fitchett and Handzo, *Spiritual Assessment, Screening and Intervention* (1998), provides a helpful summary of several important models for spiritual screening and assessment. Fitchett's *Assessing Spiritual Needs* (1993b, especially Chapter 7, 105–29) also provides a critical discussion of three popular models for spiritual history-taking and assessment, including the nursing diagnosis spiritual distress.

2. Volume 15, Number 1 (1999) of *Chaplaincy Today*, the journal of the Association of Professional Chaplains, contains a symposium on Screening for Spiritual Risk. See especially the following papers in that symposium: Fitchett, "Screening for Spiritual Risk." 2–12; and Fitchett, "Selected Resources for Screening for Spiritual Risk." 13–26. Hodges, "Spiritual Screening," 30–40; and Wakefield, Cox, and Forrest, "Seeds of Change," 41–50.

PATTY'S VISIT WITH ANDREA

One of the best ways to learn how to do spiritual assessment is to see it applied to a case. We have chosen the case of a patient, whom we call Andrea, from Patty's ministry to illustrate how a chaplain, clergy person or other spiritual care provider can use spiritual assessment to inform and guide his or her spiritual care. This is Patty's report of her second visit with Andrea.

It was a busy, stressful Saturday on-call and I had just finished talking about advance directives with a patient on the oncology unit where I work when one of the nurses, Marnie, said, "I need your help with something. We're going outside for a while. Do you have a few minutes to spare?" "Sure," I responded, as I followed Marnie into a patient's room.

The patient was Andrea, a fifty-six-year-old woman with breast cancer which has metastasized to her bones. She has been hospitalized this time for over six weeks, and has been experiencing one complication after another from her treatment. Her prognosis is not good and she knows it. Her husband is so fearful that he will not allow her to talk to him about her dying. Andrea's depression seems to grow each passing day. Nothing can comfort or distract her for very long.

I had one previous visit with Andrea. During that visit Andrea looked down and would not discuss her feelings with me. She looked like she wanted to give up. She said she wanted nothing to do with religion. She vehemently refused prayer and through her tears asked to be left alone. Her husband, holding her hand, asked for some privacy. I left with a great sense of hopelessness and loss.

On this Saturday, Andrea was too weak to sit up in a wheelchair, so Marnie had gone to great lengths to borrow a moving bed from the transplant unit and to make all the other necessary preparations for this trip.

Marnie: I asked Patty to help take you out for a while. She just happens to be the only one available right now, so she was 'volunteered' for the job, OK?

Andrea: Oh, you don't want to bother with this, do you? (Andrea seemed none too thrilled with Marnie's choice of helpers.)

Patty: Oh, it's no bother, Andrea. I have lots of time today. I'm on-call, and nothing is happening right now. So I'll just go along for the ride.

Andrea was ready. Marnie and I wheeled the bed down the hallway toward the elevators.

Andrea: (Incredulously) Where are we going? I thought you just meant that you were taking me out of the room. Where are we going?

Marnie: Oh, we're just taking a little trip outside, that's all.

As the rest of the plan sunk in, the change in Andrea's face was remarkable. Suddenly, she had a look in her eyes of anticipation, amazement and hope that had not been there before. The trip through the lobby and down the elevators to the main doors was fun. We joked about getting the bed to move as we wanted. We all began to smile, a lot.

At last we were outside. It was a gorgeous spring day. The sun was shining, not a cloud in the blue sky. The wind was brisk, but warm and inviting. We maneuvered the bed so that Andrea could see some tulips planted on the hospital grounds and an adjacent field with lots of green grass. In a small way I was able to appreciate the feeling of being out in the fresh air since by that time I had been on-call and inside the hospital for many hours. I could just imagine how this would feel to someone who had been inside for six weeks.

I didn't have to imagine very hard though, because it was written all over Andrea's face. She raised her face to the sun, eyes closed, as the spring breeze caressed her face. The smile on her lips told the story more than her words or mine ever could. We just stood by and took it all in, all three of us. Marnie and I made some causal remarks about the weather, the flowers, the grass, but we really didn't need to say a word. After a few minutes, Marnie sat down on a picnic bench behind us.

Andrea: This is so wonderful, so, so wonderful. (Tears formed in the corners of her eyes. They didn't seem only like sad tears, more a mixture of sad and happy.) I have been so depressed. I am just so confused about all of this, you know? Patty, I did everything right. I exercised. I ate right. I watched my cholesterol. I got mammograms regularly. I did everything they say you're supposed to do, and what happens? I get cancer anyway. (Pause.) I guess it has caused me to lose faith.

Patty: It would be hard not to lose faith. It just doesn't seem fair does it?

Andrea: NO! It isn't fair. Not at all. I did everything right. Everything I was supposed to do for my health. I walked. I exercised a lot. I did everything I was supposed to do.

And I worry so much about my husband. We don't have any kids. Who will take care of him? I'm going to leave him alone. How will he be after I die?

I know I'm dying. He doesn't like to talk about it, but I know I am. What do I have to look forward to? More treatment, more days in the hospital? For what? I'm just not sure. I'm not sure of anything. Except that I'm angry. I'm SO VERY ANGRY at God for doing this. So very angry.

Patty: I understand what you mean. Why? Why should you have to suffer like this?

Andrea: That's right! Why? Why me? I just can't figure it out. And I get so depressed that I just want to give up on life altogether, you know? And I'm so very angry at God. So angry. I refuse to speak to Him. You know what I mean?

Patty: Yes. I do know. I happen to be angry at God right now myself.

Andrea: You are?

Patty: Yes. My twenty-three-year-old son was just in a serious auto accident and nearly died. I asked the same questions you did. Why? Why my son? What had he done to deserve this? He's a good kid, doing all the right things, and now this. He might have died. And I was furious, absolutely furious at God for allowing it to happen. I wanted to know why. I guess we don't get to have those answers though.

Andrea: Oh, so you DO know! And you got angry about it too? Wow. Someone like you.

Patty: Well, I do feel the anger too.

Andrea: So you know what it's like to be so very angry inside that you cannot even speak to God? You can't even pray, right? I just refuse to speak to God. I'm so very angry that I refuse even to speak. I'm not trying anymore; he's not listening anyway.

Patty: I went through a period of time when I wouldn't speak to God either. Lately though I have seemed to want to go ahead and BE angry. I mean, God is God, right? God made me. I guess I think He ought to be able to handle the fact that I'm angry. In some ways, I think He ought to hear about it. I guess I think God knows about my anger anyway. So I just let Him have it! It feels kind of good, too, to let it all hang out so to speak. But that's what has been right for me, it might not necessarily be so with you.

Andrea: (She looks reflective for a long while in some silence. I wait for her to speak.) It feels so good to be able to say this to someone, to say the words, you know? I really appreciate your understanding. It helps me to know that someone else feels like this. I guess I thought I shouldn't have these feelings at all, like I wasn't being faithful, and that just made me feel worse. It really helps me to know you do understand. Just to say this to someone feels so good. I've been holding it all inside for so long. So very long.

Patty: I think I would be angry if I were in your place.

Andrea: Yes. It's hard to survive this illness and all its effects. For a while I was able to keep up my spirits, but I am really struggling now. I guess I realize that the battle is being lost, and I am needing to find out how to die. How I need to die, that's what's on my mind.

Patty: How do you think you need to die?

Andrea: I think I have to stop treatment and go home. I don't want any more treatment. I want to die with some dignity. What is this life I have right now, anyway? What kind of life is it when the biggest thing I can look forward to is some more treatment and more pain? I don't want to keep on going like this.

Patty: Do you think you can say this to your husband sometime? I know he's very scared about losing you.

Andrea: Yes, he is. And I have not wanted to tell him that I want to give up. He is so insistent that I try, that I not give up.

Patty: It must be hard to keep up the pretense.

Andrea: Yes (she sighs), it's very hard. It takes all the energy I've got to keep him from seeing how depressed I really am. And crying? Forget about it. I do my crying when he's not there.

Patty: That sounds very lonely.

Andrea: Yes, it is. (The tears form in her eyes once more, but only for a moment.) But right now, I'm here. I'm out in the sunshine. This feels so very good to me! Where's Marnie, where'd she go?

Patty: She's sitting right behind us on the picnic bench, just enjoying the sun.

From where I stand I can see Marnie. I smile at her, and she gives me a knowing smile right back. Once again, I am reminded of that singular moment of time, feeling the sunshine, the wind, seeing the flowers. For a few more precious moments, we all are silent, just taking in the sights, smells, and sounds of creation. It was an unforgettable moment of beauty, peace, and transcendence.

Andrea: I guess it must be getting time to go back. I just can't tell you how much this has meant to me, you know! I didn't even know that she was planning on taking me all the way outside. (She smiles widely.) What a tremendous gift! I can't believe she did this!

Patty: Yes, I agree. This has been a wonderful gift. Marnie is a very special person, isn't she? You know, Andrea, I guess if I really look hard, I can find grace here. I mean, to me, if I wanted to be able to find God somewhere, I could find God in Marnie and the incredible gift she has given you in this moment. I mean, that's gotta be grace, that she would go to such great lengths to do this one very loving, very kind act of caring. I feel very fortunate to have been here to be part of it, very fortunate.

Andrea: Yeah. You're right. This is the best I've felt for a long, long while. Such a little thing, to enjoy the fresh air for just a few minutes. And yet, it has been so very, very good for me. I can't thank her enough. Marnie, where are you?

At this, Marnie comes up to receive a hug from Andrea. As I watch them, I am the one with tears in my eyes.

REFLECTION

Before we begin work on a spiritual assessment of Andrea or any other case, it is helpful to take a minute to reflect on our emotional response. Our feelings about a patient can color our assessment. It is best to be aware of them so we can take their effect into account. What feelings were evoked for you as you read the conversation between Andrea and Patty? I (Patty) had felt shut out and helpless in my first visit with Andrea. The day of the surprise trip outside, as I caught hold of what Marnie had in mind, I remember being slightly anxious about Andrea's acceptance of my inclusion in the plan. Soon I was swept up in the adventure of it all. Once outside, I could feel the palpable presence of a sacred moment in the making. As I watched and listened, I felt so sad for Andrea, not just because of her illness but because of the circumstances surrounding her at this moment of her life. She was trapped inside a hospital with too much treatment, suffering, and pain and not enough fresh air, acceptance, and sunshine. I remember being truly humbled by participating in this grace-filled moment. I also admired, and still do, Marnie's kindness, compassion, and action.

At first, I (George) found myself sharing in the surprise and excitement of the ride from Andrea's room to the hospital's garden. Then I felt very sad as I read about Andrea's anger, confusion, and loneliness. I also was touched by Andrea's gratitude and her hug for Marnie. This is a complex and intense case and it may evoke many different, strong feelings for different caregivers. As we formulate any spiritual assessment or care plan it is important to be aware of the way such feelings may influence our work.

SPIRITUAL ASSESSMENT OF ANDREAA

As can be seen in Table 8.1, the "7-by-7" model for spiritual assessment has two major sections.[3] The first section is the holistic assessment in which we begin with a review of the *medical dimension* of the case. The medical dimension is the central feature in Andrea's case. She has metastasized breast cancer and her recent treatment has been fraught with complications. She is beginning to recognize that her prognosis is not good. "I know I'm dying," she says early in the visit and later she confirms this, "I guess I realize that the battle is being lost." As with many patients, the progression of her illness, the change in the proportion of good days and bad days, leads Andrea to recognize this difficult truth. "What kind of life is it when the biggest thing I can look forward to is some more treatment and more pain?" The case gives us the impression that her conversation in the garden with Patty is one of the first times Andrea has verbalized this reality, that she is just beginning to shift from understanding herself as someone battling her disease to someone who needs to "find out how to die."

Table 8.1 The "7-by-7" Model for Spiritual Assessment

Holistic Assessment	Spiritual Assessment
Medical dimension	Belief and meaning
Psychological dimension	Vocation and obligations
Family systems dimension	Experience and emotions
Psychosocial dimension	Courage and growth
Ethnic, racial, cultural dimension	Ritual and practice
Social issues dimension	Community
Spiritual dimension	Authority and guidance

The second dimension of the holistic assessment is the *psychological dimension*. In Andrea's case this dimension is also very important. Patty observes that during her six weeks of treatment and complications, "Andrea's depression seemed to grow each passing day." The depth of Andrea's depression moved Marnie to go to great lengths to get her a breath of fresh air and a few moments of sunshine. In her conversation in the garden, Andrea also shares intense angry feelings, confusion, and some grief. Her recognition that "the battle is being lost" has evoked many intense emotions in Andrea.

3. For a more thorough description of the "7-by-7" model for spiritual assessment see Fitchett, *Assessing Spiritual Needs*.

Next we review the *family systems dimension*. Andrea is married; she and her husband have no children. We do not know if there are other important family members in the picture. Patty observes that "her husband is so fearful that he will not allow her to talk to him about her dying." Andrea indicates the toll this is taking on her, "It takes all the energy I've got to keep him from seeing how depressed I am." It is clear that the communication problems in this key relationship are adding to Andrea's distress.

The *psychosocial dimension* is the next holistic dimension that we review. In this case we have little additional information to help us understand who Andrea is besides being a patient with advanced cancer. Further psychosocial information may help us better understand Andrea's needs and the resources she may have to help her cope at this difficult time.

Religion and spirituality are often profoundly intertwined with *race, ethnicity, and cultural background*, so it is important to include these dimensions in our holistic assessment. Andrea is Caucasian, but no other ethnic or cultural aspects of her case have emerged thus far.

The *social issues dimension* may be less familiar than the five dimensions we have just reviewed. It is the place where we examine the effects of social policies and institutions on Andrea and her situation. Most approaches to diagnosis or assessment focus on the individual, or perhaps the individual in her family system. We include this dimension to remind us that we live in a social context and that features of that context sometimes make things easier or harder for the people we are working with, like Andrea. In this case, as we know it thus far, there do not appear to be any major social issues that are complicating matters for Andrea.

The seventh and last dimension of the holistic assessment is the spiritual dimension that is also the second major division of the "7-by-7" model for spiritual assessment. We will examine seven specific spiritual dimensions in this portion of the assessment. The first spiritual dimension is *beliefs and meaning*. What are Andrea's key religious or spiritual beliefs and what gives her life meaning and purpose? We don't yet know Andrea's religious background, but based on what she shares with Patty it appears that she holds beliefs in an omnipotent, just God that are common teachings in many different Christian traditions. At this time we do not know what other religious or spiritual beliefs may be important to Andrea.

Part of the religious/spiritual crisis that often results from serious illness is a crisis in a person's sense of meaning and purpose. At this point it is hard to say what gives Andrea's life meaning and purpose. In recent weeks she has sacrificed a lot of her own emotional comfort to care for her husband; as she thinks about her death she is anxious about "Who will take care of him?" Her relationship with her husband may be a significant source of meaning and purpose for Andrea. As we get to know her better we may get a fuller picture of both her key beliefs, what gives her life meaning and purpose, and the effects of her worsening health on this dimension of her life.

The second spiritual dimension we consider is *vocation and obligations.* Here, we explore the moral dimension of a person's life. What duties and obligations does Andrea hold for herself and others? Is her changing health causing changes in her sense of duties and obligations? This appears to be a key dimension in our understanding of Andrea's spiritual needs and resources, with six moral themes evident in her conversation with Patty.

The first moral theme Andrea expresses is confusion about what she should do. She finds herself not "sure of anything," really struggling now "to keep up my spirits." She is asking herself if it is her duty to battle, to fight her illness and keep her spirits up, or may she begin to "find out how to die"? Andrea is not alone in asking this question. Many patients who contend with life threatening illnesses come to a point where they recognize the diminishing returns of additional treatment and wonder if it is permissible to shift their focus from an effort to cure their illness to living comfortably until death.

For many patients, this moral decision is not theirs to make alone. It must be addressed in the context of felt duties to others, especially family members and caregivers. The second theme in the moral dimension of Andrea's story is that she confronts this decision in the context of her care for her husband. She knows that thinking about her possible death is difficult for him. "I have not wanted to tell him that I want to give up. He is so insistent that I try, that I not give up." Andrea feels an obligation to her husband, and perhaps her caregivers, to continue treatment and not give up prematurely. At the same time, she feels the time may have come to focus on getting ready to die with dignity. The tension between these choices may be accompanied by a feeling of guilt, of letting her husband and/or healthcare team down if she opts for a palliative approach.

Andrea also struggles to protect her husband from her distress. "And crying? Forget about it. I do my crying when he's not there." How can Andrea continue the duty she feels to care for and protect her husband in light of her declining health?

For Andrea and for many others, just as there is a good way to live, there is a good way to die. The third theme in the moral dimension of Andrea's story is her interest in learning how to die. When Patty asks her, "How do you think you need to die?" it becomes evident that Andrea has some clear, specific images of what her dying should be like. It should be marked by dignity that will be facilitated by no further futile, painful treatment and the peace and security of her home.

The fourth theme that emerges in our assessment of Andrea's moral dimension is more explicitly religious. She is enraged that God is being unfair to her. She believes that God should reward a good life with health and longevity. However, God has not rewarded her good life, her exceedingly good life, with good health. God is treating her unfairly, unjustly. Andrea says, "I'm so very angry at God. So angry. I refuse to speak to Him." The intensity of her anger towards God and her turning away from God suggests that Andrea feels God has betrayed her, broken a promise or covenant Andrea felt existed between them.

Andrea's anger with God raises the fifth theme in the moral dimension of her story. "I guess I thought I shouldn't have these feelings at all, like I wasn't being faithful, and that just made me feel worse." It is very common for religiously affiliated and active people to feel that faithfulness precludes anger with God. Andrea's internalization of this belief suggests a depth of earlier religious training that appears to stand in contrast to her current rejection of religion.

Andrea's belief that God should reward her because of her good behavior points to the sixth and final theme in the moral dimension of her story—grace. Unlike the preceding moral themes, Andrea is not raising questions about grace, the term in the Christian tradition that refers to the unearned love of God. We don't hear about experiences of grace in Andrea's life in the small portion of her story that she shares with Patty. Rather, she appears to operate out of the belief that you should get what you earn, what you work for. Patty points out that Marnie's efforts to arrange the visit to the garden might be a moment of grace. Andrea seems to have experienced it as such, "What a tremendous gift!" It would help to know how rare such moments have been in Andrea's life.

The third spiritual dimension we consider is *experience and emotion*. This is where we consider whether the person reports any direct spiritual experiences and, if so, what impact they have had upon them. In this conversation Andrea doesn't report any direct spiritual experiences. Perhaps this contributes to her belief that you only get what you have earned. People often need to develop trust in a caregiver before they are comfortable sharing any spiritual experiences they have had. We might learn more about this as we get to know Andrea better.

The fourth spiritual dimension in our model is *courage and growth*. Here, we look at whether there has been, or appears likely to be, any change in the way the person makes meaning and finds purpose in life. For example, has Andrea had an experience of radical doubt, an experience of the dark night of the soul, in which there was a profound change in her faith. Andrea's anger with God, her feeling that God is not being fair and not listening to her are frequently important elements in experiences of deep spiritual crises and transformations, elements of what has been described as "searching faith" (Westerhoff 1976, especially Chapter Four, 79–103). However, by deciding not to talk to God, "I'm not trying anymore, He's not listening anyway," Andrea has suspended the process of entering into and resolving her spiritual crisis.

The fifth spiritual dimension which we review is *rituals and practices.* What rituals and practices shape and express Andrea's key beliefs and her sense of meaning and purpose in life? From the little that we know about her, it does not appear that Andrea currently has any public or private religious rituals or practices that are important to her. In fact, Patty reports that, during her first visit, Andrea "vehemently refused prayer." Andrea's current rejection of prayer may be related to her experience that God is not listening to her. We hope to clarify this as we get to know Andrea better. While Andrea may have little use for religious rituals, she may have personal practices that help her feel peaceful or centered. The pilgrimage to the hospital garden appears to have offered Andrea a refreshing moment of sunshine and catharsis. As we get to know Andrea better it will be important to learn more about any other rituals or practices that are important to her.

The sixth spiritual dimension in our model is *community.* Who are the people with whom Andrea shares her beliefs and her sense of meaning and purpose in life? With whom does she share her sense of duties and obligations? With whom does she share any rituals or practices that help her feel peaceful or centered? It appears that Andrea is not part of any formal religious community. Her story does not include any family or friends other than her husband. This key relationship also appears to be a stressful one, in which Andrea feels she must sacrifice her own needs in order to care for him. Although she initially rejected Patty, learning of their shared anger with God has been important to Andrea. "I really appreciate your understanding. It helps me to know that someone else feels like this."

The final spiritual dimension in our model is *authority and guidance.* In times of crisis and doubt to whom does Andrea turn for support and direction? We don't know Andrea well enough to answer this question confidently. Some things in her story, such as protecting her husband, suggest she may be a strong, self-reliant woman. Her response to Patty on their first visit suggests that she doesn't welcome the authority clergy traditionally represent. Yet, the case also suggests she may be open to Patty's authority when it is grounded in their shared personal experiences of distress and anger with God.

Summary of the Spiritual Assessment

As can be seen here, the process of developing a spiritual assessment using the "7-by-7" model is lengthy and complex. Here is a summary of our spiritual assessment of Andrea. A summary like this could be used in a chart note to share this spiritual assessment with other members of the care team.

> Andrea is beginning to face the reality of her death and is wondering if it is permissible for her to give up struggling and prepare to die with dignity. She is, for the most part, quite alone in this important and stressful process. Her husband is uncomfortable with her talking about dying and she feels she must protect him. Further, she feels God has been unfair in allowing her to become ill despite her exceptionally good health practices. She is enraged with God and refuses to speak to Him. While she was initially rejecting toward the chaplain as a representative of religion, today's visit to the hospital garden became the occasion of a cathartic conversation. It may mark the start of a trusting relationship in which we can work together on these important issues.

SPIRITUAL CARE PLAN FOR ANDREA

What are the implications of this spiritual assessment for spiritual care with Andrea? Based on this assessment, our care plan with Andrea would focus on five things. First, Andrea's painful isolation with her feelings, decisions, and the religious struggles associated with her progressing illness point to the need for a supportive relationship as an urgent focus for spiritual care. An important relationship between Andrea and Patty began to form in the garden, a relationship in which Andrea was able to share some of her anger, grief, and confusion. Spiritual care for Andrea should seek to strengthen this relationship, providing Andrea with a safe place in which she can share the feelings and experiences associated with her dying.

Related to this is the need to initiate efforts to develop a supportive relationship with Andrea's husband. He too may need a safe place to share his fears and concerns about his wife's health and the future. Hopefully, as he experiences understanding and support from a chaplain or other spiritual care provider, he will become more able to understand and support Andrea.

The second focus for spiritual care with Andrea is to address her grief and anger. In the past few weeks, Andrea has begun to realize that "the battle is being lost." She needs to have an opportunity to express the sad and angry feelings that accompany this realization, to mourn the loss of health, future and relationships. The visit to the garden provided an important beginning for that process. Spiritual care needs to help her continue it.

Third, we have the impression that Andrea's rejection of religion is not just an expression of anger with God for her present cancer. Its strength suggests there may have been other times in which she felt betrayal or injustice at the hands of God, or other religious authorities or institutions. We think it would be helpful to ask Andrea if there have been other times in her life when she felt God had not listened to her. One possibility is that she prayed to have children and felt God had not answered her prayer. Other possibilities include insensitive or unethical treatment from religious authorities earlier in her life. We hope that in the context of a trusting relationship with Patty, Andrea may be able to identify and address any past and present experiences of betrayal or injustice. Andrea's spontaneous and grateful response to the trip to the garden suggests she has some capacity for trust and gratitude. We hope the space for those emotions can be expanded by addressing any past and present experiences of betrayal or injustice.

The fourth focus for her spiritual care involves the moral questions she raised in the garden. Addressing these questions will also point to issues of community and authority. Andrea will need support and consultation as she begins to make plans to die with dignity. If her husband and physicians are strongly urging her to try further treatment, it may be very difficult for Andrea to reject their recommendations and assert her own preferences. Related to this, she will need help in making decisions about how and how long she can continue to protect her husband. A supportive and trusting relationship with the chaplain may be very important as Andrea considers decisions that other important persons in her life are not ready to support.

The fifth and final focus for spiritual care with Andrea is ritual. Are there rituals, in addition to pilgrimages to the garden, that will help facilitate Andrea's expression of sadness and anger, her lament? (Billman and Migliore 1999). Are there other rituals that can provide Andrea with moments of transcendence, in which she is lifted beyond the pain of her illness? The impasse in Andrea's conversation with God suggests that she does have some history of conversation with God, some history of prayer. It will be important for Patty to learn more about this and other past experiences with lament and transcendence as she tries to help Andrea find ritual support in her dying.

As we look at all the hard work we have done in developing this spiritual assessment and care plan for Andrea, it is important to remain modest. The next time Patty visits Andrea, she might learn something that will require us to completely alter our assessment of her and our care plan. Our assessments must not keep us from openness and presence to meet our patients at their point of need. They can help us be more effective and accountable for the care we provide to meet those needs.

DISCUSSION

Andrea's case raises a number of interesting points for discussion about spiritual care at the end-of-life. We will briefly consider three of them. First, Andrea's case raises the issue of providing spiritual care for a person who identifies herself as non-religious. As we can see from this case, some non-religious people may have significant religious issues that should be addressed by a trained, competent, chaplain or other spiritual care provider. In the case of other non-religious people, who may not be experiencing any significant religious or spiritual distress, spiritual care may not be needed or appropriate.

Second, Andrea's case illustrates what we have begun to call spiritual risk, that is underdeveloped or conflicted religious or spiritual beliefs that may compromise a patient's ability to cope with his or her illness (Fitchett 1999). Some aspects of religious coping, such as feeling that an illness represents God's punishment or feeling abandoned by God, described by Kenneth Pargament as negative religious coping, appear to be associated with poor adjustment to or recovery from illness (Pargament 1997; Pargament, Smith, Koenig and Perez 1998; Pargament et al. 1998; Koenig, Pargament and Nielsen 1998; see also Fitchett et al. 1999). We hope that instruments for spiritual screening will aid early identification of patients with possible spiritual risk so they can be referred to a professional chaplain or other spiritual care provider for more in-depth spiritual assessment and spiritual care as indicated. In the meantime, all caregivers should be alert to signs of persistent, conflicted religious or spiritual beliefs and make referrals for further spiritual assessment as indicated.

Third, Andrea's case raises a question of continuity of spiritual care. Who will provide spiritual care for Andrea if she is discharged to her home as she wishes? Chaplains who work primarily in in-patient settings often assume their spiritual care ends when a patient is discharged. However, in light of the issues that we described in our spiritual assessment of Andrea, it would not be in her best interest for her to have to develop a relationship with a new spiritual care provider when she goes home. The ideal solution would be for Patty to be able to continue to work with Andrea, and her husband, perhaps using a combination of home visits and phone calls.

CONCLUSION

Stories about gardens are an important part of many religious traditions. In the Christian tradition, before his crucifixion Jesus prays a prayer of lament and surrenders himself to God's will in the Garden of Gethsemane. Andrea began to express her lament in her visit to the hospital garden. Hopefully, she will be able to continue that process and arrive at a point where she too feels reconciled with God and can die with a greater sense of dignity and peace. We hope that our discussion of this spiritual assessment and care plan for Andrea will enable chaplains, clergy, and other spiritual care givers to provide more intentional and effective spiritual care for all patients and families at the end-of-life.

REFERENCES

Berg, G. E. 1994. "The Use of the Computer as a Tool for Assessment and Research in Pastoral Care." *Journal of Health Care Chaplaincy* 6:1, 11–25.

Berg, G. E. 1999. "A Statement on Clinical Assessment for Pastoral Care." *Chaplaincy Today* 14:2, 42–50.

Billman, K. D. and Migliore, D. L. 1999. *Rachel's Cry: Prayer of Lament and Rebirth of Hope.* Cleveland: United Church.

Fitchett, G. 1993a. *Spiritual Assessment in Pastoral Care: A Guide to Selected Resources.* Decatur, GA.: Journal of Pastoral Care Publications, Inc.

Fitchett, G. 1993b. *Assessing Spiritual Needs: A Guide for Caregivers* (Original edition: Minneapolis: Augsburg, 1993), Reprint edition Lima, OH: Academic Renewal, 2002.

Fitchett, G. 1999. "Screening for Spiritual Risk." *Chaplaincy Today* 15:1, 2–12.

Fitchett, G. 1999. "Selected Resources for Screening for Spiritual Risk." *Chaplaincy Today* 15:1, 13–26.

Fitchett, G. and Handzo, G. F. 1998. "Spiritual Assessment, Screening, and Intervention." In *Psycho-oncology*, edited by J. C. Holland, 790–808. New York: Oxford University Press.

Fitchett, G., Rybarczyk, B. D., DeMarco, G. A. and Nicholas, J. J. 1999. "The Role of Religion in Medical Rehabilitation Outcomes: A Longitudinal Study." *Rehabilitation Psychology* 44:4, 333–53. [Article 1 in this volume]

Hodges, S. 1999. "Spiritual Screening: The Starting Place for Intentional Pastoral Care." *Chaplaincy Today* 15:1, 30–40.

Koenig, H. G., Pargament, K.I . and Nielsen, J. 1998. "Religious Coping and Health Status in Medically Ill Hospitalized Older Adults." *Journal of Nervous and Mental Disease* 186:513–21.

Kuhn, C. C. 1988. "A Spiritual Inventory of the Medically Ill Patient." *Psychiatric Medicine* 6:2, 87–100

Maugans, T. A. 1996. "The SPIRITual History." *Archives of Family Medicine* 5:11–16.

Pargament, K. I. 1997. *The Psychology of Religion and Coping: Theory, Research, Practice.* New York: Guilford.

Pargament, K. I., Smith, B. W., Koenig, H. G. and Perez, L. 1998. "Positive and Negative Religious Coping with Major Life Stressors." *Journal for the Scientific Study of Religion* 37:710–24.

Pargament, K. I., Zinnbauer, B. J., Scott, A. B., Butter, E. M., Zerowin J. and Stanik, P. 1998. "Red Flags and Religious Coping: Identifying some Religious Warning Signs among People in Crisis." *Journal of Clinical Psychology* 54:77–89.

Pruyser, P. W. 1976. *The Minister as Diagnostician*. Philadelphia: Westminster.

Puchalski, C. M. 1999. "A Spiritual History." *Supportive Voice* 5:3, 12–13.

Shulevitz, M. and Springer, M. 1994. "Assessment of Religious Experience—A Jewish Approach." *Journal of Pastoral Care* 48:4, 399–406.

Wakefield, J. L., Cox, D. and Forrest, J. S. 1999. "Seeds of Change: The Development of a Spiritual Assessment Model." *Chaplaincy Today* 15:1, 41–50.

Westerhoff, J. H. III. 1976. *Will Our Children Have Faith?* New York: Seabury.

ARTICLE 9

Screening for Spiritual Struggle [1]

—GEORGE FITCHETT

Associate Professor and Director of Research, Department of Religion, Health, and Human Values, Rush University Medical Center Chicago, IL

—JAMES L. RISK

Executive Director, Bishop Anderson House, Assistant Professor, Department of Religion, Health, and Human Values, Rush University Medical Center, Chicago, IL.

WITH GROWING EVIDENCE OF the harmful effects of religious/spiritual (R/S) struggle, it was becoming increasingly clear that non-chaplain healthcare colleagues needed a simple tool which they could use to screen new patients for potential R/S struggle and refer to a chaplain, if necessary. In 2005, my departmental colleague Jay Risk and I collaborated on developing what became known as the Rush Spiritual Screening Protocol. Finding clinical colleagues who could consistently administer the protocol to all new medical rehab patients was a challenge. Persistence, and Jay's strong network of clinical colleagues, specifically colleagues in health psychology, paid off and we were able to test the protocol in over 170 patients. Since the publication of this article, the Rush Protocol, or a revised version, has been adopted in a number of clinical settings, both in- and out-patient. Research to test the best method for spiritual screening is continuing.

1. Fitchett, G., and J. Risk. 2009. "Screening for Spiritual Struggle." *Journal of Pastoral Care and Counseling* 63:1–2, 1–12. https://doi.org/10.1177/154230500906300104

ABSTRACT

A growing body of research documents the harmful effects of religious or spiritual struggle among patients with a wide variety of diagnoses. We developed a brief screening protocol for use in identifying patients who may be experiencing religious/spiritual struggle, as well as patients who would like a visit from a chaplain. We describe the results of a pilot study in which non-chaplain healthcare colleagues administered the screening protocol to patients admitted to an acute medical rehabilitation unit. The protocol identified 7% of the patients as possibly experiencing religious/spiritual struggle. Follow up spiritual assessments by the chaplain confirmed religious/spiritual struggle in all but one of these patients and also identified additional cases of religious/spiritual struggled not identified by the protocol. In addition to areas for future research, we describe how using a protocol to screen patients for religious/spiritual can make important contributions to spiritual care.

Recently, an older patient with Parkinson's Disease tearfully said to one of our chaplains, "My sister died six months ago. Why did God take her and leave me? I have done everything I'm supposed to do, but this disease . . ." Several years ago another of our chaplains heard these words from a middle age woman with advanced cancer, "Why? Why me? I just can't figure it out. And I get so depressed that I just want to give up on life altogether, you know? And I'm so very angry at God. So angry. I refuse to speak to Him. You know what I mean?" (Massey, Fitchett and Roberts 2004).

Painful laments, expressions of religious or spiritual struggle, such as these, are familiar to chaplains. What may be less familiar is a body of research that has developed in recent years documenting the harmful effects of such religious or spiritual struggle. Key features of religious/spiritual struggle, as measured in many of these studies, include feeling angry with God, or abandoned or punished by God (Pargament 1997; Pargament, Smith, Koenig and Perez 1998). This research has caused us to pay special attention to patients such as the two examples quoted above, whose comments indicate they may be experiencing religious/spiritual struggle.

This research includes a study of 96 medical rehabilitation patients, by Fitchett and colleagues, who reported that higher levels of religious struggle were associated with less recovery of independence in activities of daily living (Fitchett, Rybarczyk, DeMarco and Nicholas 1999). In a study of 557 hospitalized, medically ill older patients, Koenig and colleagues found that religious struggle was associated with poorer physical health, worse quality of life, and greater depressive symptoms (Koenig, Pargament and Nielsen

1998). In a two-year follow-up of this sample, Pargament and colleagues reported that patients with chronic religious struggle had poorer quality of life, greater depression, and increased disability (Pargament, Koenig, Tarakeshwar and Hahn 2004). This team also examined the effects of religious struggle on mortality among these patients. They found that religious struggle was a significant predictor of increased mortality, even after controlling for demographic, physical health, and mental health factors (Pagament, Koenig, Tarakeshwar and Hahn 2001). In a recent study, Fitchett and colleagues found that religious struggle was associated with poorer quality of life and greater emotional distress among patients with diabetes, congestive heart failure, or cancer (Fitchett et al. 2004). Other research, among both patients and community samples, gives further evidence of the adverse emotional effects of religious or spiritual struggle (Ano and Vascolcelles 2005; Berg, Fonss, Reed and VandeCreek 1995; Boscaglia, Clarke, Jobling and Quinn 2005; Burker, Evon, Sedway and Egan 2005; Exline, Yali and Lobel 1999; Exline, Yali and Sanderson 2000; Manning-Walsh 2005; McConnell, Pargament, Ellison and Flannelly 2006; Rippentrop et al. 2005; Sherman et al. 2005; Taylor, Outlaw, Bernardo and Roy 1999).

While the negative effects of religion and spiritual struggle are becoming clearer, it is less clear how best to identify patients who may be experiencing it. In an earlier study, we found that the patients most likely to request a visit from a chaplain were those with more religious resources, not those with higher needs (Fitchett, Meyer and Burton 2000 [Article 2 in this volume]). In addition to identifying patients who may be experiencing religious or spiritual struggle, it is important for chaplains to be able to identify patients who would like a visit from a chaplain. These patients may be seeking religious/spiritual support at a vulnerable time and they may be dissatisfied with the hospital if that support is not provided. Some of them may also be experiencing religious/spiritual struggle.

At the risk of some over-simplification, we might think of patients as falling into one of three groups. First, are those who might be experiencing religious or spiritual struggle, but who are unlikely to request a chaplain's visit. Second, are those who would like a visit from a chaplain, who may or may not request one, but who would be dissatisfied if they do not receive one. Finally, there may also be a group for whom religion or spirituality (R/S) is not important and who do not wish or expect a visit from a chaplain. It could potentially assist chaplains' productivity, effectiveness, and perhaps departmental satisfaction scores, if a brief method could be developed for accurately determining which patients fell into which of these three groups. Ideally, in order not to add to the workload of pastoral care departments, which rarely have the personnel to assess all newly admitted patients, such a screening or triage process would be implemented by other members of the health care team, who could then make appropriate referrals to the chaplains based on the results of their screening.

This paper reports on our effort to develop and implement such a screening protocol. The general aim of this project was to evaluate the use of a spiritual screening protocol, by non-chaplain health care staff, to identify and refer patients who may need or desire spiritual care services. The specific aims of the project were:

1. to determine the proportion of new admissions for which the health care staff were able to implement the screening protocol,

2. to determine the proportion of screened patients who might be experiencing spiritual struggle,

3. to compare the identification of potential cases of spiritual struggle made on the basis of the screening protocol with the results of a chaplain's spiritual assessment interview, and,

4. to determine the proportion of screened patients who requested spiritual care services.

The project had two additional aims. The first was to identify barriers, if any, to health care staff's implementation of the spiritual screening protocol. Additionally, we noted that the most frequent complaint about spiritual care from our patient/family satisfaction surveys was that a request had been made for a chaplain to visit, but no one ever came. We assumed use of the protocol might affect patient/family satisfaction with spiritual care by increasing referrals and follow-up of those patients who wished to see a chaplain. Consequently, the final aim of the study was to examine the effect of use of the protocol on patient/family satisfaction with spiritual care.

METHODS

The Screening Protocol

Several assumptions informed the development of the screening protocol. We assumed that people who were experiencing religious or spiritual struggle would not report that in a brief history-taking interview with someone they did not know well or trust. Thus, screening for spiritual struggle would have to be indirect.

We also assumed that simply asking a patient if religion or spirituality was important might elicit a negative response, "No," that could be misinterpreted as a neutral lack of interest in R/S. Thus, we included a follow-up question for those who reported that R/S was not important, "Was there ever a time when religion/spirituality was important to you?" to identify patients for whom R/S had once been important but who reported it was no longer important. We considered this change a potential red flag for religious/spiritual struggle warranting a more in-depth assessment by a chaplain. We also assumed there could be religious/spiritual struggle among those who reported that R/S was important to them. For those who said R/S was important, we included the follow-up question, "How much strength and comfort would you say that you get from your religion/spirituality right now?" to help identify those who might be getting less strength and comfort from their faith than they felt they needed, another red flag signaling the need for a follow-up chaplain assessment. Finally, we assumed that the protocol questions would have to be simple and brief if busy healthcare colleagues, not trained in spiritual care, would agree to use them routinely.

Figure 9.1 shows the screening protocol we developed. Based on the patient's responses to these protocol questions, the staff who administered the protocol would take one of three different actions: 1) Screening indicates possible spiritual struggle, refer for in-depth spiritual assessment by chaplain; 2) No indication of spiritual struggle, however, chaplain visit requested, refer for routine spiritual care, which may uncover religious/ spiritual struggle; or 3) No indication of religious struggle, no chaplain visit requested, no further action needed.

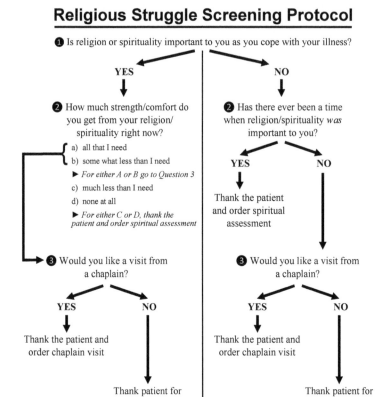

Figure 9.1

Protocol Administration

Our pilot study of the use of the screening protocol had three phases, with different health care colleagues administering the protocol in each phase. In Phase I, Patient Care Technicians (PCTs, formerly referred to as nursing aides) performed the screening. Problems with PCT turnover and inconsistency in administering the protocol led to Phase II in which medical residents administered the protocol. The problems with inconsistency in administering the protocol were worse with the residents than with the PCTs. This led to Phase III in which colleagues in the Department of Behavioral Sciences (psychology interns and staff psychologists) agreed to administer the protocol as part of their assessment of all new admissions to the study unit. We provided initial training, and follow-up consultation regarding any questions, to all the staff who administered the protocol. The three phases of the study had different durations, from two to four months.

The protocol was intended to be administered on the day of the patient's admission. In some cases it was administered on the second day. During Phase I, the PCTs gave unit clerks a sheet indicating the action required. The clerks entered this information into the computer which sent the appropriate orders for chaplain follow up. In Phase II, the protocol was added to the medical residents' computerized physician orders which sent the appropriate orders for chaplain follow-up. During Phase III, the psychology interns and staff kept a centralized log of the results of the screening. The log was checked daily by one of the chaplains who provided the appropriate follow-up.

Where the results of the screening indicated possible spiritual struggle, the unit chaplain (JLR), who is board certified by the Association of Professional Chaplains, made a follow-up visit, usually by the following day, to conduct an in-depth spiritual assessment. This assessment was designed to determine if the patient was experiencing spiritual struggle and, if indicated, to provide follow-up spiritual care that addressed that struggle. The chaplain used his professional judgment to determine the presence of spiritual struggle. Indicators that informed his judgment included the patient's painful expression of feeling abandoned by God, punished by God, or angry with God.

Study Sample

We tested the screening protocol on an 18 bed acute medical rehabilitation unit at Rush University Medical Center in Chicago. Patients on this unit were admitted for rehabilitation related to amputation, neurological disease, stroke, deconditioning, and orthopedic surgeries, including spine surgery and joint replacements. Lengths of stay varied from a few days to several weeks.

Analysis

We recorded all patients admitted to the study unit during the months in which the protocol was being administered. We recorded the category in which they were placed by the screening protocol. We also recorded the results from any chaplain's visit, either from follow-up visits where the protocol indicated possible spiritual struggle, or from visits in response to requests for routine spiritual care. Finally, we compared the responses to three questions about emotional and spiritual care from the patient/family satisfaction surveys for the twelve months prior to the study and the thirteen months of the pilot study.

This project was reviewed by the institutional review board of Rush University Medical Center. Because it was a study of a departmental quality improvement project involving minimal risk, it was determined that written informed consent was not required from the patients who were involved.

RESULTS

The main findings from the study are reported in Table 9.1. From the table it can be seen that the psychology residents were the most consistent in administering the protocol (screened 79% of all new admissions) and the medical residents were the least consistent (screened 22% of all new admissions). In the two phases where there was reasonable consistency in protocol administration, Phases I and III, the protocol questions identified 12 patients, 7% of those actually screened in those two phases, as potentially experiencing spiritual struggle. The chaplain's follow-up assessments confirmed spiritual struggle in 11 of these 12 cases (92%). In both those phases, among those not identified as having potential spiritual struggle, approximately two-thirds of the patients requested a chaplain visit and/or communion.

Table 9.1 **Results from Spiritual Struggle Screening Protocol**

Screening Adminis- tered By	Number (%) of New Admissions Screened	Cases of Spiritual Struggle		Other Spiritual Care Requests	
		Identi- fied by Screening	Con- firmed by Chaplain Assessment	Request Chaplain Visit	Request Commu- nion
PCT	78/159 (49%)	4/78 (5%)	4/4 (100%)	51/78 (65%)	22/78 (28%)
Medical Resident	10/46 (22%)	0/10 (0%)	N/A	2/10 (20%)	0
Psychology Staff	85/108 (79%)	8/85 (9%)	7/8 (88%)	52/85 (61%)	8/85 (9%)

PCT = Patient Care Technician

During and after each phase of the study we conducted interviews with the staff who were administering the screening protocol. In those interviews we asked about barriers to administering the protocol. In Phase I, the PCTs reported feeling overwhelmed by other tasks and unable to administer the protocol because of time constraints. From the interviews with them, it appeared the PCTs sometimes misunderstood and failed to correctly follow the protocol. In Phase II, the turnover of the medical residents made consistency in following the protocol very difficult. The resident's heavy work load was a barrier as was their lack of training about the importance of spiritual struggle. In Phase III, we heard reports from the psychology interns and staff that they sometimes diverged from the protocol questions and inferred patient's level of spiritual struggle from other information obtained in their interviews.

Three questions about emotional and spiritual care are included in the Medical Center's patient/family satisfaction survey; 1) "Staff addressed emotional needs," 2) "Staff addressed spiritual needs," 3) "Satisfaction with the Chaplain." Table 9.2 shows the proportion of patients and families who gave responses of "good" or "very good" to these questions in the twelve-month period prior to the pilot study and the thirteen-month period after the start of the pilot study. As can be seen from the table, there was little change in satisfaction scores for the questions about emotional needs and about satisfaction with the chaplain. In contrast, there was a 17% increase in the proportion of "good" or "very good" responses for the question about staff addressing spiritual needs, a change that was, statistically, marginally significant (2-sided Fisher's Exact Test, $p=0.06$). An alternative perspective is that there was a notable decrease in the proportion of responses of "very poor," "poor," or "fair" for this survey item, from 21% in the preceding year, to 4% in the thirteen months after the protocol was initiated.

Table 9.2 **Patient/Family Satisfaction Scores Before and During Pilot Study**

Survey Item	Responses of "Good" or "Very Good"*	
	Before Pilot Study (Jan 2004–Dec 2005)	During and After Pilot Study (Jan 2006–Jan 2007)
Staff addressed emotional needs	87/100 (87%)	27/29 (93%)
Staff addressed spiritual needs**	56/71 (79%)	25/25 (96%)
Satisfaction with the Chaplain	64/69 (93%)	20/22 (91%)

*The balance of the responses were "Very Poor," "Poor," or "Fair."
**Difference in responses marginally significant (2-sided Fisher's Exact Test, $p=0.06$).

DISCUSSION

While we had some difficulty finding staff colleagues who could administer the screening protocol consistently, when it was administered to patients on this medical rehabilitation unit 7% of those screened were identified as having potential spiritual struggle. Follow-up spiritual assessment visits by the unit chaplain confirmed the presence of spiritual struggle in all but one of these cases. In the technical language of screening, the protocol demonstrated a positive predictive value of 92%; the use of the protocol by the staff led to identification of only one false positive case of spiritual struggle.

During Phase II, when it became apparent that there was little consistency in the medical residents' administration of the protocol, the unit chaplain made rounds to newly admitted patients and administered the screening protocol to 36 of 46 new admissions (78%) not screened by the residents. Of the 36 patients screened, based on the protocol, four (11%) were identified as possibly experiencing spiritual struggle. Spiritual assessment interviews with those four patients confirmed they were experiencing spiritual struggle.

Also, in Phase II, during the course of his rounds with other patients on the unit, the chaplain discovered two patients who were experiencing spiritual struggle who had not been identified as such via the use of the protocol, that is, two cases which were false negatives. The chaplain identified other false negative cases, five each in Phases I and III of the study. These were patients who had requested a chaplain visit, and in response to the protocol question had reported they were receiving "somewhat less" strength and comfort than they needed right now from their R/S. When he visited them, the chaplain assessed they were experiencing religious/spiritual struggle that was understated by their choice of the response "somewhat less."

How does the proportion of patients identified by the protocol as potentially experiencing religious/spiritual struggle compare with published reports of the prevalence of religious/spiritual struggle? In our study of 96 medical rehabilitation patients, we found 12% had high levels of religious struggle (Fitchett, Rybarczyk, DeMarco and Nicholas 1999 [Article 1 in this volume]). In their study of the 239 older medical patients, Pargament and colleagues reported 26% had at least some positive response to one of seven questions about religious struggle at baseline and two years later (Pargament, Koenig, Tarakeshwar and Hahn 2004). In our study of a mixed group of 238 medical in- and out-patients, we found 15% had moderate or high levels of religious struggle (Fitchett et al. 2004 [Article 3 in this volume]). Based on these reports, the 7% of medical rehabilitation patients identified in this pilot study, via the protocol, as potentially having spiritual struggle is quite low. This suggests that the protocol is not identifying all the potential cases of spiritual struggle, that it yields a number of false negatives. It is also possible that among medical rehabilitation patients, for example hip or knee joint replacement patients, there are many for whom the outlook is generally positive and the likelihood of spiritual struggle is low.

Our observations about the barriers that created inconsistency in the staff's administration of our screening protocol were similar to those that have been reported by others, including lack of time, lack of training, discomfort with the topic, and role concerns (Ellis, Vinson and Ewigman 1999; Kristeller, Rhodes, Crippe and Sheets 2005; Taylor 2002). Kristeller and colleagues (2005) designed a project that provided oncologists with a protocol for inquiring about their patient's spirituality. They found that having a detailed protocol and training, including role-playing, led to high levels of physician comfort in using the protocol. Use of the protocol also did not prolong the patient visit. Better training may have helped overcome some of the barriers to nurses or physicians consistently administering our screening protocol.

We observed a different issue in our conversations with the psychology interns and staff who administered the protocol in Phase III. Being tied to the exact words of the protocol felt limiting to them and they sometimes inferred whether patients were experiencing religious/spiritual struggle based on other comments made during the interview. They also felt it might compromise the patient's trust in them if, in cases where patients described religious or spiritual struggle, they did not get the patient's permission to make a referral to the chaplain.

Regarding the effects of implementing the screening protocol on patient/family satisfaction, we consider the results presented here to be preliminary. We compared satisfaction scores from the year prior to the implementation of the protocol with those from the thirteen months beginning with the start of Phase I. However, between Phase I and II, there was a three-month gap with no administration of the protocol, and over all three phases, the protocol was administered to only 55% of the newly admitted patients. A more precise evaluation of the impact of the protocol on patient/family satisfaction would compare the satisfaction of those to whom the protocol was administered and those to whom it was not. In light of this, we have reserved comment about the fact that satisfaction scores were higher on only one of the three questions during the year after we began administering the protocol.

Three levels of inquiry about patient's R/S needs and resources have been described: spiritual screening, spiritual history-taking, and spiritual assessment (Massey, Fitchett and Roberts 2004). Few acute care hospitals have sufficient chaplaincy staff to implement spiritual history-taking or in-depth spiritual assessment for all newly admitted patients. The two-step model described here with, 1) spiritual screening by non-chaplain staff, followed-up by 2) in-depth spiritual assessment by the chaplain, where indicated by the screening, appears to be a good way to make use of limited chaplaincy personnel. It has also been recommended for nurses (Taylor 2002).

We wish to note that this is not the first screening protocol developed by chaplains to be published, nor is it the only one to focus on religious/ spiritual struggle. A partial list of other models includes articles describing two other screening models (Hodges 1999; Wakefield, Cox and Forrest 1999) that appeared in a Symposium, "Screening for Spiritual Risk" in *Chaplaincy Today*, the Journal of the Association of Professional Chaplains (Volume 15, Number 1, 1999). Prior to that, Paul Derrickson described using trained volunteers and beginning pastoral care students to visit newly admitted patients and make referrals where indicated (Derrickson 1994–1995). Greg Stoddard (1993) wrote about training staff to identify patients in spiritual distress. Martin Montonye (1994–1995) described the development of a form nursing staff could use to communicate patients' descriptions of their religious/spiritual needs. George Handzo (1998) described a two-level, interdisciplinary model of screening cancer patients for distress, including spiritual distress. What is unique about the present report is the more complete documentation of the results from implementing the protocol.

The 1999 *Chaplaincy Today* Symposium also included an article describing six instruments that could be used to screen for what was then called spiritual risk (Fitchett 1999b). Among those was Gary Berg's eight-item Spiritual Injury Scale, first presented as part of his computerized spiritual assessment and used in many VA [Eds. V Veterans Affairs] hospitals (Berg 1994, 1999). Several other instruments described in that paper, including the Brief RCOPE, developed by Kenneth Pargament and colleagues (1998), the Index of Religiosity (Idler 1987), and the FACIT—Sp (Peterman, Fitchett, Brady, Hernandez, & Cella, 2002), were developed for research purposes. We think that, although they are sometimes confused (O'Connor et al. 2005), spiritual screening and spiritual assessment are clinical activities that are distinct from research. In light of the useful screening protocols that have been published, including the present one, we no longer recommend the research instruments described in the 1999 *Chaplaincy Today* Symposium (Fitchett 1999b) as useful tools for clinical practice.

In addition to those previously mentioned, several limitations of the present study should be kept in mind. Our estimate of those who were screened in each phase of the study does not take into account patients who, because of confusion, dementia, or other conditions, could not be screened.

We do not know how many such patients there were in each phase. By not collecting that information we have underestimated the proportion of cognitively-able, newly admitted patients, who were screened.

The chaplain's in-depth spiritual assessment of patients who were identified, by the protocol, as having religious/spiritual struggle permits us to estimate the false positives that come from this screening. But because the chaplain did not visit and assess all the newly admitted patients during each phase, we cannot estimate the proportion of false negatives that might be associated with the protocol. As discussed above, we are sure there are some, that is patients who were experiencing religious/spiritual struggle, who were not identified as such by their responses to the protocol questions. A future study should include both the screening protocol and an in-depth spiritual assessment interview to permit a more thorough evaluation of the protocol. Finally, we are aware that this pilot project only tested the protocol on one medical rehabilitation unit. We have no information on how useful the protocol would be in contexts of greater patient acuity, such as intensive care units, or shorter lengths of stay.

Future research regarding the screening protocol includes, as previously mentioned, comparing it to a chaplain's in-depth spiritual assessment for every patient, as well as testing its usefulness among more diverse groups of patients. In addition, we would like to know more about the staff barriers to administering the protocol, and whether health care colleagues in addition to psychologists could be trained and motivated to administer the protocol consistently. Additionally, we continue to be interested in the many different forms that religious/spiritual struggle might take and in how people cope with it. In the course of this study, experiences with several patients made us especially curious to learn how to identify and assist patients who may be experiencing unacknowledged religious/spiritual struggle.

One colleague suggested that we modify the follow-up question for those who say that R/S is not important to them. The suggestion was to ask "Was there a time before the present illness when religion or spirituality was important to you?" instead of, "Has there ever been a time?" Our colleague felt the change would help keep the focus on religious/spiritual struggle associated with the present illness. Our experience, however, is that some of the struggles we have heard about from our patients were not related to the present illness, and not a small number had their origins in situations that were years old (Bradshaw and Fitchett 2003). In light of that we feel the present wording of that question works best.

However, in light of this study, we have revised the responses to the question about how much strength and comfort the patient is presently getting from their R/S. A colleague suggested having only three response options for the question would simplify the protocol. Additionally, as discussed earlier, we found a number of patients who had responded, "Somewhat less than I need" to this question, whom the chaplain later found to be experiencing religious/spiritual struggle. In the revised version of the protocol we have dropped the response, "Much less than I need," and we now treat responses of either, "Somewhat less than I need," or "None at all" as signs of potential religious/spiritual struggle and indicators of a need for referral to the chaplain for in-depth spiritual assessment.

As we noted at the beginning of this article, there is a growing body of evidence that points to the negative impact of religious/spiritual struggle on quality of life and emotional adjustment to illness. It may also compromise recovery and mortality. In light of this, it is important to be able to quickly identify, and refer for spiritual care, patients who may be experiencing religious/spiritual struggle. The results of this pilot study suggest that our screening protocol is a useful tool for identifying patients who may be experiencing religious/spiritual struggle. It is simple. Staff from other health professions can be taught to implement it. The protocol may miss some patients who are experiencing religious/spiritual struggle, but we only saw one false positive case during the study. In addition, the protocol enables staff to quickly identify patients who wish to receive spiritual care. Consistent referral and spiritual care for those patients may provide them with the spiritual support they desire and ensure greater satisfaction with spiritual care services.

In closing, we wish to emphasize three other benefits from using a screening protocol such as the one described here (Fitchett 1999a). First, using a screening protocol can improve stewardship of the professional chaplain's time. In most departments of spiritual care, there are many pressures on the time of professional chaplains. Chaplains can spend less time in case-finding when health care colleagues use a screening protocol to identify patients who wish to see the chaplain and patients who may need to see the chaplain.

Second, a screening protocol such as this one can be very useful in documenting the need for spiritual care. The protocol can help chaplains document the proportion of patients who request spiritual care, and the proportion of patients who may need spiritual care. Having information about the proportion of patients in a specific service area who may be experiencing religious/spiritual struggle is like having information about the acuity of R/S needs of those patients. It can provide a rational basis for discussions about the number of staff chaplains that are needed to meet the R/S needs of those patients.

Third, there is strong pressure to provide evidence about the benefits of spiritual care. Because it may be difficult to measure the impact of spiritual care among all patients, chaplains should begin with studies that examine the impact of spiritual care among patients identified as experiencing religious/spiritual struggle. Colleagues in grief counseling faced similar pressure to demonstrate the benefits of their work. It was only when their studies focused on people with evidence of complicated grief that research showed the benefits of their interventions (Parkes 2001). Similarly, given the evidence of the harmful effects of religious/spiritual struggle, providing spiritual care to patients experiencing religious/spiritual struggle may make a measurable difference in their quality of life, emotional adjustment to illness, and possibly their recovery and survival.

REFERENCES

Ano, G. G. and Vascolcelles, E. B. 2005. "Religious Coping and Psychological Adjustment to Stress: A Meta-analysis." *Journal of Clinical Psychology* 61:461–80.

Berg, G. E. 1994. "The Use of the Computer as a Tool for Assessment and Research in Pastoral Care." *Journal of Health Care Chaplaincy* 6:1, 11–25.

Berg, G. E. 1998. "A Statement on Clinical Assessment for Pastoral Care." *Chaplaincy Today* 14:2, 42–50.

Berg, G. E., Fonss, N., Reed, A. J. and VandeCreek, L. 1995. "The Impact of Religious Faith and Practice on Patients' Suffering from a Major Affective Disorder: A Cost Analysis." *Journal of Pastoral Care* 49:4, 359–63.

Boscaglia, N., Clarke, D. M., Jobling, T. W. and Quinn, M. A. 2005. "The Contribution of Spirituality and Spiritual Coping to Anxiety and Depression in Women with a Recent Diagnosis of Gynecological Cancer." *International Journal of Gynecological Cancer* 15:755–61.

Bradshaw, A. and Fitchett, G. 2003. "'God, Why Did This Happen To Me?' Three Perspectives on Theodicy." *Journal of Pastoral Care and Counseling* 57:179–89.

Burker, E. J., Evon, D. M., Sedway, J. A. and Egan, T. 2005. "Religious and Non-religious Coping in Lung Transplant Patients: Does Adding God to the Picture Tell us More?" *Journal of Behavioral Medicine* 28:513–26.

Derrickson, P. E. 1994–1995. "Screening Patients for Pastoral Care: A Preliminary Report." *The Caregiver Journal* 11:14–18.

Ellis, M. R., Vinson, D. C. and Ewigman, B. 1999. "Addressing Spiritual Concerns of Patients: Family Physicians' Attitudes and Practices." *Journal of Family Practice* 48:105–9.

Exline, J. J., Yali, A. M. and Lobel, M. 1999. "When God Disappoints: Difficulty Forgiving God and Its Role in Negative Emotion." *Journal of Health Psychology* 4:365–79.

Exline, J. J., Yali, A. M, and Sanderson, W. C. 2000. "Guilt, Discord, and Alienation: The Role of Religious Strain in Depression and Suicidality." *Journal of Clinical Psychology* 56:1481–96.

Fitchett, G. 1999. "Screening for Spiritual Risk." *Chaplaincy Today* 15:1, 2–12.

Fitchett, G. 1999. "Selected Resources for Screening for Spiritual Risk." *Chaplaincy Today* 15:1, 13–26.

Fitchett, G., Meyer, P. and Burton, L. A. 2000. "Spiritual Care in the Hospital: Who Requests It? Who Needs It?" *Journal of Pastoral Care* 54:2, 173–86. [Article 2 in this volume]

Fitchett, G., Murphy, P. E., Kim, J., Gibbons, J. L., Cameron, J. R., and Davis, J. A. 2004. "Religious Struggle: Prevalence, Correlates and Mental Health Risks in Diabetic, Congestive Heart Failure, and Oncology Patients." *International Journal of Psychiatry in Medicine* 34:179–96. [Article 3 in this volume]

Fitchett, G., Rybarczyk, B. D., DeMarco, G. A. and Nicholas, J. J. 1999. "The Role of Religion in Medical Rehabilitation Outcomes: A Longitudinal Study." *Rehabilitation Psychology* 44:4, 333–53. [Article 1 in this volume]

Handzo, G. F. 1998. "An Integrated System for the Assessment and Treatment of Psychological, Social, and Spiritual Distress." *Chaplaincy Today* 14:30–37.

Hodges, S. 1999. "Spiritual Screening: The Starting Place for Intentional Pastoral Care." *Chaplaincy Today* 15:30–40.

Idler, E. L. 1987. "Religious Involvement and the Health of the Elderly: Some Hypotheses and an Initial Test." *Social Forces* 66:226–38

Koenig, H. G., Pargament, K. I. and Nielsen, J. 1998. "Religious Coping and Health Status in Medically Ill Hospitalized Older Adults." *Journal of Nervous and Mental Disease* 186:513–21.

Kristeller, J. L., Rhodes, M., Cripe, L. D. and Sheets, V. 2005. "Oncologist Assisted Spiritual Intervention Study (OASIS): Patient Acceptability and Initial Evidence of Effects." *International Journal of Psychiatry in Medicine* 35:329–47.

Manning-Walsh, J. 2005. "Spiritual Struggle: Effect on Quality of Life and Life Satisfaction in Women with Breast Cancer." *Journal of Holistic Nursing* 23:120–40.

Massey, K., Fitchett, G. and Roberts, P. A. 2004. "Assessment and Diagnosis in Spiritual Care. In *Spiritual Care in Nursing Practice*, edited by K. L. Mauk and N. K. Schmidt, 209–42. Philadelphia: Lippincott, Williams and Wilkins.

McConnell, K. M., Pargament, K. I., Ellison, C. G. and Flannelly, K. J. 2006. "Examining the Links between Spiritual Struggles and Symptoms of Psychopathology in a National Sample." *Journal of Clinical Psychology* 62:1469–84.

Montonye, M. 1994–1995. "Patient-centered Caring: Identifying Religious Needs." *The Caregiver Journal* 11:33–37.

O'Connor, T. S., Meakes, E., O'Neill, K., Penner, C., Van Staalduinen, G. and Davis, K. 2005. "Not Well Known, Used Little and Needed: Canadian Chaplains' Experiences of Published Spiritual Assessment Tools." *Journal of Pastoral Care and Counseling* 59:1–2, 97–107. doi.org/10.1177/154230500505900110

Pargament, K. I. 1997. *The Psychology of Religion and Coping: Theory, Research, Practice.* New York: Guilford.

Pargament, K. I., Koenig, H. G., Tarakeshwar, N and Hahn, J. 2001. "Religious Struggle as a Predictor of Mortality among Medically Ill Elderly Patients: A Two-Year Longitudinal Study." *Archives of Internal Medicine* 161:15, 1881–85.

Pargament, K. I., Koenig, H. G., Tarakeshwar, N. and Hahn, J. 2004. "Religious Coping Methods as Predictors of Psychological, Physical and Spiritual Outcomes among Medically Ill Elderly Patients: A Two-Year Longitudinal Study." *Journal of Health Psychology* 9:6, 713–30.

Pargament, K. I., Smith, B. W., Koenig, H. G. and Perez, L. 1998. "Patterns of Positive and Negative Religious Coping with Major Life Stressors." *Journal for the Scientific Study of Religion* 37:4, 710–24.

Parkes, C. M. 2001. "A Historical Overview of the Scientific Study of Bereavement." In *Handbook of Bereavement Research: Consequences, Coping, and Care*, edited by M. S. Stroebe, R. O. Hansson, W. Stroebe and H. Schut, 25–45. Washington, DC: American Psychological Association.

Peterman, A. H., Fitchett, G., Brady, M. J., Hernandez, L. and Cella, D. 2002. "Measuring Spiritual Well-being in People with Cancer: The Functional Assessment of Chronic Illness Therapy—Spiritual Well-Being Scale (FACIT—Sp)." *Annals of Behavioral Medicine* 24:49–58.

Rippentrop, E. A., Altmaier, E. M., Chen, J. J., Found, E. M. and Keffala, V. J. 2005. "The Relationship between Religion/Spirituality and Physical Health, Mental Health, and Pain in a Chronic Pain Population." *Pain* 116:311–21.

Sherman, A. C., Simonton, S., Latif, U., Spohn, R. and Tricot, G. 2005. "Religious Struggle and Religious Comfort in Response to Illness: Health Outcomes among Stem Cell Transplant Patients." *Journal of Behavioral Medicine* 28:359–67

Stoddard, G. A. 1993. "Chaplaincy by Referral: An Effective Model for Evaluating Staffing Needs." *The Caregiver Journal* 10:37–52.

Taylor, E. J. 2002. *Spiritual Care: Nursing Theory, Research, and Practice.* Upper Saddle River, NJ: Pearson Education, Inc.

Taylor, E. J., Outlaw, F. H., Bernardo, T. R. and Roy, A. 1999. "Spiritual Conflicts Associated with Praying about Cancer." *Psycho-Oncology* 8:386–94.

Wakefield, J. L., Cox, R. D., and Forrest, J. S. 1999. "Seeds of Change: The Development of a Spiritual Assessment Model." *Chaplaincy Today* 15:41–50.

ARTICLE 10

Development of the PC–7, a Quantifiable Assessment of Spiritual Concerns of Patients Receiving Palliative Care Near the End of Life [1]

—GEORGE FITCHETT

Department of Religion, Health, and Human Values, Rush University Medical Center, Chicago, IL

—ANNA LEE HISEY PIERSON

Advocate Aurora Good Samaritan Hospital, Downers Grove, IL

—CHRISTINE HOFFMEYER

Advocate Aurora Lutheran General Hospital, Park Ridge, IL

—DIRK LABUSCHAGNE

Department of Religion, Health, and Human Values, Rush University Medical Center, Chicago, IL

—AOIFE LEE

Spiritual Care, Rush Oak Park Hospital, Oak Park, IL

1. G. Fitchett, A. L. H. Pierson, C. Hoffmeyer, D. Labuschagne, A. Lee, S. Levine, S. O'Mahony, K. Pugliese, and N. White. 2019. "Development of the PC–7, a Quantifiable Assessment of Spiritual Concerns of Patients Receiving Palliative Care Near the End of Life." *Journal of Palliative Medicine*. doi: 10.1089/jpm.2019.0188.

—STACIE LEVINE
Section of Geriatrics and Palliative Medicine, Department of Medicine, University of Chicago Medicine, Chicago, IL

—SEAN O'MAHONY
Section of Palliative Medicine, Department of Internal Medicine, Rush University Medical Center, Chicago, IL

—KAREN PUGLIESE
Spiritual Care and Education, Northwestern Medicine, Central DuPage Hospital, Winfield, IL

—NANCY WAITE
Evanston Hospital, NorthShore University Health System, Evanston, IL

THIS IS MY MOST recent publication in this collection. It was published twenty years after Article 1 and twenty-six years after I described the 7x7 model for spiritual assessment in Assessing Spiritual Needs. *The PC-7 takes a very different approach to spiritual assessment than the 7x7 model (see Article 8). Specifically, it is a quantifiable model for describing unmet spiritual concerns in a specific patient group, those receiving palliative care at the end of life. As we say in the article, we were inspired by the SDAT model for spiritual assessment in geriatric medical rehabilitation developed by a Swiss team led by Stephanie Monod. Further research is underway to examine the validity and reliability of the PC-7. The model is the result of work by a team of chaplains who came together to work on an interdisciplinary palliative education project. When I suggested we also see if we could develop a better model for spiritual assessment in palliative care they were all in. Thus, somewhat like the initial team that helped launch chaplain case studies (see Article 6), the PC-7 is the result of the work of a team of chaplains that identified a need in our profession and collaborated over several years to address it.*

ABSTRACT

Background:

Attending to the religious/spiritual (R/S) concerns of patients is a core component of palliative care. A primary responsibility of the chaplain is to conduct a thorough assessment of palliative care patients' R/S needs and resources. Problems with current approaches to spiritual assessment in all clinical contexts, including palliative care, include limited evidence for their validity, reliability, or clinical usefulness; narrative content; and lack of clinical specificity.

Objectives:

The aim of our work was to develop an evidence-based, quantifiable model for the assessment of unmet spiritual concerns of palliative care patients near the end of life.

Design:

The PC–7 model was developed by a team of chaplains working in palliative care. Phase 1 used literature in the field and the chaplains' clinical practice to identify key concerns in the spiritual care of palliative care patients. Phase 2 focused on developing indicators of those concerns and reliability in the chaplains' rating of them.

Results:

Key concerns in the model include the following. Need for meaning in the face of suffering; need for integrity, a legacy; concerns about relationships; concern or fear about dying or death; issues related to treatment decision making; R/S struggle; and other concerns. An approach to scoring the patients' degree of unmet spiritual concerns was adapted from the literature. Assessing cases from the chaplains' practice led to high levels of agreement (reliability).

Conclusion:

Using the PC–7 model, chaplains can describe and quantify the key spiritual concerns of palliative care patients. Further research is needed to test its validity, reliability, and clinical usefulness.

Key words: Chaplain care; Palliative care; Spiritual assessment; Spiritual care

INTRODUCTION

The importance of attending to religious and spiritual concerns in palliative care is widely recognized in practice guidelines and consensus statements. (National Consensus Project for Quality Palliative Care 2018). It is also generally recognized that chaplains are the spiritual care specialists on the palliative care team, and one of their primary responsibilities is conducting assessments of the patients' religious/spiritual (R/S) needs and existing resources (Puchalski et al. 2009). While the limitations of chaplains' documentation of their spiritual assessments have been described (Aslakson et al. 2017; Johnson et al. 2016; Lee, Curlin and Choi 2017), the limitations of current approaches to spiritual assessment have received only brief attention (Balboni et al. 2017).

Current approaches to spiritual assessment in all clinical contexts, not just palliative care, are marked by three major limitations. The first is that, with few exceptions, most published models for spiritual assessment were designed to be used in multiple clinical contexts—what we call the "one-size-fits-all" approach (Fitchett 1993/2002; Lucas 2001; Pruyser 1976; Shields, Kestenbaum and Dunn, 2015). These models were developed before the growth of research about R/S issues associated with different clinical conditions, for example, oncology (Canada and Fitchett 2015; Peteet and Balboni 2013). Research now permits the development of more efficient and research-informed condition-specific models for spiritual assessment. This includes spiritual assessment in palliative care focused on the spiritual concerns of these patients who have been identified through research (Balboni et al. 2017).

The second limitation is that most models for spiritual assessment are based on narrative. Many chaplains prefer a "conversational approach" to spiritual assessment and have been uncomfortable with models that "attempt to measure or quantify spirituality, religiosity, or spiritual injury" (Lewis 2002, 5). Because it is essential that chaplains develop the ability to describe the effects (outcomes) of their care (Handzo et al. 2014), models for spiritual assessment must have a quantitative component, which could be combined with narrative summaries. The Spiritual Distress Assessment Tool (SDAT), developed by Monod and colleagues (Monod et al. 2012), demonstrates that a quantifiable approach to assessing unmet spiritual needs is possible.

The third limitation is the lack of a standard, evidence-based approach to spiritual assessment in palliative care or in any clinical context. The existing evidence is limited, but it suggests that most chaplains use their own model for spiritual assessment or a model developed in their local spiritual care department (O'Connor et al. 2005). Thus, at best, the level of evidence supporting most models for spiritual assessment is expert opinion. The lack of evidence-based models for spiritual assessment raises questions about the quality of this central spiritual care activity. This lack of standardization makes it harder for clinical colleagues to understand the R/S dimension of the patient's experience and why it may be relevant for the patient's overall care. It also limits the research that can be conducted about spiritual assessment and spiritual care.

The aim of this project was to develop an evidence-based model for spiritual assessment, specific to adult palliative care, that quantified the patients' level of unmet spiritual concerns and that could be widely adopted.

METHODS

The project was carried out by a team of seven Chicago-area chaplains working in different institutions in palliative care and related areas (e.g., intensive care units, chaplaincy research). Some team members were relatively new to chaplaincy and palliative care (one to two years of experience); others were experienced palliative care spiritual care providers and leaders in the development of specialty certification in palliative care for chaplains. The team came together as part of a multiyear palliative care education initiative, The Coleman Palliative Medicine Training Program (Levine et al. 2017).

There were two phases in the development of the PC–7 model for spiritual assessment in palliative care. The first phase focused on identifying a set of key themes or central spiritual issues and related indicators for patients receiving palliative care. The themes and indicators were generated from a review of relevant literature, from a series of case discussions, and from the clinical experience of the team members. The second phase focused on developing inter-rater reliability in using the model to score patients' unmet spiritual needs. This was accomplished through monthly discussions of case studies provided by members of the team.

Chaplains working in palliative care address a wide variety of concerns of both patients and their loved ones (Jeuland, Fitchett, Schulman-Green and Kapo 2017; Massey et al. 2015). The team felt that, for our initial effort, it was unrealistic to develop a model for spiritual assessment that addressed all of these situations; therefore, we developed a model for spiritual assessment that focused only on the patient who was receiving palliative care. Although family members are often the focus of a palliative care chaplains' attention, the model does not focus on assessing the spiritual needs of family members. It was further decided that the model would focus only on palliative care patients who were near the end of life (e.g., patients facing decisions about discontinuing curative treatment); themes were not developed for all patients who receive palliative care consultation (e.g., patients being seen for pain control who are not near the end of life).

RESULTS

Developing the themes and indicators

Our initial spiritual assessment model contained five themes. Four of the themes came from the work of Steinhauser and colleagues on quality of life at the end of life. That team's investigations began with qualitative interviews in which patients with advanced illness were asked to describe factors associated with a good death (Steinhauser et al. 2000). Those accounts were used to develop an initial version of the QUAL—E, an instrument designed to assess quality of life at the end of life for patients with advanced illness (Steinhauser et al. 2002). Further psychometric testing of the QUAL—E (Steinhauser, Clipp, Bosworth and McNeilly 2004) identified four domains, two of which—life completion and preparation for the end of life—we found to be relevant for our work. Four of the initial themes in our spiritual assessment model were derived from items assessing these domains. They were Need for Meaning, Need for a Legacy, Concerns about Family, and Fear about Dying. We added a fifth theme, R/S Struggle, based on the work of Pargament and colleagues (Pargament, Smith, Koenig and Perez 1998) and the evidence about the prevalence and harmful effects of R/S struggle or R/S pain (Delgado-Guay 2016; Exline 2013).

In each monthly conference call, we used the most current version of the model, updated after each call to reflect consensus about alterations, to assess a case brought by a member of the team. A total of 14 patients were discussed; they included men and women, middle age and older, white and African American, and most reporting a Christian religious affiliation. All of these were hospitalized patients with advanced illness who had been referred for palliative care and assistance in planning goals of care.

In early discussions, we realized the similarity between two of our themes and the stages of adult and late life development in the work of Erik Erikson (Erikson and Erikson 1997). Specifically, the theme Need for Meaning was related to Erikson's description of Integrity, and the theme Need for Legacy was related to Erikson's description of Generativity. We also realized the similarity between our theme Need for Meaning and Elizabeth MacKinlay's description of the spiritual tasks of aging (MacKinlay and Trevitt, 2007). These monthly case discussions also led to the addition of one more theme, Issues Related to Making Decisions about Treatment. We also added a theme for Other Dimensions of Spiritual Concern that were not encompassed in the other themes.

Our team discussions led to the elaboration of the indicators for each theme. The indicators serve to clarify the kinds of R/S concerns that are part of each theme. The indicators also include notes that differentiate apparently similar R/S concerns so that the chaplain does not give a score to more than one theme for any particular patient's R/S concern. There have been 11 iterations of our model for spiritual assessment; many iterations only had minor revisions to the indicators. Table 10.1 shows the current model.

Table 10.1 Chaplain Assessment of Explicit Spiritual Concerns of Patients in Palliative Care

Theme	Indicators (these indicators are meant to be suggestive, not exhaustive of the associated themes)
Need for meaning in the face of suffering	• The patient is having difficulty coming to terms with changes in things that gave meaning to life (e.g., grief related to key relationships, illness, frailty, dependency). • The patient expresses despair or hopelessness about these changes. • (The focus here is on coming to terms with illness, loss, diminished quality of life, or other diminishment. If the issue is about the meaning of their life, then score under Legacy.)
Need for integrity, a legacy, generativity	• The patient questions the meaning of life—whether the life he or she has lived has meaning. • Patient has painful regret about some or all of life lived. (If the regret is about a relationship where reconciliation is possible, then score under Concerns about relationships.) • The patient questions whether he or she has made a positive contribution to loved ones, others, or society. • The patient has tasks that must be completed before he or she is ready to die. (If the tasks are interpersonal, score under Concerns about relationships.) • Reminiscing about their life is painful for the patient. • The patient is distressed about having lived an imperfect life. (If the regret, conflict, or discomfort focuses on current illness, score under Need for meaning in the face of suffering.)
Concerns about relationships: family and/or significant others	• The patient has unfinished business with significant others (e.g., need to overcome estrangement, need to express forgiveness, need for reconciliation, and unfulfilled expectations about others). • (Regrets about relationships where reconciliation is unlikely should only be scored under Legacy.) • The patient has concerns about the family's ability to cope without him or her. • The patient has concerns that he or she is a burden to family/friends. • The patient expresses isolation or loneliness.

Concern or fear about dying or death	• The patient has concerns about dying or being unready for death. This may include explicit hesitation, reluctance, or avoidance to consider or discuss mortality, or associated issues. (This refers to a general sense of unreadiness. If the unreadiness is expressed in terms of specific tasks, score under Need for integrity. If the unreadiness is expressed in terms of unfinished interpersonal tasks, score under Concerns about relationships.) • The patient is impatient for death. • The patient is concerned to participate in important events before death; the patient is concerned that illness or death will prevent participation in important events. • The patient is torn between letting go and fighting on. • The patient has uncertainty or fear about life after death (afraid of damnation; concerned about reunion with loved ones). • The patient has fear of pain or of pain in dying.
Issues related to making decisions about treatment	• The patient needs assistance with value-based advance care planning. • The patient is confused or distressed about end-of-life treatment or about making choices about end-of-life treatment.
R/S struggle	• The patient wonders whether he or she is being abandoned or punished by God. • The patient is concerned about God's judgment, forgiveness, and/or love. • The patient questions God's love for him or her. • The patient feels God is not answering prayers (e.g., asking to die soon). • The patient expresses anger with God. • The patient is alienated from formerly meaningful connections with religious institutions or leaders.
Other dimensions	• The patient identifies a need for assistance to perform important rituals, religious or otherwise. • Other spiritual concerns.

R/S, religious/spiritual.

Scoring unmet spiritual concerns

We adopted the approach to scoring unmet R/S concerns or needs from the SDAT developed by Monod and colleagues (Monod et al. 2012; Monod, Rochat, Büla and Spencer 2010). The SDAT was developed for use in

geriatric medical rehabilitation; it uses five themes identified by Monod and colleagues for that context (Monod 2010). As we have described, we developed seven different themes that were relevant for our clinical focus, care for patients receiving palliative care near the end of life. The SDAT assigns a score from 0 to 3 representing the chaplain's assessment of the level of the patient's unmet R/S concern or need (0=no evidence of unmet need, 1=some evidence of unmet need, 2=substantial evidence of unmet need, and 3=evidence of severe unmet need) for each of the themes in the spiritual assessment model. The approach to scoring in the SDAT is to limit the score to a patient's explicit expression of R/S concern, need, or distress (e.g., "I feel that I am a burden to my family"). In our work, we found that this focus on explicitly expressed concern was in tension with chaplains' training to be attentive to unexpressed distress or concern. Discussion of this issue led us to create an additional scoring option 0*. The 0* score indicates that there is no explicit evidence of R/S concern, but the chaplain feels further assessment is needed to confirm this.

The focus on unmet R/S needs or concerns in the SDAT model appears to ignore chaplains' assessment of patients' R/S resources as well as their needs. This is not the case; the chaplains' assessment of the patient's R/S resources is taken into account in evaluating the extent to which an R/S concern or need is unmet, that is, beyond the patient's current available personal or interpersonal R/S resources. Thus, a patient who expresses a substantial R/S concern about unfinished business with a family member who also expresses having the ability to reach out and engage that person might be scored 1 (some evidence of unmet need). A patient with a similar concern who, for example, expresses reluctance to reach out and engage the person might receive a score of 2 (substantial evidence of unmet need). In our model, a score of 2 or 3 for any theme implies a level of unmet R/S concern or need that should be addressed in a care plan and follow-up care (Lucas 2001; Massey et al. 2015).

Our discussions led to several additional clarifications for assigning scores for unmet R/S concerns or needs. First, we assign a score that represents where the patient is at the end of the visit. If there has been change in the level of concern during the visit (decreased or increased), that can be noted in a narrative chart note. Second, prior knowledge of the patient, and especially their ability to cope and other resources available to them, may be used to assign a value for spiritual concerns that have been expressed. Third, where multiple indicators of R/S need or concern for one theme are evident, we assign the score for the indicator of greatest need. For example, unfinished business with family or friends and concerns that one is a burden to them are both indicators of potential concerns about relationships.

A patient may indicate painful concern about unfinished business with a loved one (scored 3, evidence of severe unmet need) and also wonder if he or she has become a burden to other loved ones (scored 1, some evidence of unmet need). In such a case, the patient would be assessed 3 for concern about relationships.

Spiritual assessment method

Like the original SDAT, our PC–7 model for spiritual assessment is based on an interview with the patient. The interview is not intended to use structured discussion of the themes or indicators in the model; most chaplains prefer open-ended interviews that are responsive to the patients' concerns (O'Connor et al. 2005; Monod, Rochat, Büla and Spencer 2010). The original SDAT model (Monod, Rochat, Büla and Spencer 2010) includes interview questions designed to clarify if there are any unmet R/S needs that have not been spontaneously mentioned in the interview. At present, we have not developed similar questions for the PC–7. When one or more of the themes in the PC–7 have not been mentioned in an open-ended interview, chaplains might comment on them, noting that other patients have had concerns in these areas. The chaplain can then inquire whether they are a concern for the patient being interviewed. While the clinical situation frequently does not allow multiple conversations over several days, when the chaplain has had the opportunity to become more familiar with the patient's background, concerns, and coping resources, our spiritual assessments are likely to be more thorough.

Developing reliability

A key concern with developing an interviewer rating of the level of R/S concerns or needs is the reliability associated with the model, especially inter-rater reliability. Within our team, inter-rater reliability improved to 100%. Factors associated with our improved inter-rater reliability include the following: clarifying the indicators of R/S concern or need, adding the 0* scoring option, and the other scoring clarifications noted above.

Reliability of the PC–7 model was further tested during a national webinar in February 2018, hosted by the Association of Professional Chaplains (APC), in which 154 chaplains participated. In the webinar, after presenting the model, a case vignette was presented and participants used the model to score the spiritual assessment for the case. Table 10.2 shows the participants' scores for the case (recoded to [0–1] no to some concern vs. [2–3] substantial or severe concern). As can be seen in Table 10.2, for four of the seven themes, more than 90% of the participants agreed there was no or some spiritual concern, and for a fifth theme, 84% of the participants agreed there was substantial or severe concern. We find this a remarkable level of agreement after only a 15–20-minute introduction to the model and the case. We are hopeful that with more extensive training, including practice using the model for spiritual assessment of cases, high levels of inter-rater reliability will be evidenced among chaplains using the model. The Supplementary Data include the case example used in this webinar, the assessments of the case by members of our team, and a brief discussion of those assessments. In addition to this webinar, the model was presented in two workshops attended by 100 chaplains each at the 2017 national conferences of the APC and the National Association of Catholic Chaplains (NACC). The workshops followed a format similar to the webinar with similar levels of reliability for scoring the case vignettes that were presented. The workshop participants also expressed enthusiasm for having a quantifiable model for assessment specific to patients receiving palliative care near the end of life.

Table 10.2 **Chaplains' Scores for Spiritual Concerns for Webinar Vignette ("Mildred")**

	Scores	
Theme	0–1	2–3
Need for meaning ($n = 117$)	92%	8%
Need for integrity, a legacy ($n = 154$)	92%	8%
Concerns about family ($n = 149$)	16%	84%
Concern about dying ($n = 148$)	68%	32%
Issues related to treatment decisions ($n = 151$)	63%	37%
R/S struggle ($n = 149$)	97%	3%
Other dimensions ($n = 148$)	98%	2%

Scores are dichotomized: 0–1 = no or some spiritual concern; 2–3 = substantial or severe spiritual concern.

DISCUSSION

A key concern in developing a model for spiritual assessment in palliative care is whether the model encompasses the R/S needs or concerns that are encountered most frequently in this clinical context; that is, does the model have face validity? Our evidence for the face validity of the PC–7 model comes from three sources. The first source is the consistency of the themes in the model with existing theoretical and empirical literature about spiritual issues at the end of life (Benito et al. 2014; Leget 2017). The second source is the use of case examples taken from the clinical practice of the team members to inform the development of the key themes in the model. The third source is the positive response to the PC–7 model from colleagues who have participated in the workshops and webinar where it has been presented. Discussions in these sessions did not identify any major themes that were missing from the model.

Limitations of the PC–7 model include those we have previously noted. While the focus of palliative care is addressing the needs of patients with serious illness, our model is limited to palliative care patients who are facing the end of life. In addition, palliative care, as well as spiritual care within palliative care, seeks to address the needs of both patient and loved ones, while our model focuses only on the R/S needs of the patient. We felt these limitations provided necessary focus for the development of this new approach to spiritual assessment in palliative care. We hope future work will address them. Colleagues have also noted that the theistic assumptions in the indicators for R/S struggle may limit the validity of the theme for nontheistic patients. These indicators were drawn from the items in the negative religious coping subscale of the Brief RCOPE (Pargament, Smith, Koenig and Perez 1998). Until recently, this has been the most widely used measure of R/S struggle among patients with diverse conditions (Exline 2013). For example, among patients with advanced illness, higher levels of R/S struggle have been associated with poorer quality of life (Tarakeshwar 2006). Revisions to these indicators should be considered in future research especially in light of new measures of R/S struggle (Exline, Pargament, Grubbs and Yali 2014) and spiritual pain (Delgado-Guay 2016) that have been reported.

The PC–7 model requires further testing for reliability and validity; the work of Monod and colleagues (Monod et al. 2012) examining the reliability and validity of the SDAT provides a model for this research. Research is needed that examines the validity and reliability of the PC–7 model in culturally diverse samples, including those from non-Christian faiths and those who have no religious affiliation. The PC–7 model was developed based on hospitalized patients; research is also needed about its validity and reliability in outpatient, home care, and hospice contexts. Furthermore, while the PC–7 model has been enthusiastically received by chaplaincy colleagues, systematic research is needed into chaplains' experience and comfort using the model. In addition, research is needed to determine whether palliative care colleagues in other disciplines (physicians, nurses, and social workers) find the model provides them with the information they need about the patient's R/S needs and concerns and provides it in an efficient way (Choi, Chow, Curlin and Cox 2018). Once proven reliable and valid, the PC–7 model can be used to identify the prevalence and intensity of unmet R/S needs and concerns among patients at the end of life and in research testing the effects of spiritual care interventions that address those needs.

CONCLUSION

After reviewing chaplain documentation of care for patients in the ICU, Aslakson and colleagues recommended that the profession "explore ways of having more explicit and standardized documentation of spiritual assessment content in both chaplain and/or palliative care notes" (Aslakson et al. 2017, 654). Here, we report the development of the PC–7, an evidence-based model for spiritual assessment in palliative care that addresses these recommendations and other limitations of current approaches to spiritual assessment, such as their one-size-fits-all approach and narrative method.

ACKNOWLEDGEMENTS

We express our thanks to the Coleman Foundation for their support of the Coleman Palliative Medicine Training Program (https://colemanpalliative.org/), which brought our team together and enabled our initial work on this model for spiritual assessment in palliative care. We also acknowledge our gratitude for the assistance of Kristen Schenk in preparing the article for publication.

FUNDING INFORMATION

This research did not receive any specific grant from funding agencies in the public, commercial, or not-for-profit sectors.

AUTHOR DISCLOSURE STATEMENT

No competing financial interests exist.

SUPPLEMENTARY MATERIAL

Supplementary Data

REFERENCES

Aslakson, R. A., Kweku, J., Kinnison, M., Singh, S. and Crowe II, T.Y. 2017. "Operationalizing the Measuring What Matters Spirituality Quality Metric in a Population of Hospitalized, Critically Ill Patients and their Family Members." *Journal of Pain and Symptom Management* 53:3, 650–55.

Balboni, T. A., Fitchett, G., Handzo, G. F., Johnson, K. S., Koenig, H. G., Pargament, K. I., Puchalski, C. M., Sinclair, S., Taylor, E. J. and Steinhauser, Karen E. 2017. "State of the Science of Spirituality and Palliative Care Research Part II: Screening, Assessment, and Interventions." *Journal of Pain and Symptom Management* 54:3, 441–53.

Benito, E., Oliver, A., Galiana, L., Barreto, P., Pascual, A., Gomis, C. and Barbero, J. 2014. "Development and Validation of a New Tool for the Assessment and Spiritual Care of Palliative Care Patients." *Journal of Pain and Symptom Management* 47:6, 1008–18.e1. doi.org/10.1016/j.jpainsymman.2013.06.018

Canada, A. L. and Fitchett, G. 2015. "Religion/Spirituality and Cancer: A Brief Update of Selected Research." In *Psycho-Oncology*, 3rd ed., edited by J. C. Holland, W. S. Breitbart, P. B. Jacobsen, M. J. Loscalzo, R. McCorkle and P. N. Butow, 503–8. New York: Oxford University Press.

Choi, P. J., Chow, V., Curlin, F. A. and Cox, C. E. 2018. "Intensive Care Clinicians' Views on the Role of Chaplains." *Journal of Health Care Chaplaincy* 5:3, 1–10. doi: 10.1080/08854726.2018.1538438

Delgado-Guay, M. O., Chisholm, G., Williams, J., Frisbee-Hume, S., Ferguson, A. O. and Bruera, E. 2016. "Frequency, Intensity, and Correlates of Spiritual Pain in Advanced Cancer Patients Assessed in a Supportive/Palliative Care Clinic." *Palliative and Supportive Care* 14:4, 341–48. doi: 10.1017/S147895151500108X

Erikson, E. H. and Erikson, J. M. 1997. *The Life Cycle Completed: Extended Version with New Chapters on the Ninth Stage of Development.* New York: W.W. Norton & Co.

Exline, J. J. 2013. "Religious and Spiritual Struggles." In *APA Handbook of Psychology, Religion, and Spirituality (Vol 1): Context, Theory, and Research*, edited by K. I., Pargament, J. J. Exline and J. W. Jones, 459–75. New York: American Psychological Association.

Exline, J. J., Pargament, K. I., Grubbs, J. B. and Yali, A. M. 2014. "The Religious and Spiritual Struggles Scale: Development and Initial Validation." *Psychology of Religion and Spirituality* 6:5, 208–22. doi: 10.1037/a0036465

Fitchett, G. 1993/2002. *Assessing Spiritual Needs: A Guide for Caregivers* (Original edition: Minneapolis: Augsburg, 1993), Reprint edition Lima, OH: Academic Renewal, 2002.

Handzo, G. F., Cobb, M., Holmes, C., Kelly, E. and Sinclair, S. 2014. "Outcomes for Professional Health Care Chaplaincy: An International Call to Action." *Journal of Health Care Chaplaincy* 20:2, 43–53. doi.org/10.1080/08854726.2014.902713

Jeuland, J., Fitchett, G., Schulman-Green, D. and Kapo, J. 2017. "Chaplains Working in Palliative Care: Who They Are and What They Do." *Journal of Palliative Medicine* 20:5, 502–08.

Johnson, R., Wirpsa, M. J., Boyken, L., Sakumoto, M., Handzo, G., Kho, A. and Emanuel, L. 2016. "Communicating Chaplains' Care: Narrative Documentation in a Neuroscience-spine Intensive Care Unit." *Journal of Health Care Chaplaincy* 22:4, 133–50.

Lee, B. M., Curlin, F. A. and Choi. P. J. 2017. "Documenting Presence: A Descriptive Study of Chaplain Notes in the Intensive Care Unit." *Palliative and Supportive Care* 15:2, 190–96.

Leget, C. 2017. *Art of Living, Art of Dying: Spiritual Care for a Good Death.* London: Jessica Kingsley.

Levine S, O'Mahony S, Baron A, Ansari, A., Deamant, C., Frader, J., Leyva, I., Marschke, M. and Preodor, M. 2017. "Training the Workforce: Description of a Longitudinal Interdisciplinary Education and Mentoring Program in Palliative Care." *Journal of Pain and Symptom Management* 53:4, 728–37. doi.org/10.1016/j.jpainsymman.2016.11.009

Lewis, J. M. 2002. "Pastoral Assessment in Hospital Ministry: A Conversational Approach." *Chaplaincy Today* 18:2, 5–13. doi.org/10.1080/10999183.2002.10767 203

Lucas, A. M. 2001. "Introduction to the Discipline for Pastoral Care Giving." In *The Discipline for Pastoral Care Giving*, edited by L. VandeCreek and A. M. Lucas, 1–33. Binghamton, NY: Haworth.

MacKinlay, E. B. and Trevitt, C. 2007. "Spiritual Care and Ageing in a Secular Society." *The Medical Journal of Australia* 186:S10, 74–S76.

Massey, K., Barnes, M. J., Villines, D., Goldstein, J. D., Hisey Pierson, A. L., Scherer, C., Vander Laan, B. and Summerfelt, W. T. 2015. "What Do I Do? Developing a Taxonomy of Chaplaincy Activities and Interventions for Spiritual Care in Intensive Care Unit Palliative Care." *BMC Palliative Care* 14:10, 1–8. Accessed August 17, 2020, https://bmcpalliatcare.biomedcentral.com/track/pdf/10.1186/s12904–015-0008–0 Reprinted in *Evidenced-Based Healthcare Chaplaincy*, edited by G. Fitchett, K. B. White and K. Lyndes, 66–81. London: Jessica Kingsley, 2018.

Monod, S., Martin, E., Spencer, B., Rochat, E. and Büla, C. 2012. "Validation of the Spiritual Distress Assessment Tool in Older Hospitalized Patients." *BMC Geriatrics* 12:13. doi.org/10.1186/1471–2318-12–13

Monod, S., Rochat, E., Büla, C.J., Jobin, G., Martin, E. and Spencer, B. 2010. "The Spiritual Distress Assessment Tool: An Instrument to Assess Spiritual Distress in Hospitalised Elderly Persons." BMC *Geriatrics* 10:88. doi: 10.1186/1471–2318-10–88

Monod, S., Rochat, E., Büla, C. and Spencer, B. 2010. "The Spiritual Needs Model: Spirituality Assessment in the Geriatric Hospital Setting." *Journal of Religion, Spirituality and Aging* 22:4, 271–82. doi: 10.1080/15528030.2010.509987

National Consensus Project for Quality Palliative Care. 2018. *Clinical Practice Guidelines for Quality Palliative Care*, 4th ed. Richmond, VA: National Coalition for Hospice and Palliative Care.

O'Connor, T. S., Meakes, E., O'Neill, K., Penner, C., Van Staalduinen, G. and Davis, K. 2005. "Not Well Known, Used Little and Needed: Canadian Chaplains' Experiences of Published Spiritual Assessment Tools." *Journal of Pastoral Care and Counseling* 59:1–2, 97–107. doi.org/10.1177/154230500505900110

Pargament, K. I., Smith, B. W., Koenig, H. G. and Perez, L. 1998. "Patterns of Positive and Negative Religious Coping with Major Life Stressors." *Journal for the Scientific Study of Religion* 37:4, 710–24.

Peteet, J. R. and Balboni, M. J. 2013. "Spirituality and Religion in Oncology." *CA: Cancer Journal for Clinicians* 63:4, 280–89.

Pruyser, P. W. 1976. *The Minister as Diagnostician*. Philadelphia: Westminster.

Puchalski, C., Ferrell, B., Virani, R., Otis-Green, S., Baird, P., Bull, J., Chochinov, H., Handzo, G., Nelson-Becker, H., Prince-Paul, M., Pugliese, K. and Sulmasy, D. 2009. "Improving the Quality of Spiritual Care as a Dimension of Palliative Care: The Report of the Consensus Conference." *Journal of Palliative Medicine* 12:10, 885–904.

Shields, M., Kestenbaum, A. and Dunn, L. B. 2015. "Spiritual AIM and the Work of the Chaplain: A Model for Assessing Spiritual Needs and Outcomes in Relationship." *Palliative and Supportive Care* 13:1, 75–89.

Steinhauser, K. E., Bosworth, H. B., Clipp, E. C., McNeilly, M., Christakis, N. A., Parker, J. and Tulsky, J. A. 2002. "Initial Assessment of a New Instrument to Measure Quality of Life at the End of Life." *Journal of Palliative Medicine* 5:6, 829–41. doi. org/10.1089/10966210260499014

Steinhauser, K. E., Clipp, E. C., Bosworth, H. B. and McNeilly, M. 2004. "Measuring Quality of Life at the End of Life: Validation of the QUAL—E." *Palliative and Supportive Care* 2:1, 3–14.

Steinhauser, K. E., Clipp, E. C., McNeilly, M., Christakis, N. A., McIntyre, L. M. and Tulsky, J. A. 2000. "In Search of a Good Death: Observations of Patients, Families, and Providers." *Annals of Internal Medicine* 132:10, 825–32.

Tarakeshwar, N., Vanderwerker, L. C., Paulk, E., Pearce, M. J., Kasl, S. V. and Prigerson, H. G. 2006. "Religious Coping is Associated with Quality of Life of Patients with Advanced Cancer." *Journal of Palliative Medicine* 9:3, 646–57. doi: 10.1089/ jpm.2006.9.646

Mildred

A Case Study for Assessment of Spiritual Concerns of
Patients Receiving Palliative Care Near the End of Life

THIS CASE EXAMPLE IS intended to illustrate the application of the PC–7
model to an actual case of a palliative care patient. This case comes from
one of the members of our team who was working as the chaplain on an
inpatient palliative care team.

THE CASE

"Mildred" (a pseudonym) is a 59-year-old woman with Stage IV rectal
cancer with metastases to the liver. She has already received four different
lines of chemotherapy. The palliative care team discussed Mildred during
morning rounds. Some team members expressed concern about her oncologist's plan to discuss further chemotherapy with Mildred. The oncologist had defended this plan, noting that Mildred's performance status was
good and she wanted to receive more treatment. Later in the day, before
visiting Mildred, I reviewed her chart and read a note from her oncologist,
who had met with Mildred that morning. He had informed Mildred that
based on recent test results, further chemotherapy was contraindicated.
The oncologist also raised the issue of code status with Mildred, but she
did not wish to discuss that with him.

My conversation with Mildred began with a discussion of completing a Health Care Power of Attorney (HCPOA). Mildred wanted to appoint her daughter, and we completed the paperwork together.

P = patient, C = Chaplain

P1: So, is this the same as a DNR?

C2: No, it is different. (I explain the difference to her.)

P3: That's what my oncologist talked with me about this morning . . .

C4: About your code status?

P5: Yes, and my oncologist said I can't receive any more chemo.

C6: (gently) What was it like hearing that?

P7: Well, hard! I cried a little after we were done.

C8: That's understandable. It's difficult news to receive.

P9: I'm feeling better now.

C10: You had some time to process it?

P11: I think I'll keep needing to process it. I was diagnosed in 2013, so it's been more than three years now. It's strange how cancer can become a way of life. You just start living with it. Coming in to clinic. Receiving treatment, doing a little better. Feeling weaker, needing to come to the hospital again. For a while I couldn't do the infusions anymore, and I had to take pills. But they had a lot of side effects, so I needed to stop.

C12: That's lot to go through . . . And then this morning, your oncologist said no more chemo.

P13: I'm not giving up hope. I've been fighting this for so long. . . (she pauses for a few seconds and starts smiling). My daughter's son is three months old now.

C14: What made you think of him just now?

P15: I want to be a part of his life. And I have other grandchildren.

C16: Has your family been a source of support during all of this?

P17: Oh, yes. I have a son and a daughter who are here in Chicago, and then another son in Florida.

C18: How have they been dealing with you being sick?

P19: They are holding up well. They keep telling me, "Don't lose hope!"

C20: How do you think will they react to the news you heard today?

P21: It's hard for me to imagine telling them. They've been going through this with me. My daughter is currently living with me, so she's been very helpful and supportive.

C22: Is there anything else in your life that helps you through this? (she seems unsure how to answer) For example, some people find religion helpful.

P23: I am religious. I was raised Christian, and I go to services. Two of my children are very religious, more than I am. But it doesn't play a big role in my life.

C24: How do you make sense of what's happening to you?

P25: If it's God's will, this is what I have to go through.

C26: I hear you. People have different beliefs about God's involvement in our lives, but sometimes things happening can make us angry, or make us ask "why?" Have you ever felt like that?

P27: I felt like that with my mom. I felt angry. My mom passed away in 2015. She was sick for a while, and she was in her 80s. But still, when it came time for us to decide what to do, we wanted the doctors to do everything. And in the end, she was intubated and couldn't talk. And I can't know for sure, but I think she was suffering. That's not something I would want for myself. I don't want to be on machines. But I don't feel like that (referring to the anger she felt) now. This is just something I have to go through.

C28: It sounds like your experience with your mom might have given you insight into what you would want regarding your own care. (I explain further that this relates to her code status. Mildred agrees that I could share these wishes with our palliative care MD, who was going to follow up later in the day.) But I want to go back to your emotions during your mother's illness. Right now, you don't feel anger or questioning like you did during your mother's illness?

P29: No, I don't. Cancer is different for different people. My cousin was diagnosed in November and died the following February. It happened so fast! His family didn't have time to prepare for it. I want my children to prepare themselves. But it will be hard, because they've been through this with me for so long. I'm afraid they wouldn't want to hear the news.

C30: I hear that the idea of telling your children is quite daunting to you.

P31: (She nods, and remains quiet for a moment.) I don't want to lose hope, but I'm also thankful. (She smiles again.) I have nine grandchildren and they are all boys (she laughs). They all came over to my house for the holidays, and it was chaos!

C32: Oh, I can imagine! So your son from Florida also came up to be with you?

P33: Yes, that's something I like to do—get everyone under the same roof, and just appreciate the opportunity for us all to be together. It has been such a long time since we all were able to be together.

A nurse enters the room and announces that Mildred has to be taken elsewhere for a test. I thank Mildred for her time and arrange to drop off a copy of her HCPOA. I also mention that our palliative care physician will follow up. Mildred was discharged early the next morning, and I didn't get to follow up with her.

[Note, before reading the team's assessment of Mildred, some readers may wish to pause and use the model template to score to the case and then compare their scores and underlying rationale to those of our team.]

THE TEAM'S ASSESSMENT

Each of the seven members of our team read this case study and then gave a score for Mildred for each of the themes in the PC–7 model. In a conference call, we shared our scores and discussed the things we noted in the case report that informed them. Supplementary Table 10.S1 shows the team members' scores for Mildred's spiritual concerns. As can be seen in the Table, with one exception, all of the team members gave Mildred low scores (1 or less) for explicit spiritual concerns for each of the themes in the model. The total scores for Mildred's spiritual concerns for all of the team members were also low, ranging from 0 to 3 on a scale that could range from 0 to 21. Below, we report additional information about the team members' evaluation of each of the themes in the model.

Table 10.S1 **Team Scoring of Explicit Spiritual Concerns of "Mildred"**

	C_1	C_2	C_3	C_4	C_5	C_6	C_7
Need for meaning	0	0*	0	1	0	0	0
Need for integrity, a legacy	0	0	0	0	0	0	0
Concerns about family	0*	1	1	0*	1	1	2
Concern about dying	0*	0	0	1	0*	1	1
Issues related to treatment decisions	0*	0	0	0	1	1	0
Religious/Spiritual struggle	0	0	0	0	0	0	0
Other dimensions	0	0	0	0	0	0	0
Sum	0	1	1	2	2	3	3

Scoring spiritual concerns: 0 = no evidence of spiritual concern; 0* = no evidence of spiritual concern, further assessment needed to be sure; 1 = some evidence of spiritual concern; 2 = substantial evidence of spiritual concern; 3 = evidence of severe spiritual concerns. C1–C7 refer to the seven chaplain raters.

Theme 1: Need for meaning

The team members were mostly in agreement that Mildred gave no evidence of concerns about finding meaning in the face of her declining health (5 scores of 0). They noted that Mildred appeared to have initially been distressed when her oncologist shared the news that no further treatment was available, but by the time the chaplain saw her, she did not appear to be upset about this. In making this assessment, the team members pointed to Mildred's comment in P31, "I don't want to lose hope, but I'm also thankful." One member scored 1 for this theme, indicating that mild concern was present but that Mildred appeared to have the resources to address the concern. Another member of the team gave a score of 0*. This team member was concerned that Mildred changed the subject after saying in P31 "I don't want to lose hope." This chaplain felt it was important to follow up with Mildred the next day to explore possible feelings of hopelessness.

Theme 2: Need for integrity, a legacy

The team members were unanimous in assessing that Mildred gave no evidence of concern about the meaning of her life or of regrets about it. In fact, she shares her sense of gratitude for her life (P31).

Theme 3: Concerns about family

The team members were somewhat divided in their assessment of Mildred's concerns about her family. Two team members saw no explicit concerns about family but wanted an opportunity for further conversation about this to be sure of their assessment (score 0*). Four team members gave a score of 1 for this theme, indicating they saw mild concern but sensed Mildred would be able to address it. These team members pointed to Mildred's comments in P21, "It's hard for me to imagine telling them [her family]." They also noted that Mildred was aware that not appearing to lose hope was important to her family (P19). Observing these concerns and Mildred's desire to be part of her grandson's life (P15), one member of the team gave Mildred a rating of 2 (moderate spiritual concern) for this theme.

Theme 4: Concern about dying

The team members also varied in their views about this theme from no concern (score of 0) to mild concern (score of 1). In their assessments, the team members focused on Mildred's comment in P11, "I think I'll need to keep processing it [the oncologist's report about no further treatment]," and in P13, "I'm not giving up hope. I've been fighting this for so long," indicating possible ambivalence between letting go and fighting on. Some team members felt these comments did not indicate concern (score 0), while others saw them as evidence of mild concern (score 1); several members of the team did not see explicit concern but wanted an opportunity to assess again to be sure (score 0*).

Theme 5: Issues related to treatment decisions

Again, for this theme, the team members varied in their assessment from no concern to mild concern. Most members of the team felt that Mildred's description of her mother's possible suffering at the end of her life (P27) and her statement, "That's not something I would want for myself. I don't want to be on machines," indicated she was clear about her own treatment preferences. Several members of the team noted that agreeing to a DNR order can be a stressful confrontation with decisions about care at the end of life, and they wanted an opportunity to reassess after Mildred had made that decision.

Theme 6: Religious/spiritual struggle and Theme 7: Other concerns

The team members were unanimous in observing no spiritual concerns for either of these dimensions.

SUMMARY

This case illustrates the application of the PC–7 model to the case of Mildred, a woman with advanced cancer who was being seen by a palliative care team. Overall, the members of our team saw little explicit spiritual concern in Mildred. Where spiritual concern was noted, with one exception, the team members rated it as mild (score of 1) indicating they felt Mildred had the personal and interpersonal resources to address those concerns and no further spiritual care was indicated. The exception was for the theme concerns about family where one of the chaplains on the team gave a score of 2, indicating a moderate level of concern that this chaplain would address in future conversations with Mildred. However, even within the overall low ratings of spiritual concern, the variation in team members' assessments of Mildred should be noted. That is, while for three of the themes the team members were unanimous in assessing no concern, for three other themes, the members' assessments included no concern, no concern but reassess, and mild concern. While further research is needed, we think this range of variation in assessment using the PC–7 model will be common. Furthermore, we believe that similar variation within the none-to-mild range of spiritual concern (scores of 0, 0*, 1) or within the moderate-to severe range of spiritual concern (scores of 2 or 3) indicates an acceptable level of reliability for the PC–7 model.

Part II

COMMENTARY

1

Religious or Spiritual Care

Identifying and addressing the breadth
of spiritual needs

—CHERYL HOLMES
Chief Executive Officer, Spiritual Health Association, Melbourne, Australia

INTRODUCTION

GEORGE FITCHETT'S CONTRIBUTION TO spiritual care is considerable and
his research, publications, mentoring, and vision have influenced much of
what has occurred in the field for decades. As the Chief Executive Officer
for the Spiritual Health Association located in Australia, my task is to provide leadership for the development of spiritual care in health. So much
of current research and practice has been informed by George's work. This
growing body of evidence and knowledge continues to inform the strategic
directions we develop in Australia. At the same time there are significant
questions for the field that have been shaped and reshaped by the changing
contexts within which spiritual care occurs. So much has changed and yet
the fundamental questions remain concerned with issues of what we do,
how we do it, and the difference it makes to the people who receive our care.
In this commentary I want to consider how George's work has influenced
the way we think about these questions, what this means for us now and the
directions needed for the future.

I write from within the Australian context and so it is important to provide some information about the religious and spiritual demographics of this country. The most recent Australian Bureau of Statistics census data showed increasing religious diversity (Hinduism was the fastest growing religion) and an increase in those reporting "no religion." For the first time this was the largest cohort (31%), above any denomination or religious group (Australian Bureau of Statistics 2016). A national study undertaken by McCrindle Research reported growing numbers of people who identify as "spiritual but not religious" (14%) (McCrindle 2017). When the McCrindle study was undertaken the 2016 census data was not yet available so the data from the 2011 census was used. By separating out the "spiritual but not religious" group, the overall numbers of those who identified as Christian went from 61 percent to 45 percent. I would assume that the 2016 census data would continue that trend with increasing numbers of "spiritual but not religious" and decreasing numbers of those identifying as Christian. It is within this multi-faith, multi-cultural and secular context that spiritual care in Australia must respond to the central questions that continue to be addressed through research and changing practices.

WHAT WE DO

Fitchett's recent review provides a clear overview of the current research defining what it is that chaplains do (Fitchett 2017). Foundational for these activities is the skill required to identify the spiritual needs that have informed the chaplain's response. That is, before there can be an intervention an assessment is required. Fitchett's work has been foundational in this area (Fitchett 1993; Fitchett and Roberts 2003 [Article 8 in this volume]). Yet the development of tools for screening and assessing spiritual needs continues with varying degrees of validity and use (Fitchett 2014).

There seems to be a number of tensions impacting this development. The first is the tension between the medical and the psycho-social-spiritual models of care. Chaplains do not want an assessment that becomes a written exercise to gather information (a check-list as it were) at the expense of being present to nurturing a relationship (O'Connor et al. 2005). The second tension relates to the language of "religious" and "spiritual." The conflation of religious and spiritual that occurs in the literature is particularly problematic in the Australian context—though I am sure we are not alone in this. Is there a difference between religious struggle and spiritual struggle? At times these terms are used separately and at times they are conflated to simply R/S struggle or screening (Fitchett and Risk 2009 [Article 9 in this volume]). Determining the language, we use is essential because of what it conveys to our patients/clients and also to our professional colleagues. It is important though that the use of terms such as "spiritual" and "spirituality" are not being used as the Trojan horse to get religion into the market place. The development of the Chaplaincy Taxonomy has been significant in this conversation and, in the Australian context, the use of the Spiritual Intervention Codes in documentation has enabled increasing clarity and consistency (Massey et al. 2015; Spiritual Health Association 2019). If we define spiritual struggle mostly in terms that relate to theistic concepts, then we are potentially missing and even alienating a growing section of the community who do not identify with a religious tradition.

Another question that needs to be asked is whether the attempt to broaden the reach of spiritual care has placed us in a perpetual cycle of trying to define what it is we do within what is an amorphous catchall term that we have constructed as a domain of care. Having said that, we must recognize that all the domains of care are constructed, whether physical, psychological, emotional, social or spiritual. We know that we cannot divide the human person into these distinct and separate spheres. The human person is an integrated whole and yet in order to ensure care of the "whole person" we have needed to remind those within the medical model that we are more than just physical beings. The identification of these domains of care has enabled us to locate spirituality within the health care model.

There are those who have warned against the adoption of a generic spirituality detached from religion (Pattison 2001; Koenig 2008). This misrepresents the movement towards an inclusive understanding of "spirituality" that recognizes that spiritual needs and resources come in many shapes and forms. Those working, researching and writing in the field (and issuing warnings) are often those who hold a religious worldview and have, until recent times, shaped chaplaincy care. This is where the question of whose needs are being met becomes important and the concept of person-centered care, an essential aspect of healthcare, provides a framework in which to formulate a response. As I have already noted, increasing numbers of people describe themselves as "spiritual but not religious," for them this language means something and we need to understand this (Mercandante 2014). What matters to the people in receipt of our care must inform the tools used for screening and assessment to be truly person-centered. Fitchett's review of recent research brings together significant findings on what chaplains do, the contribution of spiritual care to patient experience and outcomes, and identifies the breadth of spiritual needs in palliative and end of life care (Fitchett 2017). Further research to identify spiritual needs and understandings of spiritual care has been undertaken since that collection was published (Selman et al. 2018). As screening and assessment tools increasingly define areas of spiritual concern and need (inclusive of religious concerns and needs), chaplains may better be able to refine and articulate what they do. Proving this makes a difference will continue to be a focus for future research.

MEASURING WHAT WE DO

In 2014 a number of international colleagues called for chaplains to focus on outcomes to highlight the value of spiritual care's contribution to people's health and wellbeing (Handzo et al. 2014). Once again it is important to recognize that Fitchett's recent overview outlines research undertaken on a number of outcome measures including, patient satisfaction (the majority of studies fall into this category), anxiety, depression, and quality of life (Fitchett 2017). The impact of care for patients/clients in health care generally is increasingly, being measured through Patient Reported Outcome Measures (PROM), and interest in PROM has gained traction globally (Williams et al. 2016). The development of the Scottish Spiritual Care PROM provides the possibility for patient reported outcomes following chaplaincy interventions (Snowden and Telfer 2017).

There are a number of questions arising from this research, and Fitchett raises an important one that applies to all research on outcomes. How is the care provided by the chaplain different from care that could be given by other religious providers or health professionals? (Fitchett 2011 [Article 6 in this volume]). In other words, how do we know that the outcomes are related to the spiritual care and what was the specific care that produced the required outcome? We find ourselves back at the conundrum of what it is that chaplains actually do.

It is at this point that the potential of case study research becomes evident. One of the strengths of case studies is that they provide an opportunity to look at the whole process of spiritual care from screening and assessment, to interventions and outcomes. Together with Steve Nolan, Fitchett has added considerably to the number of case studies available to the field (Fitchett and Nolan 2015, 2018), and he has clearly identified the benefits and realms of influence for case study research (Fitchett 2011, 2018; Fitchett and Grossoehme 2012 [Article 7 in this volume]).

Fitchett has identified case studies as a pathway towards more advanced research that would be acceptable in the research hierarchy, i.e., randomized controlled trials (RCT) (Fitchett 2011 [Article 6]). I am not convinced we should be aiming towards conducting RCTs, and I want to highlight the integrity I see in case study research for spiritual care. If questioning of the medical model provided a rationale for spiritual care, then perhaps case studies provide a way to question how knowledge is privileged in the health care system. Increasingly, research methodologies make way for the voice of the researcher and recognize that objectivity is not always objective (Romanyshyn 2013). In the plethora of research methodologies, case studies give voice to what matters in spiritual care: the stories and narratives of both patients/clients and the chaplain, that form the connecting threads. Case study research has shown us that spiritual care interventions are fundamentally about relationships. These are not interventions for the development of "how to" manuals; they are stories around which language, narratives and meta-narratives can be developed. This is where we can begin perhaps to create the meta-narratives of the "spiritual but not religious." Are there recurring themes, concerns, needs that are identifiable in the case studies reported?

This deeper analysis of the growing number of case studies could provide rich data about the nature of peoples' spiritual concerns and spiritual struggle (outside of purely religious concerns) and provide further shape to the interventions and outcomes important to the increasing numbers of people receiving care who do not have a religious affiliation. We also need to think about whose voice is being heard. There is a growing recognition that patients/clients are partners in their health care and need to have a voice in shaping not only the care they receive but the processes and programs delivering that care (Horvat 2019). Case study research may provide an avenue to partner with patients/clients about the spiritual care they receive. Case studies co-authored by chaplains and their patients/clients could really change the way we understand spiritual care.

RELIGIOUS CARE OR SPIRITUAL CARE

In his closing reflections on a number of case studies, Fitchett reminds us that we live in a time of less connection to religious institutions and he sees an opportunity here for chaplains as "sources of spiritual care" (Fitchett 2018, 269). In Australia there is not only less connection to religious institutions but a growing antipathy and even anger towards these institutions. This stems from a number of places including the recent damning report from the Royal Commission into Institutional Responses to Child Sexual Abuse (2017), and the current debates in Australia on Freedom of Religion. A recent opinion piece in an Australian newspaper reflects this antipathy:

> now, as in the past, they assume the right to impose their faith
> on others. Far from being denied a "voice" in the public square,
> they have a megaphone. What irks them is that fewer of us are
> listening. (Szego 2019)

This angst is not confined to Australia and questions about the need for re-ligious endorsement of chaplains has been raised elsewhere (Swift 2014). The adoption of the language of spiritual care has enabled us to rebrand ourselves and to carve out a broader remit for ourselves, to lay claim to a domain of care essential to whole person care. Yet our research and prac-tice has not wholly embraced the opportunities of these changes, as can be seen in the continued mixing of the language of religious/spiritual, as discussed previously.

How we use language matters and there is a growing need for us to become clear about our terminology. Once again, this could be guided by listening to the voices of those in receipt of our care.

In the paper co-authored with Daniel Grossoehme, Fitchett reports research that identifies the importance of chaplains visiting as remind-ers "of God's care and presence" and the importance of chaplains visiting at "times of particular anxiety or uncertainty" (Fitchett and Grossoehme 2012, 391 [Article 7]). One of these is clearly religious, the other not neces-sarily so. These different emphases may begin to flesh out ways to define religious and spiritual, recognizing that at times they may overlap and at other times they will be very distinct. Fitchett also reports the ways in which the chaplain might reduce anxiety through "reinforcing reassuring religious beliefs, repeating familiar religious rituals, and empathic listen-ing" (Fitchett and Grossoehme 2012, 394 [see Article 7]). Only one of these interventions sits outside a religious framework. Perhaps spiritual interventions to reduce anxiety could consist of reinforcing reassuring beliefs and values, creating meaningful rituals, reestablishing important connections and empathic listening. Our initial screening questions need to take into account the breadth of religious, non-religious and spiritual expressions as recommended by Savage (2019).

We need to get more serious about identifying what the distinctions look like so that we are better able to respond to and identify both religious and spiritual needs. The language we use and our definitions matter. They matter to our research and to our practice. Fitchett has discussed his con-nection with a definition of pastoral care used by Roy Bradley (recognized as the father of Clinical Pastoral Education in Australia). Bradley describes pastoral care as "the art of keeping the mystery of God present to humanity through redemptive relationships" (Bradley 1997, 18). This is a beautiful and meaningful description, but once again the limitations of the language for those outside a religious and theistic framework are obvious. We might perhaps describe spiritual care as "the art of keeping the mystery of love (or hope) present to people in and through meaningful connections." In the end this is not about religious care or spiritual care. These belong together for some people and are completely distinct for others. Spiritual care needs to be inclusive of the spiritual needs and concerns that matter most to the people who receive our care and for whom it is important. This includes the religious, the non-religious, the spiritual but not religious and any other permutation that may evolve. In the end spiritual care will only continue to find a place in health care if we can demonstrate that we are addressing the real concerns and needs of people and making an essential contribution to their health and wellbeing.

CONCLUSION

One of the questions raised in this contribution has centered on our attempt as a profession to carve out a broader remit for our work through embracing the language and concept of spiritual care. There is probably a range of opinions about whether this has hindered or enhanced the profession, but there could be no doubt that it has created confusion both within it and outside it. While religious affiliation declines, Fitchett notes that people "still seek to locate themselves in relation to something transcendent and loving" (Fitchett 2018, 269). One of the tensions for chaplains is that, as so many of us come from a religious tradition it is difficult to think outside of those structures, even when we really believe we are capable of it. We are unable to see our unconscious bias (and language). This is where we need critical friends and partners. The growth in non-religious spiritual care practitioners here in Victoria, Australia, gives us an opportunity to think through our language, definitions, research and practice. We need also to form stronger partnerships with those who use spiritual care services, our professional colleagues and patients/clients.

There can be no doubt about the contribution Fitchett has made to the field of chaplaincy and spiritual care. His work, along with that of other researchers, has brought us to the table and given us a language and a voice within health care, but we need to continue to adapt and to take up new opportunities that arise in the changing landscape of health care. We need to continue to define and redefine what we do and how we do it in ways that challenge the dominant medical model that privileges certain knowledge over other ways of knowing. Case studies bring us back to research that has integrity with spiritual care, emphasizing story, narrative and reflexivity. Case studies take up the challenge of identifying the outcomes of spiritual care and there is increasing potential for these to include the voice of the patient/client.

There are many challenges ahead. While research in the Australian context is increasing it is still limited and so we continue to look to our friends and colleagues around the world to inform our strategic directions, research and practice. George Fitchett has been a significant mentor, friend and colleague in this work.

REFERENCES

Australian Bureau of Statistics. 2016. "Census Data—Religion." Accessed August 17, 2020, http://www.abs.gov.au/AUSSTATS/abs@.nsf/mediareleasesbyReleaseDate/7E65A144540551D7CA258148000E2B85?OpenDocument

Bradley, R. 1997. *What Are We Doing in Supervision?* Presentation given at the conference, *Clinical Pastoral Education Beyond 2000* (August 28), Heidelberg, Victoria, Australia: Austin and Repatriation Medical Centre.

Fitchett, G. 1993/2002. *Assessing Spiritual Needs: A Guide for Caregivers* (Original edition: Minneapolis: Augsburg, 1993), Reprint ed. Lima, OH: Academic Renewal, 2002.

Fitchett, G. 2011. "Making Our Case(s)." *Journal of Health Care Chaplaincy* 17:1, 3–18. [Article 6 in this volume]

Fitchett, G. 2014. "Assessing Spiritual Needs in a Clinical Setting." Presentation given at the *European Conference on Religion, Spirituality and Health* (May 22), Malta.

Fitchett, G. 2017. "Recent Progress in Chaplaincy Related Research." *Journal of Pastoral Care and Counseling* 71:163–75.

Fitchett, G. 2018. "Afterword: Case Studies and Chaplaincy Research." In *Case Studies in Spiritual Care: Healthcare Chaplaincy Assessments, Interventions and Outcomes,* G. Fitchett and S. Nolan, 259–71. London: Jessica Kingsley.

Fitchett, G. and Nolan, S. eds. 2015. *Spiritual Care in Practice: Case Studies in Healthcare Chaplaincy.* London: Jessica Kingsley.

Fitchett, G. and Nolan, S. eds. 2018. *Case Studies in Spiritual Care: Healthcare Chaplaincy Assessments, Interventions and Outcomes.* London: Jessica Kingsley.

Fitchett, G. and Grossoehme, D. 2012. "Health Care Chaplaincy as a Research-Informed Profession." In *Professional Spiritual and Pastoral Care: A Practical Clergy and Chaplain's Handbook,* edited by S. Roberts, 387–406. Woodstock, VY: SkyLight Paths. [Article 7 in this volume]

Fitchett, G. and Risk, J. 2009. "Screening for Spiritual Struggle." *Journal of Pastoral Care and Counseling* 63:1–2, 1–12. [Article 9 in this volume]

Fitchett, G. and Roberts, P. A. 2003. "In the Garden with Andrea: Spiritual Assessment in end of life care." In *Walking Together: Physicians, Chaplains and Clergy Caring for the Sick,* edited by C. M. Puchalski, 23–31. Washington, DC: The George Washington Institute for Spirituality and Health. [Article 8 in this volume]

Handzo, G. F., Cobb, M., Holmes, C., Kelly, E. and Sinclair, S. 2014. "Outcomes for Professional Health Care Chaplaincy: An International Call to Action." *Journal of Health Care Chaplaincy* 20:43–53.

Horvat, L. 2019. *Partnering in Healthcare: A Framework for Better Care and Outcomes.* Melbourne, Australia: Safer Care Victoria.

Koenig, H. G. 2008. "Concerns about Measuring 'Spirituality' in Research." *Journal of Nervous and Mental Disease* 196:349–55.

Massey, K., Barnes, M. J., Villines, D., Goldstein, J. D., Hisey Pierson, A. L., Scherer, C., Vander Laan, B. and Summerfelt, W. T. 2015. "What Do I Do? Developing a Taxonomy of Chaplaincy Activities and Interventions for Spiritual Care in Intensive Care Unit Palliative Care." *BMC Palliative Care* 14:10, 1–8. Accessed August 17, 2020, https://bmcpalliatcare.biomedcentral.com/track/pdf/10.1186/s12904-015-0008-0 Reprinted in *Evidenced-Based Healthcare Chaplaincy*, edited by G. Fitchett, K. B. White and K. Lyndes, 66–81. London: Jessica Kingsley, 2018.

McCrindle, M. 2017. *Faith and Belief in Australia: A National Study on Religion, Spirituality and Worldview Trends.* Baulkham Hills, Australia: McCrindle Research Pty Ltd.

Mercandante, L. A. 2014. *Belief without Borders: Inside the Minds of the Spiritual but not Religious.* New York, United States of America, Oxford University Press.

O'Connor, T. S., Meakes, E., O'Neill, K., Penner, C., Van Staalduinen, G. and Davis, K. 2005. "Not Well Known, Used Little and Needed: Canadian Chaplains' Experiences of Published Spiritual Assessment Tools." *Journal of Pastoral Care and Counseling* 59:1–2, 97–107. doi.org/10.1177/154230500505900110

Pattison, S. 2001. "Dumbing Down the Spirit." In *Spirituality in Health Care Contexts*, H. Orchard, 33–46. London: Jessica Kingsley.

Romanyshyn, R. D. 2013. *The Wounded Researcher: Research with Soul in Mind.* New Orleans, LA: Spring Journal, Inc.

Royal Commission into Institutional Responses to Child Sexual Abuse. 2017. *Final Report.* Canberra, Australia: Commonwealth of Australia. Accessed August 17, 2020, https://www.childabuseroyalcommission.gov.au/final-report

Savage, D. 2019. *Non-Religious Pastoral Care: A Practical Guide.* Abingdon and New York: Routledge.

Selman, L. E., Brighton, L. J., Sinclair, S., Karvinen, I., Egan, R., Speck, P., Powell, R. A., Deskur-Smielecka, E., Glajchen, M., Adler, S., Puchalski, C., Hunter, J., Gikaara, N., Hope, J. and the InSpirit Collaborative. 2018. "Patients' and Caregivers' Needs, Experiences, Preferences and Research Priorities in Spiritual Care: A Focus Group Study across Nine Countries." *Palliative Medicine* 31:1, 216–30.

Snowden, A. and Telfer, I. 2017. "Patient Reported Outcome Measure of Spiritual Care as Delivered by Chaplains." *Journal of Health Care Chaplaincy* 23:4, 131–55.

Spiritual Health Association. 2019. *Spiritual Care in Medical Records: A Guide to Reporting and Documenting Spiritual Care in Health Services.* Abbotsford, Australia: Spiritual Health Association.

Swift, C. 2014. *Hospital Chaplaincy in the Twenty-First Century: The Crisis of Spiritual Care on the NHS*, 2nd edition. Abbingdon: Ashgate.

Szego, J. 2019. "Discrimination Bill Saves the Religious Lobby from Themselves." *The Age*, September 1. Accessed August 17, 2020, https://theworldnews.net/au-news/discrimination-bill-saves-the-religious-lobby-from-themselves

Williams, K., Sansoni, J., Morris, D., Grootemaat, P. and Thompson, C. 2016. "Patient-Reported Outcome Measures: Literature Review." Sydney: Australian Commission on Safety and Quality in Health Care. Accessed August 17, 2020, https://www.safetyandquality.gov.au/sites/default/files/migrated/PROMs-Literature-Review-December-2016.pdf

2

Test All Things Spiritual; Hold On to What Is Concrete

Towards a hermeneutic of story and statistics

—Martin Walton

Professor Emeritus, Spiritual Care and Chaplaincy Studies, Protestant Theological University, Groningen, The Netherlands

Test all things; hold on to what is good.

1 Thessalonians 5:21

LANGUAGE ISSUES

Most chaplains have narratives about times when their care made a difference to a patient or a loved one. Stories rarely change attitudes toward spiritual care. For some, that is because stories cannot be quantified. For others, stories represent a different language. Christian scriptures tell how the apostle Paul began his defense by speaking to the people of Athens in language they already understood (Acts 17). In contemporary health care, the language is evidence-based practice. Chaplains need to be able to speak that language to be understood and professionally valued by our peers. (Fitchett and Grossoehme 2012 [Article 7 in this volume])

In diverse ways the articles of George Fitchett and his co-authors in this reader contribute to the conversation between different contexts, with their respective discourses, in other words, their use of language and specific vocabularies The wide range of subjects, the prudent procedures, and the careful formulations, shape an impressive witness to the attempt to be good stewards of the calling and opportunities of chaplaincy care in all of its facets (Fitchett and Grossoehme 2012 [Article 7]). These articles examine relations between religion and health; they investigate the occurrence of religious struggle and coping; they seek the "lost," that is, they seek to identify those with high needs and high levels of struggle but few resources; they explore aspects of chaplaincy training; they discuss issues of chaplains' allotment of time; and they address any number of theoretical and conceptual issues, all for the sake of weighing the evidence for the effectiveness of chaplaincy. That search for evidence of effect of chaplains' care (which, the authors emphasize, is not to be confused with the beneficial effects of patients' religiousness as such) is a central driving concern. That is also the case, albeit indirectly, in a reflection on spiritual struggle and growth among CPE students, as it becomes clear that their spiritual path is directly related to their ability to meet the needs of patients.

My reflections can be no more than comments in the margins of the extraordinary legacy of George Fitchett, to whom I owe much. Basically, I want to do only one thing here and that is to reflect on the relationship between the two languages indicated in the quote above, taken from the penultimate article in this Fitchett reader. In order to do so, I will look at some of the basic concepts of chaplaincy care that play a role in this reader and elsewhere and suggest some shifts in terminology. Before doing so, I will first offer some comments on the hermeneutics of pastoral and chaplaincy care, and then on the normative and idealistic nature of the profession of chaplaincy. I will then make four suggestions for shifting the emphasis from rather abstract, idealistic terms to more concrete, behavioral terms. Finally, I will indicate how these terms can come together in a perspective that helps to meet the challenges of research.

TOWARDS A HERMENEUTIC OF STORY AND STATISTICS

Behind most every statistic that can be gathered in chaplaincy research, there is a story. The story may be about how the sharing of her predicament and struggle with a chaplain lowered the anxiety of a patient. The story may be about how working through personal values and private concerns in conversations with a chaplain contributed to shared medical decision making, resulting in an ability to face the imminence of death, resulting in turn in abstinence from aggressive treatment and an earlier coming of death. The story may be about a ritual that helped someone find forgiveness, or perhaps a ritual that finally channeled intense anger regarding memories of misuse, resulting in both instances in a sense of relief and more control of behavior. It is important to note that such stories underlie statistical measures of lowered anxiety, reduced end of life treatment costs and behavioral changes in complex care settings as a result of chaplaincy care.

The discourse of story, narrative, not only provides a way of speaking of which chaplains are particularly fond of using in telling about their profession, but it is also to a great extent their manner of speaking in the actual process of providing care. It is also the way that patients speak in sharing their situation. In addition, narrative enables chaplains to relate the life and situation of patients to the resources of religion, worldview and cultural traditions. In fact, pastoral and chaplaincy care has often been conceptualized in terms of relating the story of a person to the stories of tradition, as a hermeneutical narrative enterprise. Charles Gerkin revitalized Anton Boisen's term the "Living Human Document" in order to emphasize that the personal story of a patient deserves the same respectful and careful reading as does a holy text (Gerkin 1984). Just as there is an interpretive hermeneutics of holy texts and cultural symbols, there should also be an insightful hermeneutics of the living reality of a human life. Such a hermeneutics involves a close reading of an individual human story and its predicament (Gerkin 1984). It may require the patient revelation and reading of a very long story. It may need to include, as Bonnie Miller McLemore indicated with the term "Living Human Web," a thorough analysis of the context (Miller McLemore 1996). The reading may, for all sorts of reasons, have to limit itself to discernment of a concise utterance or poetic expression in the context of a very brief exchange. In whatever way or whichever setting, the challenge for pastoral and chaplaincy care is to make connections between the meaning expressed in an individual story and the meanings and values of religious and cultural traditions. That can be done by means of expressive resources and figures of identification, metaphorical images and symbolic renderings, comparison and contrast.

The present situation of chaplaincy care is that it also has to relate to the "meaning systems" of medical and social sciences, to the gathering of evidence for the effectiveness of care and to the "vocabulary" of research and statistics. In the hermeneutic of personal story and tradition it is the concept of narrative that provides a coherent vision and tools or means for making connections. The question I want to ask here is, how we might relate the primary frame of reference of chaplaincy, that is, its native habitat (narrative, tradition, experience, relations, etc.) with the secondary frame of the context in which chaplaincy seeks to be at home (intervention, standardization, outcome, effect, evidence, etc.). (For the concepts primary and secondary frame of reference, see Mooren 2009.) Or, to put it another way, what could be the terms and means of a hermeneutic for relating stories and statistics.

In their co-authored article, Fitchett and Daniel Grossoehme (2012 [Article 7]) refer to four possible relations between science and religion that have been outlined by Ian Barbour (1990): *conflict*, that requires choosing sides; *independence*, that allows each to go its own way in parallel worlds; *dialogue*, that looks for points of contact between distinct discourses; and *integration*, that seeks a coherent vision with allowance for distinction. The first two possible relations or models would leave the differing perspectives of story and statistics essentially unconnected and unchanged. Not only do those models fail to address the challenges chaplaincy faces, they ultimately bear no fruit. The latter two are more interactive and also seem interrelated. No coherent vision can be formulated without identifying points of contact and no effective dialogue can take place without some perspective on the whole.

The questions that arise then are: (1) what might the points of contact might be? and (2) what would constitute a sufficiently coherent vision in order to develop a hermeneutic of story and statistics? The quote at the beginning of this chapter suggests a shift from the discourse (or "language," as Fitchett and Grossoehme, put it) of narrative to the discourse ("language") of evidence-based practice. It is reminiscent of the position of Anne Vandenhoeck (2007) that chaplains need to be multi-lingual. But how is that multi-linguality to express itself if chaplains are not to live in two different worlds and alternately speak two unreconciled and independent languages? How might the discourses of narrative and the discourses of evidence interact with each other?

I will focus in what follows on the discourse and vocabulary of chaplaincy. To make the picture complete one might also ask questions about the discourse and assumptions of evidence-based practice in health, the reliance on standardized care situations that often fail to account for the complexity of real life situations, the generalizations from select populations to other populations despite differences of sex, age, ethnic and class background, and the difficulties of integrating ethical standards for good personalized care into random controlled trials. I think these concerns are real, but they have been addressed elsewhere (see, for example, Council for Public Health and Society 2017). My concern here is, therefore, with the vocabulary and assumptions of chaplaincy practice.

CHAPLAINCY AS AN IDEALISTIC AND IDEOLOGICAL PROFESSION

Chaplaincy care involves fundamental values and ideals. It is person centered based upon a relational anthropology; it is attentive to subjective and cultural perspectives; and it often includes advocacy of dignity and self-determination. It is tied to constitutional rights with regard to freedom of religion and expression. It often expresses itself in terms of assumed "universals" on spirituality, religion, and the search for meaning, that also bear a transcendent reference. One can speak, therefore, of a "normative professionalism" (Kunneman 2006) that expresses itself in the care, not just of persons, but also of values. Such normative professionalism, which is shared with other person-oriented professions, creates for chaplaincy a double relationship to health care. As allies in the care practices of health institutions, chaplains seek first to contribute to the wellbeing and health of patients. Secondly, chaplains relate critically and constructively to the very foundations of care in ethical and cultural reflection on the institutions and setting in which they work. Why do we provide care as we do? What are the religious and cultural roots of the ways in which we provide care? Are our care practices respectful of the integrity and dignity of persons? What are the motivations and inspirations of professionals in providing care? What are the fundaments of interdisciplinary care and shared decision making? How is ethical deliberation practiced on the work floor?

Normative professionalism, and the resulting double relationship to care practices, lends to chaplaincy an idealistic and ideological character. That character is a strength of the profession in its attentiveness to persons in vulnerable predicaments and in the preservation of fundamental values. At the same time such ideological normativity can be a hindrance if the idealist language, in terms of person-centeredness, presence, relationship, dignity, and spirituality, gets in the way of specific and concrete descriptions of what chaplains actually do. The ideological and ideal terms can themselves be a hindrance if they hide the way in which the ideals are embodied in specific acts of chaplaincy care and in interactions with patients and professionals. The description of outcomes in experiential and spiritual terms can be a hindrance if it fails to appreciate the bodily and behavioral effects that chaplaincy care can render. The ideals become abstractions, or remain so for others, if they cannot be related to observable interactions and effects.

In the critique of the vocabulary of chaplaincy care that follows, I do not mean to discredit terms like presence or relationship. However, my approach will, for the sake of argument, be critically dialectical in my advocacy of a shift in terminology. My suggestions are heuristic in nature, and I do not presume that they in themselves can solve the problems or resolve the challenges with regard to chaplaincy and evidence-based care. I do think that such shifts in terminology and focus can help to concretize the language used in chaplaincy and facilitate points of contact between story and statistic and help, in turn, to formulate a coherent vision. For that reason, although I do take issue with some of the terms that Fitchett and Grossoehme employ, I would like to think that my suggestions contribute to their central concerns with regard to chaplaincy research.

SHIFTING THE TERMS IN TALKING ABOUT CHAPLAINCY

Shift One. From "relationship" to "interaction"

In the spiritual care plan developed for Andrea, Fitchett and Patricia Roberts accentuate with repetition the need for a supportive, trusting relationship of the chaplain with Andrea (Fitchett and Roberts 2003 [Article 8 in this volume]). What if they had evaluated in more detail the verbatim encounter between Roberts (chaplain) and Andrea (patient)? In that encounter, we see Roberts maintaining a careful distance in respecting the resistance on the part of Andrea. We read how Roberts employs counseling techniques, expressing empathy and interest, in order to illicit emotional responses from Andrea. We see Roberts naming and framing the friction between Andrea and her husband. We read how Roberts employed self-disclosure to establish rapport with Andrea. We hear Roberts introducing theological perspectives on God that include an invitation for Andrea to address her anger to God rather than avoiding God. We hear Roberts framing the opportunity provided by the care provider, Marnie, to go outside as itself a gift and an opportunity.

We also see Andrea responding that it is good for her to be able to talk about all the issues with Roberts, that she is turning towards accepting that the "battle" is being lost, that she can name the friction with her husband, that she is surprised by a new possible perspective on her anger towards God, that she enjoys the outdoors and affirms the use of the term "gift."

There are the beginnings of tears. There is a smile. Marnie gets a hug. What else might Roberts have observed on posture and expressiveness?

Through all of the interactions and interventions described in the verbatim, a relationship with Andrea is established. In the responses of Andrea, certain outcomes can be perceived. The description of interactions and of their concrete effects tells us, in fact, much and many times more about what Roberts actually did and how one goes about establishing a trusting, supporting relationship than emphasizing the importance of the relationship itself.

In addition to talking about (the importance of) relationship chaplains need to observe, describe and evaluate their interactions. The terminology of relationship is too general to guide actual practice. It also does not help in situations in which the nature of the relationship is problematic due to resistance, in the case of Andrea, with regard to gender and cultural differences, or in situations in which misuse of the relationship takes place. Focus on the specific interactions provides information more drawn from observation and more easily communicable. It can also help to develop (criteria for) specific interventions.

Shift Two. From "presence" to "posture"

In his article, "CPE and Spiritual Growth" (Fitchett 1998–1999 [Article 5 in this volume]), we witness how CPE student Gilbert wrestles with the issue of the baptism of a deceased child. His supervisor offers new perspectives but leaves Gilbert to arrive at his own conclusions. Eventually, after "a long and painful journey," Gilbert lets go of his theological objections. He tells his supervisor, "all I could think about was being there for them, caring for them." The commentary that follows is framed in terms of presence.

> Gilbert was now able to be present to the family and able to meet their needs for he was able to let go of his anxiety of doing the right thing by the church and was able to be pastorally present to the family. He was able to claim his responsibility to provide ministry to this family as he best thought fit. (Fitchett 1998–1999 [Article 5])

If we look at what Gilbert wrote of his care in his final evaluation, we see, however, that verbal expressions other than "being there" also play a crucial role: sitting, watching, hearing, asking, baptizing, speaking, facing, deciding, and taking away "a barrier to being my present" (Fitchett 1998–1999 [Article 5]).

Just as in the case of Roberts, these verbs tell us much more than simply the description "presence" reveals. They tell us *how* Gilbert was present in specific interactions. The possibility of those interactions seems to be grounded in what the supervisor sees as "taking responsibility," allowing the concrete need to prevail above ecclesial convention. In other words, the key to the case might be the different (theological) position and (pastoral) posture Gilbert was able to assume after his "long and painful journey."

In the same article, CPE student Jean relates the following:

> As my verbatims clearly showed, I was continually feeling that I wasn't doing the pastoral care work right and I had difficulty just being with people even though that is what I most want to be able to do for myself and have others do for me. (Fitchett 1998–1999 [Article 5])

Here again presence is assumed to be the clue, even though we are not told what she was not doing right. We are told that Jean was burdened by heavy expectations. We then hear how she is touched by the theme of grace. The suggestion seems to be that the theme of grace enabled Jean to assume a different posture towards the weight of the expectations and thus also in her chaplaincy encounters.

The use of the word posture, that also implies observable physical aspects, allows for a more specific description of what is going on within the person of the chaplain, and between the chaplain and the other person than the term presence. Several of the verbs that Gilbert uses are receptive or even passive: sitting, watching, hearing, being asked, facing. I end up wishing I had a video registration of Gilbert in order to see his physical posture and expressions during those receptive activities. Presence is too general a term to investigate. Trying out different postures can lead to specific care strategies that can be tested and compared.

Shift Three. From "experience" to "expression"

In the spiritual assessment on Andrea (Fitchett and Roberts 2003 [Article 8]), there is an interesting passage on the experience of grace.

> We don't hear about experiences of grace in Andrea's life in the small portion of her story that she shares with Patty [Roberts]. Rather, she appears to operate out of the belief that you should get what you earn, what you work for. Patty points out that Marnie's efforts to arrange the visit to the garden might be a moment

> of grace. Andrea seems to have experienced it as such, "What a
> tremendous gift!" (Fitchett and Roberts 2003 [Article 8])

On the basis of Andrea's expression, or exclamation that the visit to the garden was a tremendous gift, Roberts suggests that Andrea experienced a moment of grace. However, we know very little of Andrea's actual experience.
We do know she is angry with God. But when Roberts offers her a different
perspective on that anger, she simply says that it is good to be able to talk.
When the subject of the non-communication with her husband leads to
tears, Andrea changes the subject. We can surmise that there is a lot going
on in Andrea that she is not (yet) talking about, or able to talk about, but we
know little about her inner experience. What we do see and hear is what she
expresses verbally and non-verbally.

The focus on experience plays a role at other places in the spiritual
assessment as well. And to be sure, it is one of the strengths of chaplaincy
care, and one of the key elements of counseling skills, that close attention
is paid to what persons experience, how they see their situation, and how
they relate to it. What we can factually observe, however, is what persons
express, verbally and non-verbally. The language of experience is very much
subject to interpretation by others, or even by oneself. Staying closer to what
persons factually express, not "understanding" them too quickly but inviting them through counseling to express more, allows the other to express
themselves more precisely, and moves the chaplain to be more specific in his
or her observations and descriptions, not allowing interpretation to prevail
above observation and registration.

Shift Four: From "spirituality" to "meaning" and "value"

Spirituality is a predominant term in contemporary chaplaincy care. Some
attribute to spirituality universal character ("Everyone has a spirituality,"
Swinton 2001), but the terminology of spirituality is not universally employed. If we look at Articles 4 and 2, we see several terms that play a role
in research: spirituality, religion, meaning, peace, faith, religious coping.
The terms "religion" and "spirituality" are often used as functional equiva-
lents, but religion, especially in relation to the protective function of religion (Fitchett, Rybarczyk, DeMarco and Nicholas 1999 [Article 1 in this
volume]) and religious coping, seems to be better documented in research
than spirituality. Religiosity can contribute to meaning (Canada, Murphy,
Fitchett and Stein 2016 [Article 4 in this volume]), but spirituality can
also be defined in terms of meaning (Fitchett, Rybarczyk, DeMarco and
Nicholas 1999 [Article 1]). Faith, defined as a global framework of beliefs

(the term is taken from Park et al. 2008), is considered to be more dispositional and deserves more recognition for its influence than is generally attributed to it Canada, Murphy, Fitchett and Stein 2016 [Article 4]), but its relation to religion or religiosity is not clearly defined. These comments are not so much meant as criticisms as to point out what the state of affairs is with regard to key terms of chaplaincy and chaplaincy research. The terms are fluid and variously defined. Religion has never been a well-defined term. The term spirituality, despite its strong Christian roots and less than universal reception, has migrated from designating a practice within religion to becoming a universal designator. The fluidity of the concepts raises the question about the perishable date of the terminology will be in times of increasing secularization and religious individualization, religious plurality, and multiple religious belonging.

It is interesting how the term "meaning" is variously employed in the literature as a defining element of spirituality, as a contributor to quality of life, and as an experiential outcome of coping and/or spiritual care. This suggests to me that meaning may be the bottom line. Humankind's search for meaning (Frankl 2006), whether ultimate or penultimate, seems to have a better claim on universality than spirituality. The search for meaning also lies at the heart of Gerkin's pastoral hermeneutic (Gerkin 1984). Furthermore, questions of meaning are very close to the actual practice of chaplaincy conversation. Asking what an event means to someone, exploring what their dear ones mean to them, and simply counseling, "That means a lot to you, doesn't it!" are common exchanges in chaplaincy encounters. At times meaning is almost synonymous with value, which likewise finds common conversational expression. "That's so precious." "They are worth more to me than anything else in the world." "That runs against your deepest values."

Speaking about meaning and value is closer to the everyday practice of chaplaincy care and provides more of a common vocabulary than speaking about spirituality. That at least holds for my own context in a secularized country like the Netherlands. I think that speaking about meaning is generally also more concrete. Fitchett's self-disclosure at the beginning of Article 5 suggests that it is not religion as such, not the tenets of religion in themselves, but the workings and effects of religion, the searching and owning of faith, the accompaniment in issues of meaning and value, that are of vital importance, and that have a concreteness and specificity to them that is often missing in the language used to speak of spirituality and spiritual care.

VISION

There may be other shifts in emphasis that can be helpful, but these four examples may suffice for the present purposes. The common thread is an emphasis on concreteness and specificity for the sake of points of contacts with the discourse of evidence and statistics. I suggest that the shifts allow chaplains to look with new eyes and in more detail at their own practice for the sake of quality improvement. The shifts can aid chaplains in describing the specific interactions and interventions that lead to certain outcomes. They enable chaplains to share the ways of speaking of other health care professionals with regard to observable effects on physical bearing and wellbeing and confirmable outcomes, expressed both verbally and non-verbally. They enable chaplains to use the everyday terms like "meaning" and "value" for communication in interdisciplinary settings. They suggest that measures of key outcomes can be derived from described effects of chaplaincy care in case studies. They can lead chaplains to seek confirmation of observed or suspected outcomes from patients themselves, from those around them and from health care colleagues. The shifts lend to the practice of chaplaincy an observable and a describable concreteness that can be more readily translated into research procedures. And they provide a way of thinking about chaplaincy that facilitates transferring results of research into practice.

That is a lot to claim, claims that ultimately can only be—and need to be—proven in practice. For the primary criteria in the testing of all things spiritual is the fruits thereof. Fruits are as concrete as taste and smell, color and texture, as they are expressed in behavior, posture, body language and verbal utterances, or in measures of patient reported outcome and wellbeing. It is to be expected that the most prevalent effects of chaplaincy care will be related to the primary discourse of chaplaincy: narrative and autobiographical competence, renewed faith and trust, experiencing grace and letting go, or more concretely: directing anger to God in prayer, naming a visit to a garden a gift, experiencing physical release in a ritual of forgiveness or protest, or learning to speak the word "dying" out loud.

It is likely that those fundamental effects will have functional counterparts in effects on stress levels, behavior, end of life treatment decisions, etcetera. The fruits will then be multiplied. They also need to be harvested in research results and sturdy statistics. The harvesting is not for the sake of chaplains, but for the sake of patients and for the sake of quality improvement, that is, for the sake of the benefits of what chaplains have to offer people. Chaplains are called to discern which spiritual care is helpful, which is not, and what might be potentially harmful (O'Connor and Meakes 1998). That requires detailed observation and systematic attention. Just as grounded theory is a disciplined and structured form of hermeneutics and close reading, so is the use of statistical measures and comparisons a structured and systematic form of discernment.

To that end it helps to understand the profession of chaplaincy as an embodied practice, a practice that affects not just the spirits and souls of persons, but also their bodies, postures and interactions, not just their experiences but also their expressiveness. To the theological justifications that Fitchett and Grossoehme identify, *tikkun olam*, stewardship and the acquisition of knowledge (Fitchett and Grossoehme 2012 [Article 7]), I would add the notions of embodiment and of testing the fruits of the spiritual.

When I first became a chaplain in 1993, I had the feeling that the guiding principal was taken from the biblical book of Judges: "every man did what was right in his own eyes" (Judges 17:6 and 21:25 New American Standard Bible). One of the most important contributions of George Fitchett to the field of chaplaincy is something that may not draw attention at first. It is reflected in the fact that seven of the nine articles are co-authored. Collaboration and professional solidarity are key elements of his transformative enterprise: cooperating in research, enabling others to do research, facilitating research literacy and transference of research practice, helping chaplains to better allot their time in order to seek the struggling and the lost and ultimately enabling chaplains to have a better story, so that their stories are not just illustrations but can be integrated into a hermeneutic of story and statistics.

REFERENCES

Barbour, I. 1990. *Religion in an Age of Science,* San Francisco.

Canada, A. L., Murphy, P. E., Fitchett, G. and Stein, K. 2016. "Re-examining the Contributions of Faith, Meaning, and Peace to Quality of Life: A Report from the American Cancer Society's Studies of Cancer Survivors–II (SCS–II)." *Annals of Behavioral Medicine* 50:1, 79–86. [Article 4 in this volume]

Council for Public Health and Society (Raad voor Volksgezondheid en Samenleving, Netherlands. 2017, *No Evidence without Context. About the Illusion of Evidence-based Practice in Healthcare,* The Hague. Accessed August 17, 2020, https://www. raadrvs.nl/documenten/publications/2017/6/19/no-evidence-without-context.-about-the-illusion-of-evidence-based-practice-in-healthcare

Fitchett, G. 1998–1999. "CPE and Spiritual Growth." *Journal of Supervision and Training in Ministry* 19:130–46. Reprinted in *Expanding the Circle: Essays in Honor of Joan Hemenway,* edited by C. F. Garlid, A. A. Zollfrank and G. Fitchett, 213–34. Decatur, GA: Journal of Pastoral Care Publications, Inc. 2009. [Article 5 in this volume]

Fitchett, G. and Grossoehme, D. 2012. "Health Care Chaplaincy as a Research-Informed Profession." In *Professional Spiritual and Pastoral Care: A Practical Clergy and*

Chaplain's Handbook, edited by S. Roberts, 387–406. Woodstock, VY: SkyLight Paths. [Article 7 in this volume]

Fitchett, G. and Roberts, P. A. 2003. "In the Garden with Andrea: Spiritual Assessment in End-of-Life Care." In *Walking Together: Physicians, Chaplains and Clergy Caring for the Sick*, edited by C. M. Puchalski, 23–31. Washington, DC: The George Washington Institute for Spirituality and Health. [Article 8 in this volume]

Fitchett, G., Rybarczyk, B. D., DeMarco, G. A. and Nicholas, J. J. 1999. "The Role of Religion in Medical Rehabilitation Outcomes: A Longitudinal Study." *Rehabilitation Psychology* 44:4, 333–53. [Article 1 in this volume]

Gerkin, C. V. 1984. *The Living Human Document. Revisioning Pastoral Counseling in a Hermeneutical Mode*. Nashville: Abingdon.

Frankl, V. E. 2006. *Man's Search for Meaning. An Introduction to Logotherapy*. Boston: Beacon.

Kunneman, H. 2006. "Horizontale Transcendentie en Normatieve Professionalisering: De Casus Geestelijke Verzorging." In *Geloven in Het Publieke Domein. Verkenningen van een Dubbele Transformatie*, edited by W. B. J. H. van de Donk e.a., 367–95. Amsterdam: Amsterdam University Press.

Miller-McLemore, B. J. 1996. "The Living Human Web: Pastoral Theology at the Turn of the Century." In *Through the Eyes of Women: Insights for Pastoral Care*, edited by J. S. Moessner 9–26. Minneapolis: Augsburg Fortress.

Mooren, J. H. (2009³). *Geestelijke Verzorging en Psychotherapie*. Utrecht: Baarn-Ambo.

O'Connor, T. S. and Meakes, E. 1998. "Hope in the Midst of Challenge: Evidence-based Pastoral Care." *Journal of Pastoral Care* 52:4, 359–67.

Park, C. L., M. R. Malone, D. P. Suresh, D. Bliss and R. I. Rosen 2008. "Coping, Meaning in Life, and Quality of Life in Congestive Heart Failure Patients. *Quality of Life Research*. 17:1, 21–26.

Swinton, J. 2001. *Spirituality and Mental Health Care: Rediscovering a "Forgotten" Dimension*. London: Jessica Kingsley.

Vandenhoeck, A. 2007. *De Meertaligheid van de Pastor in de Gezondheidszorg. Resultaatgericht Pastoraat in Dialoog met het Narratief-hermeneutisch Model van C.V. Gerkin*, Leuven.

3

Spiritually Mature
and Evidence-Based Chaplains

Commentary on Fitchett's "CPE and Spiritual Growth"

—DAVID FLEENOR

Director of Education, Center for Spirituality and Health, Mount Sinai Health System, New York

INTRODUCTION

I TOOK MY FIRST unit of Clinical Pastoral Education (CPE) in 1998, the year George Fitchett wrote "CPE and Spiritual Growth" (Fitchett 1998–1999 [Article 5 in this volume]). It was for me, as he writes, "a profound, life changing experience." I was in my second year of a Master of Divinity degree at a Pentecostal seminary in Tennessee, which required me to take a unit of CPE. I had heard my classmates talk about their experiences, which sounded frightening and intriguing all at once. Being in my mid-twenties and somewhat naive, I thought, since I had to do this, it would be a good idea to use a summer CPE program as an opportunity to vacation in an exotic city for three months. I applied to several programs halfway across the country in Colorado, which at that time was the most exotic place I could think of. As a backup plan, I applied to the local program in Chattanooga, Tennessee. I did not receive even one reply from the CPE programs in Colorado, but, thankfully, was admitted to the local site. It didn't take me long to understand why the programs in faraway places did not respond. I soon learned what they already knew: CPE is no vacation!

As I read Fitchett's article, I was reminded of how challenging and transformative my initial CPE experience was. Now, as a CPE certified educator, I hope to foster similarly transformative experiences that facilitate my students' spiritual and professional growth. Yet, I wonder, given the educational requirements for chaplains today, how might we continue to foster spiritual growth while training evidence-based chaplains?

In what follows, I affirm Fitchett's thesis that CPE can facilitate spiritual growth, and I share how it did so for me. I then observe that Fitchett's research efforts have helped lead to the spiritual growth of the entire profession of health care chaplaincy. I conclude by sharing my vision of what education and training for spiritually mature and evidence-based health care chaplains could look like.

SPIRITUAL GROWTH THROUGH CPE

I entered CPE with my head and heart full of doubts about my Pentecostal faith. I had graduated from a Pentecostal college and was enrolled in a Pentecostal seminary. I was a Pentecostal minister who had led youth groups and preached revivals. Yet, I was no longer convinced that I believed many of the central tenets of my faith or belonged to that community.

In CPE, I had my first experience with an ecumenical peer group and CPE certified educator, who practiced Christianity in ways I had never seen nor heard of before, and it was disorienting. I was astounded the day I listened to my more liberal Christian peers talking about how excited they were that the Dali Lama would be the commencement speaker at their school. How in the world, I wondered, could a Christian school invite a Buddhist spiritual leader to be the commencement speaker? I'll never forget the day I heard one of my peers, a Methodist minister, proclaiming that she did not believe Jesus was God. That was the last straw. I marched into my Baptist CPE certified educator's office, sat down, looked him straight in the eyes with as much intensity as I could muster, and said, "You believe Jesus is God, don't you?" Our eyes locked, a pregnant pause ensued, and, wisely, he did not answer. I don't remember his exact response. I only remember that he did not flinch in the face of my intense questioning. He gave me space to ask the question, explore why it was important to me, and search for my answers, and he cared for me through that scary and painful process. To this student, it did, as Fitchett wrote, "feel strange and uncomfortable" to question my core beliefs (Fitchett 1998–1999 [Article 5]). It felt like "unfaith" and "betrayal," but it was a part of the process of spiritual growth as I moved from "affiliative faith" to "searching faith" (Fitchett 1998–1999 [Article 5]). And my CPE certified educator did exactly what Fitchett recommended—he helped me name the questions (Fitchett 1998–1999 [Article 5]).

I had also entered into CPE with a deep, unconscious longing for connection. My family of origin had not been able to teach me how to connect in the ways that I needed. It was my CPE certified educator who modeled for me what human connection looked and felt like. He made eye contact, held silence, paid attention, and saw me. I could tell by his questions, invitations, challenges, and affirmations that he connected with me. Connection was unfamiliar, yet transformative. I later realized that connection with him was not only for my healing and spiritual growth but also a model for how to facilitate healing in spiritual care relationships. Indeed, I learned that connection is central to how chaplains do their jobs.

Similar to the way Fitchett left the Reformed tradition of Christianity and found his way to the Quaker community, I left Pentecostalism for the Episcopal Church. My journey echoes his when he writes, "I had to leave . . . to see if the sacred, as I was coming to know it from my experience, could be found dwelling in another place" (Fitchett 1998–1999 [Article 5]). I found the sacred in three places: the hospital, CPE, and the Episcopal Church. At the end of my first CPE unit, I knew in my heart that I wanted to be a hospital chaplain, a CPE certified educator, and an Episcopal priest. I graduated in 1999 with a Master of Divinity degree and went straight into a CPE residency. I began the process of becoming an Episcopal priest, which meant I would have to go to an Episcopal seminary for Anglican studies, which I did a few years later. Following that, I began CPE supervisory education. It took a little over a decade, and by 2010 I had achieved all three of my vocational aspirations. Nurtured by CPE and the Episcopal Church, I moved from searching faith to owned faith. I resonate deeply with Fitchett's experience of CPE and the people he interviewed. CPE was transformative for me and indeed a time of unmatched spiritual growth.

The primary questions I asked during CPE were about myself—questions about my identity, beliefs, and sense of belonging, which were all critical to my spiritual growth. There was also a secondary set of questions I began asking during that unit of CPE about how I practiced ministry as a chaplain. Those questions would take on far more significance than I could have ever imagined. I spent much of my time in CPE trying to figure out, among other things, what does a chaplain do? While it sounds like a question that should be easily answered by any introductory course, it was not. My CPE certified educator and peer group invited me to reflect on the question, to look within, and find the answer for myself. While that approach was incredibly helpful concerning questions of identity, belief, and belonging, it did not help answer this more practical question of what chaplain's do.

At the risk of being criticized for avoiding my pain and my patients' pain, I sneaked off to the hospital library to see what others had written on this question. Unbeknownst to me, I had become a researcher, and this was my first research question: what do chaplains do as members of a health care team? I was not trying to become a researcher. I simply wanted to have more confidence in what I was doing (and supposed to be doing) as a chaplain intern when I visited patients. I was grateful to learn that I wasn't the first person to ask this question.

In 1991, in the *Southern Medical Journal*, physician Cecil Sharp wrote, "The hospital chaplain is a relatively new member of the health care team, and there is little objective information on the chaplaincy's role in the hospital" (Sharp 1991, abstract). Writing about chaplaincy in the neonatal intensive care unit, Sharp then posed the following questions: "Can the hospital chaplain be useful to parents or staff who work where life and death often hang in the balance? Should the chaplain's role be objectively defined?" (Sharp 1991, 1482). In 1993, George Handzo asked a similar question when he wrote, "Where do chaplains fit in the world of cancer care?" (Handzo 1993, 29). I was comforted to learn that I was not the only one who had wondered about the tasks and goals of a health care chaplain. The question was very much alive. And it remains a living question to this day. From 2007 to 2017, various authors published at least seven articles and one book with titles that included some variation of the words "What do chaplains do?" (Cadge, Calle and Dillinger 2011; Handzo et al. 2008; Jeuland, Fitchett, Schulman-Green and Kapo 2017; Massey et al. 2015; Mowat and Swinton 2007; Vanderwerker et al. 2008).

Throughout CPE, I grew personally and professionally but learned little about scientific research, which is all too common. Most chaplains have no formal training in scientific research and report feeling anxious and inadequate when it comes to involvement with it (Murphy and Fitchett 2009). Sneaking into that hospital library as a CPE student, I was unaware that I was wading into the waters of a babbling brook that would become a tide of change in health care chaplaincy as the field sought to become evidence-based.

SPIRITUAL GROWTH OF THE PROFESSION OF HEALTH CARE CHAPLAINCY

Fitchett's focus on fostering spiritual growth in CPE students would widen to facilitating the spiritual growth of the entire profession of health care chaplaincy by engaging in and promoting scientific research. Using John Westerhoff's (2000) model to assess the field around the time when Fitchett wrote this article, the profession was in a stage of *searching faith*. While we have moved significantly as a field over the last two decades, I believe that we appropriately remain in this stage. Fitchett (1998–1999) describes this phase as "a time of questioning the faith of our family" (Westerhoff 2000, 134). Westerhoff describes it as a phase characterized by doubt or critical judgment, experimentation, and commitment to a cause or person. The key characteristics of *searching faith* may be seen in the field's movements over the last several decades.

Doubts and debates emerged within the profession as chaplains, embedded in an ever-changing health care context, began asking questions about identity and practice, such as, who are we in this context and what is our role here? Cadge describes the field in a state of stress in the 1990s as "healthcare became increasingly evidence-based and bureaucratic" (Cadge 2019, 51). Because of long-standing doubts about its continued viability, the field of health care chaplaincy worked for years to prove its worth to health care administrators with marginal success. Amid these doubts, some chaplaincy leaders called for changes that included adopting evidence-based approaches (Carey and Newell 2002; VandeCreek 2002b). Others inside the profession argued such changes would fundamentally alter chaplains' professional identity and self-understanding (VandeCreek 2002a; VandeCreek 2011). These internal debates, characteristic of *searching faith,* continue today.

Experimentation, as Westerhoff (2000) argues, is central to *searching faith*. As Cadge (2019) points out, the field experimented with joint conferences and attempts at mergers, but to no avail. Such experiments were premature attempts to alleviate the discomfort of transition and growth of a profession. And as I write this, leaders of major professional chaplaincy organizations are actively engaged in conversations about joint conferences and mergers.

A small but growing voice of reformers led by Larry VandeCreek and others set out to save the profession by committing themselves to the cause of evidence-based practice. Evidence-based practice emerged in medicine in the 1970s and became normative for health care. Whereas chaplains learn humanities research in their theological training, other health care professionals learn scientific research and have a different epistemology than chaplains. Chaplains work from the understanding that authoritative sources of knowledge include tradition, personal experiences, role modeling, and intuition. (Hundley 1999). Other health care professionals rely more on evidence from scientific studies. VandeCreek and colleagues expressed the urgency for chaplains to engage in scientific research by saying that it is

> becoming so relevant that chaplains who ignore them will increasingly be thought of by these [health care] professionals as uninformed. Continued neglect of these results will imply that the knowledge base of pastoral care is out of date and other [health care] professionals will begin to regard chaplains as incompetent. Thus, we must find ways to integrate the research results of others into their clinical practice (Cadge 2019, 53)

It was apparent to chaplaincy reformers that to survive and develop chaplains would need to learn a new language, the language of scientific research, and evidence-based practice (O'Connor and Meakes, 1998; O'Connor, 2002).

No one has done more than Fitchett to engage the profession's *searching faith* by learning, practicing, teaching, and advocating for evidence-based spiritual care. His enormous influence on the field today is due, in part, to the way he went about facilitating this change. Fitchett focused on the same three features of CPE that he highlighted in his article—questions, answers, and community—to promote the growth of the profession. He respectfully asked his colleagues challenging questions from a scientific perspective about their ministries (Fitchett 2002). He did the hard work of seeking answers by earning a Doctor of Philosophy degree in Epidemiology, collaborating with interprofessional health care colleagues, conducting scientific studies, and publishing the results of their work. He conducted research with colleagues to identify chaplains' attitudes and misconceptions about research (Murphy and Fitchett 2009). With colleagues, he studied CPE residencies to determine what educational methods were being used, if any, to teach research literacy (Fitchett, Tartaglia, Dodd-McCue and Murphy 2012; Tartaglia, Fitchett, Dodd-McCue, Murphy and Derrickson 2013). He worked collaboratively outside and within the professional community of chaplains and CPE certified educators to persuade the field to embrace scientific research and thus transform our identity and practice as health care chaplains. He called upon chaplains to value research by frequently reading peer-reviewed literature; to become research literate by learning the basics of qualitative and quantitative research; and to conduct research (Fitchett 2002). By asking these questions, finding answers through scientific research, and doing so in relationship with his colleagues, Fitchett helped deepen the *searching faith* of the field and garner greater acceptance of research as an integral part of health care chaplaincy.

A VISION FOR EDUCATING SPIRITUAL MATURE AND EVIDENCED-BASED CHAPLAINS

As a result of Fitchett and his colleagues' efforts, the training and certification of chaplains have evolved a great deal in the last decade. Fitchett has argued that chaplaincy training should be guided by chaplaincy certification competencies such as proficiency with spiritual assessments, outcomes-oriented chaplaincy, and research literacy (Fitchett et al. 2012; Fitchett et al. 2015). Several CPE residencies now teach research (Tartaglia et al. 2013) and incorporate journal clubs (Fleenor et al. 2019). These evolutions are good, but more change is needed to shape health care chaplains who are spiritually mature and evidence-based.

Inspired by Fitchett and other leaders in the field who have been calling for reformations to chaplaincy education (Massey 2014; Tartaglia 2015; Wintz and Hughes 2018), I offer a vision for how health care chaplains could be educated in a way that retains CPE's focus on spiritual growth and integrates it with evidence-based practice. This vision is, admittedly, unrealistic in many ways. I offer it, though, truly as a vision, not as a roadmap, with the hope that we will, in the words of the Spanish poet, Antonio Machado, be inspired to "make the path as we walk it" (Machado 2003).

From my view there are at least three ways education for chaplains needs to change: 1) new graduate-level degrees focused mainly on chaplaincy should be developed; 2) board certification requirements should be revised to accept chaplaincy-focused graduate degrees in place of graduate theological degrees, and; 3) CPE should be reorganized to focus on contexts of practice.

New Graduate Degrees for Chaplains

Chaplaincy educators should develop new degrees that include theology and retain a focus on facilitating spiritual formation but which are not primarily theological degrees. Chaplaincy educators should look to master's degrees in social work or pastoral counseling as models for these new degrees.

The current standard, acceptable graduate degree for health care chaplains is the Master of Divinity, which requires a minimum of 72-credit hours to complete. This degree is insufficient for training spiritually mature and evidence-based health care chaplains because it focuses on Christian ministry; curricula are concentrated mostly on spiritual formation, but not on evidence-based practice; and access to these degrees may soon be too limited as theological seminaries struggle to remain financially viable.

The Master of Divinity is a degree intended historically for the formation of Christian ministers. As chaplaincy has become a more religiously diverse profession, many who aspire to become chaplains have had to spend large amounts of time and money to earn a degree that, at best, does not meet their needs and, at worst, forms them for Christian ministry, even though they belong to no religious tradition or another religious tradition altogether. Fortunately, several schools in the U.S. such as Harvard Divinity, Union Theological Seminary, and Naropa University, have developed Master of Divinity degrees that are more suitable for non-Christians who wish to become chaplains. It is time to stop requiring non-Christian students to earn a degree that does not meet their religious/spiritual educational needs.

The second problem with requiring the Master of Divinity degree is that the curriculum focuses on spiritual and religious formation (typically for Christian ministry in congregational contexts) and not on evidence-based practice in a health care context. The Association of Theological Schools (ATS) requires Master of Divinity degrees to contain program content that includes religious heritage, cultural context, personal and spiritual formation, and capacity for leadership (Association of Theological Schools 2015). While each of these areas has merit for health care chaplains, other areas of study are needed for success in a health care environment.

A new graduate chaplaincy degree with a standardized curriculum should be developed (Wintz and Hughes 2018). Such a degree should include course work, clinical experiences, and clinical supervision, similar to the educational programs in social work and counseling, which typically require 48–60 graduate credit hours and may be completed in two years. Course work should include theories of spiritual care, spiritual assessment, individual and group counseling skills, human development, research methods, ethics, world religions and spiritualties, thanatology, organizational development, and other areas.

The third problem is that theological seminaries are on the decline in the U.S. (Cadge 2019). They may no longer be viable training grounds for chaplains because of rising costs, institutional instability, and lack of expertise. Chaplaincy educators should consider partnering with colleges and universities to develop graduate degrees in health care chaplaincy. To do so, however, chaplaincy leaders first need to develop faculty who can teach in them. George Fitchett, who earned his Doctor of Philosophy degree in Epidemiology, is a model for this. Through his and Wendy Cadge's efforts through the Transforming Chaplaincy project, there is now a cadre of chaplains with Master's degrees in Public Health, some of whom are pursuing doctoral-level work in health-related research. As chaplains earn qualifications and faculty appointments at various health-related schools, new degree programs can be stocked with faculty who are knowledgeable about and experienced in health care and chaplaincy.

Changes to Board-Certification Requirements

Certifying bodies should revise their educational standards to include alternative degrees, like the ones I mentioned above. They could continue to accept graduate theological degrees, such as the Master of Divinity degree or its equivalent until new degrees that are tailor-made for health care chaplaincy have been established.

CPE Reconceived, Renamed and Reorganized

Finally, CPE, the clinical component of chaplaincy education, should be reconceived. The term "pastoral" has fallen out of favor because of its connotation with Christian history and theology (Schuhmann and Damen 2018). The word "spiritual" has become the de facto replacement because it is inclusive and better captures the zeitgeist, at least in the U.S. (Lee 2002). In many contexts of chaplaincy practice, it is awkward and clunky to continue to call the training of chaplains "clinical *pastoral* education." CPE should be renamed Spiritual Care Education (SCE) and be subdivided by the context of practice, such as health care, corrections, campus, military, etc.

Specific to the health care context, SCE should be further subdivided into two major categories based on the generalist/specialist model (Handzo and Koenig 2004; Robinson et al., 2016). Generalist health care SCE would be for health care professionals such as physicians, nurses, and social workers. The curriculum would aim to help health care professionals identify spiritual distress and how to consult and collaborate with health care chaplains, the spiritual care specialists. Specialist health care SCE would be for health care chaplains in various contexts such as inpatient hospitals, outpatient clinics, hospice, and long-term care. The curricula would include traditional aspects of CPE, such as integrating theory with practice, self-reflection, interpersonal skills, and communication skills, along with health care focused knowledge and skills such as medical terminology and documenting in the electronic medical record.

CONCLUSION

As a field, health care chaplaincy has come a long way since 1998 when Fitchett wrote "CPE and Spiritual Growth," and when I took my first unit of CPE. We are more evidence-based than ever, and more spiritually diverse and developed than at any time in our history. As we continue to engage our *searching faith*, we must continue to ask questions of ourselves and our colleagues, seek their answers by honoring multiple ways of knowing, and remain in community with one another. As we do, we will develop as spiritually mature and evidence-based professionals who reliably relieve patients' spiritual distress and facilitate their healing.

REFERENCES

Association of Theological Schools. 2015. "Degree Program Standards." Accessed August 17, 2020, https://www.ats.edu/uploads/accrediting/documents/degree-program-standards.pdf

Cadge, W. 2019. "Healthcare Chaplaincy as a Companion Profession: Historical Developments." *Journal of Health Care Chaplaincy* 25:2, 45–60.

Cadge, W., Calle, K., and Dillinger, J. 2011. "What do Chaplains Contribute to Large Academic Hospitals? The Perspectives of Pediatric Physicians and Chaplains." *Journal of Religion and Health* 50:2, 300–312.

Cadge, W., Fitchett, G., Haythorn, T., Palmer, P. K., Rambo, S., Clevenger, C. and Stroud, I. E. 2019. "Training Healthcare Chaplains: Yesterday, Today and Tomorrow." *Journal of Pastoral Care and Counseling* 73:4, 211–21.

Carey, L. B. and Newell, C. 2002. "Clinical Pastoral Education and the Value of Empirical Research: Examples from Australian and New Zealand Datum." *Journal of Health Care Chaplaincy* 12:1–2, 53–65. Reprinted in *Professional Chaplaincy and Clinical Pastoral Education Should Become More Scientific: Yes and No*, L. VandeCreek, 53–66. London: Routledge, 2011.

Fitchett, G. 1998–1999. "CPE and Spiritual Growth." *Journal of Supervision and Training in Ministry* 19:130–46. Reprinted in *Expanding the Circle: Essays in Honor of Joan Hemenway*, edited by C. F. Garlid, A. A. Zollfrank and G. Fitchett, 213–34. Decatur, GA: Journal of Pastoral Care Publications, Inc. 2009. [Article 5 in this volume]

Fitchett, G. 2002. "Health Care Chaplaincy as a Research-informed Profession: How We Get There." *Journal of Health Care Chaplaincy* 12:1–2, 67–72. [Article 7 in this volume]

Fitchett, G., Tartaglia, A., Dodd-McCue, D., and Murphy, P. 2012. "Educating Chaplains for Research Literacy: Results of a National Survey of Clinical Pastoral Education Residency Programs." *Journal of Pastoral Care and Counseling* 66:1, 1–12.

Fitchett, G., Tartaglia, A., Massey, K., Jackson-Jordan, B., and Derrickson, P. E. 2015. "Education for Professional Chaplains: Should Certification Competencies Shape Curriculum?" *Journal of Health Care Chaplaincy* 21:4, 151–64.

Fleenor, D., Terry, K., Sharma, V., and Marin, D. 2019. "Prevalence of Journal Clubs: A Survey of Clinical Pastoral Education Residencies in the United States." *Journal of Health Care Chaplaincy* 26:2, 71–86.

Handzo, G. 1993. "Where do Chaplains Fit in the World of Cancer Care?" *Journal of Health Care Chaplaincy* 4:1–2, 29–44.

Handzo, G. F., Flannelly, K. J., Kudler, T., Fogg, S. L., Harding, S. R., Hasan, Y. H., Ross, A. M. and Taylor, B. E. 2008. "What Do Chaplains Really Do? II. Interventions in the New York Chaplaincy Study." *Journal of Health Care Chaplaincy* 14:1, 39–56.

Handzo, G., and Koenig, H. G. (2004). "Spiritual Care: Whose Job Is It Anyway?" *Southern Medical Journal* 97, 12, 1242–44.

Hundley, V. 1999. "Evidence Based Practice: What Is It? And Why Does It Matter?" *Scottish Journal of Healthcare Chaplaincy* 2:1, 11–14.

Jeuland, J., Fitchett, G., Schulman-Green, D. and Kapo, J. 2017. "Chaplains Working in Palliative Care: Who They Are and What They Do." *Journal of Palliative Medicine* 20:5, 502–8.

Lee, S. J. C. 2002. "In a Secular Spirit: Strategies of Clinical Pastoral Education." *Health Care Analysis* 10:4, 339–56.

Machado, A. 2003. *There Is No Road.* Buffalo, NY: White Pine.

Massey, K. 2014. "Surfing through a Sea Change: The Coming Transformation of Chaplaincy Training." *Reflective Practice: Formation and Supervision in Ministry* 34:144–52.

Massey, K., Barnes, M. J., Villines, D., Goldstein, J. D., Hisey Pierson, A. L., Scherer, C., Vander Laan, B. and Summerfelt, W. T. 2015. "What Do I Do? Developing a Taxonomy of Chaplaincy Activities and Interventions for Spiritual Care in Intensive Care Unit Palliative Care." *BMC Palliative Care* 14:10, 1–8. Accessed August 17, 2020, https://bmcpalliatcare.biomedcentral.com/track/pdf/10.1186/s12904-015-0008-0 Reprinted in *Evidenced-Based Healthcare Chaplaincy*, edited by G. Fitchett, K. B. White and K. Lyndes, 66–81. London: Jessica Kingsley, 2018.

Mowat, H., and Swinton, J. 2007. *What Do Chaplains Do? The Role of the Chaplain in Meeting the Spiritual Needs of Patients.* 2nd ed. Aberdeen: Mowat Research Limited

Murphy, P. E., and Fitchett, G. 2009. "Introducing Chaplains to Research: 'This Could Help Me.'" *Journal of Health Care Chaplaincy* 16:3–4, 79–94.

Robinson, M. R., Thiel, M. M., Shirkey, K., Zurakowski, D., and Meyer, E. C. 2016. "Efficacy of Training Interprofessional Spiritual Care Generalists." *Journal of Palliative Medicine* 19:8, 814–21.

Schuhmann, C., and Damen, A. 2018. "Representing the Good: Pastoral Care in a Secular Age." *Pastoral Psychology* 67:4, 405–17.

Sharp, C. G. 1991. "Use of the Chaplaincy in the Neonatal Intensive Care Unit." *Southern Medical Journal* 84:12, 1482–86.

O'Connor, T. S. 2002. "Is Evidence Based Spiritual Care an Oxymoron?" *Journal of Religion and Health* 41:3, 253–62.

O'Connor, T. S., and Meakes, E. 1998. "Hope in the Midst of Challenge: Evidence-based Pastoral Care." *Journal of Pastoral Care* 52:4, 359–67.

Tartaglia, A. F. 2015. "Reflections on the Development and Future of Chaplaincy Education." *Reflective Practice: Formation and Supervision in Ministry* 35.

Tartaglia, A., Fitchett, G., Dodd-McCue, D., Murphy, P., and Derrickson, P. E. 2013. "Teaching Research in Clinical Pastoral Education: A Survey of Model Practices." *Journal of Pastoral Care and Counseling* 67:1, 1–14.

VandeCreek, L. 2002a. "Chaplain No: Should Clinical Pastoral Education and Professional Chaplaincy Become More Scientific in Response to Health Care Reform? *Journal of Health Care Chaplaincy* 12:1–2, xix–xx.

VandeCreek, L. 2002b. Chaplain Yes: Should Clinical Pastoral Education and Professional Chaplaincy Become More Scientific in Response to Health Care Reform? *Journal of Health Care Chaplaincy* 12:1–2, xxi–xxii.

VandeCreek, L. ed. 2011. *Professional Chaplaincy and Clinical Pastoral Education Should Become More Scientific: Yes and No.* New York, NY and Abingdon, Oxon: Routledge.

Vanderwerker, L. C., Flannelly, K. J., Galek, K., Harding, S. R., Handzo, G. F., Oettinger, S. M., and Bauman, J. P. 2008. "What Do Chaplains Really Do? III. Referrals in the New York Chaplaincy Study." *Journal of Health Care Chaplaincy* 14:1, 57–73.

Westerhoff, J. 2000. *Will Our Children Have Faith?* Harrisburg, PA: Morehouse.

Wintz, S., and Hughes, B. 2018. "Standardized Methods of Education within Clinical Training for Chaplaincy." *PlainViews*, 15: 1, 1–10. Accessed August 17, 2020, https://www.researchgate.net/publication/322808014_Standardized_Methods_of_Education_within_Clinical_Training_for_Chaplaincy

Reading Fitchett

A brief orientation to statistical terms used in reporting quantitative research

—Annelieke Damen and Steve Nolan

Several articles in this collection assume familiarity with the methods and techniques of quantitative research and, in particular, the statistical analysis of quantitative data. Many chaplains, whose training has traditionally been in humanities and the liberal arts, may lack this familiarity. In contrast to qualitative research—which analyzes data about human behaviors using the kinds of interpretative and hermeneutical techniques with which chaplains are more likely to be acquainted—quantitative research gathers data that can be measured and given numerical values so that it can then be analyzed using statistical techniques. It is these statistical techniques that are likely to be alien—and alienating—to many chaplains. With this in mind, we offer a brief orientation to some of the statistical terms used in quantitative research reports. The aim is not to be a primer in statistics, but simply to facilitate novice readers of quantitative research to engage with, understand and, perhaps more effectively, evaluate what they are reading in this collection, and in the wider literature. This brief orientation follows the structure of a typical quantitative research article and key terms are highlighted in bold italics; however, it does not aim to be exhaustive, and readers wanting more detailed understanding are referred to the list of further reading suggestions below.

What is most immediately striking to anyone trained in the humanities, is how much space empirical research articles devote to discussing methodology. On the face of it, this can appear to be disproportionate—even, at times, tedious—and readers may be tempted to skip the detail and go straight to what they may think will be the more interesting discussion of the research findings. However, these sometimes lengthy accounts of methodology are important because they make clear how rigorous the research has been and, thereby, enable readers to judge the likely validity of the arguably more interesting research findings.

REVIEWING THE LITERATURE

Research articles typically begin with a review of the existing literature. Literature reviews are important preliminary studies because they appraise studies relevant to the research interest, outline what is currently known and highlight areas for knowledge development. The study question, sometimes formulated as a hypothesis, follows from reviewing the literature and aims to address a gap (or gaps) identified in current knowledge, for example, Article 3 addressed a gap Fitchett's team had identified in what was known about religious struggle.

METHODOLOGY

In the methodology section, the researcher explains how they collected their data. Data is frequently gathered from patient interviews using questionnaires that measure a range of *variables* (a variable being any attribute, characteristic or quantity that can be measured or counted, for example, demographic variables, medical variables, or a measure of religion/spirituality). For example, in Article 1, Fitchett's team uses a number of *instruments* (focused questionnaires designed to understand a person's subjective experience) to measure attitudes and opinions about their religiosity, religious coping, spiritual injury, etc. A key feature common to such instruments is the *Likert scale*. Developed to measure an individual's attitudes, specifically when they know they are being studied, Likert rating scales offer a series of statements that the individual rates according to how strongly or otherwise they associate with that statement. In Article 1, interviewees were invited to rate on a 4-point Likert scale, ranging from *not at all* (o) to *a great deal* (3), their use of certain religious activities as a means of coping with their disability. The number of points a Likert scale offers for rating can vary; those used by Fitchett's teams range from 4 to 7 points.

The methods section will also contain an explanation of whether a study is ***cross-sectional***, meaning that the researchers analyze data gathered from a sample at a specific point in time (for example, Article 3), or ***longitudinal***, which involves observations of a sample repeated over time (for example, Article 1). In longitudinal studies researchers measure key variables at ***baseline*** (i.e., at the beginning of a study) and then again at predetermined follow-up points (in Article 1 this was at 4-months). The reason for this is that it allows researchers to observe change over time and to understand whether that change has been influenced by baseline factors. Sometimes a longitudinal study also reports a cross-sectional analysis of just the baseline data (see for example Article 1).

Finally the methods section will explain which statistics will be used for the analysis. Statistics describe patterns in the numerical information gathered and examine possible associations among the variables that make up the numerical information. Selecting the statistics that are used depends both on the study questions and also on the kind of data gathered. The methods section is followed by a report of the results of the statistical analyses.

STATISTICAL ANALYSIS

Mean and Standard Deviation (SD)

Most studies start their results section with a report about the participants and the variables that were used. These statistics are called ***descriptive statistics*** and frequently include values for the ***mean (M)*** (the average) and the ***standard deviation (SD)*** from the mean (how far the individual values for a variable are spread from the average). For example, in Table 1.2, the mean for public religiosity is 6.1, calculated by finding the sum of all the patients' scores and dividing that value by the total number of patients. In this case, the SD 2.4 indicates a moderate level of dispersion of the individual scores around the mean (a smaller SD would indicate the scores were less widely dispersed).

Variables: Nominal, Ordinal, and Continuous

Usually, the next step is to analyze the relationships between variables. There are many statistical tests available to do this and the choice of test will be informed by a number of factors, an important one being the type of variable that is to be examined. There are three major types of variables: ***nominal***, ***ordinal***, and ***continuous***. A nominal variable includes groups that have no particular order, for example, the variables of gender, race/ethnicity, and marital status in Table 4.1. In contrast, an ordinal variable consists of groups that do have a defined order, for example, in the same table, the education variable includes the groups "less than high school," "high school," "some college" and "college." A continuous variable can take an unlimited number of values between the lowest and highest points of measurement. Again in this table, the example is annual income.

Chi-square, T-test, ANOVA , Mann-Whitney and Kruskal-Wallis

One type of relationship researchers often examine is the difference between groups. When dealing with nominal and ordinal variables, researchers use a statistical test called the **Chi-square test**. For example, in Tables 2.4, 2.5 and 2.6, Fitchett's team used this test to understand whether requests for spiritual care were different for different groups. When dealing with continuous variables, two tests are commonly used: a **t-test** to compare two groups and an **ANOVA** *test* to compare more than two groups. For example in Table 2.3, the *t*-tests compare the mean age between those who did and did not request care; by comparison, in Table 3.1, the ANOVA test compares the mean age between three different patient groups.

These tests are appropriate when studying the differences between groups when a variable is reasonably normally distributed (the classic bell-curve distribution, Figure 1).

Classic Bell-Curve Distribution

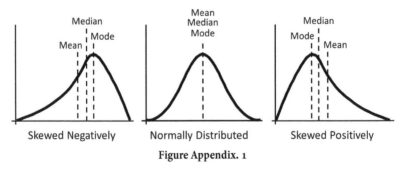

Figure Appendix. 1

However, where distribution is skewed, the **Mann-Whitney** test is preferred for a variable with two groups or the **Kruskal-Wallis** test for a variable that has three or more categories. For an example, see Table 3.3.

It is beyond the scope of this brief orientation to explain in detail how the results of these tests are interpreted. However, the indicators of statistical significance that accompany statistical tests will indicate whether there are actual differences between groups.

Statistical Significance: Probability (p)

An important question addressed by statistical tests concerns the ***statistical significance*** of the analysis, in other words, whether the result of a test is in some way meaningful or is merely the result of chance. Performing a test for statistical significance indicates the ***probability (p)*** that the result has occurred by chance. By convention, if the likelihood is 5 times in 100 or less, then it is considered unlikely that the difference has resulted by chance and the finding can, therefore, be regarded as statistically significant. This will be written as a probability of less than or equal to 0.05 ($p=<0.05$). Sometimes a note indicates that the probability in a study is even smaller (less than 1 time in 1000 likelihood that the difference is observed by chance, $p<.001$). Table 2.4, for example, shows a significant difference between those patients who request spiritual care and attend public worship never/yearly, bi- to semi-monthly, and those who attend public worship at least weekly. The difference is found in the proportion of each group. By way of comparison, in Table 2.5, the differences are not significant and, therefore, are likely to have occurred by chance. (Statistical significance is often indicated in a note at the bottom of a table and/or an asterisk sign of the results.)

Correlation (r)

When researchers want to understand the relationship between continuous variables, rather than between groups, they test for ***correlation,*** normally represented as *(r)*. (Though not named in this collection of papers, Pearson's correlation coefficient is the test most commonly used.) Values for correlations range from -1 to 1. The closer to -1 or 1 the correlation statistic is, the stronger the relationship between the two variables being examined. A negative correlation indicates an inverse relationship (where one variable increases the other decreases). In Table 1.2, Fitchett's team reports the correlation of the scores between time of admission and follow-up. Here there is a positive correlation of .84 for public religiosity, which means that the higher baseline score correlates with a higher follow-up score.

Multivariable Analysis

Testing a relationship between two variables is called *bivariate analysis.* Researchers can also conduct *multivariable analysis* using a test known as *multiple regression.*[1] Researchers distinguish between *dependent variables* (also known as outcome variables) and *independent variables*, which may influence or predict the dependent (outcome) variable. In *regression analysis,* researchers are looking at multiple predictors simultaneously to try to understand whether there is a relationship between a predictor and a dependent variable after statistically adjusting for (or controlling for) the effects of other possible predictors. In Table 1.6, Fitchett's team looked at the relationship between "Follow-up somatic autonomy," as the dependent variable, and several potential predictors (independent variables): "Admission somatic autonomy," "Race," "Diagnostic group," "Social support," "Admission depression," "Admission negative coping." In the different models (step 1, 2, and 3) the investigators looked at different relationships by adding different variables.

The relationship in a multiple regression is usually reported with a test statistic called a *standardized beta coefficient (β)*, which can show a positive or a negative relationship. For example, in Table 1.6, a positive relationship (.246*) is reported between "Admission somatic autonomy" and "Follow-up somatic autonomy," when one increases the other also increases. A negative relationship (-.229*) is shown between "Admission negative religious coping" and "Follow-up somatic autonomy," indicating that as negative religious coping increases follow-up somatic autonomy decreases. The relationship in a multiple regression can, however, also be reported with an *unstandardized beta coefficient (B)*. An unstandardized coefficient represents the amount of change in a dependent variable due to a change of one unit of an independent variable when the effects of the other variables in the model are taken into account. For example, in Table 4.4, for a one point increase in "Faith" (independent variable) the "Mental component summary" (dependent variable) increases by 0.530.

When investigators use a nominal or ordinal variable as a predictor in multiple regression models they commonly select one subgroup as the *reference group* and calculate the effects of other subgroups in reference to it. For example, in Table 3.4, the reference group for frequency of worship attendance is "never attends." Fitchett's team compared the effect of each of the other worship attendance groups to this reference group. From the table,

1. Linear regression is used when the dependent or outcome variable is continuous. Logistic regression is used when the dependent variable is dichotomous (e.g., request chaplain care "Yes" or "No").

it is apparent that, compared to those who never attend worship, among those who attend rarely or monthly there are no statistically significant differences in negative religious coping. However, the beta coefficient of -0.251 for those who attend weekly or more is statistically significant and it indicates that participants in this subgroup have lower negative religious coping scores than those in the reference group who never attend worship. It was a mistake for Fitchett's team not to specify the reference groups for gender, marital status and race in the table or text. However, none of these variables were significantly associated with negative religious coping, so important information was not omitted.

Mediation Analysis

A special type of multivariate analyses examines **mediation**. In Article 4, Fitchett and his team used mediation analysis to try to explain the relationship between "Faith" (independent/predictor variable) and "Quality of Life" (dependent/outcome variable) via the inclusion of a third variable ("Meaning" or "Peace") as a mediator variable (see Figure 1).

Cronbach's Alpha (α)

The final statistical test to note is **Cronbach's alpha (α)**. This is an important measure that indicates the reliability or internal consistency of a scale (for example, the Brief RCOPE Scale or the Spiritual Injury Scale). In other words, how well a given scale measures what it claims to measure. The α coefficient ranges from 0 to 1, and generally a higher coefficient indicates stronger reliability. The rule of thumb is that a coefficient between 0.65 and 0.9 is recommended; a coefficient less than 0.5 is usually unacceptable. In Table 1.1, Fitchett's team report the α coefficients of the scales they used.

As noted above, this brief orientation is offered to aid chaplains unfamiliar with statistical concepts and terminology to begin to engage more effectively with quantitative research articles, particularly those in this collection. The literature of statistics is voluminous but the following introductory level texts offer some next steps for interested readers.

FURTHER READING

Graham, A. 2017. *Statistics: A Complete Introduction*. London: Hodder & Stoughton.

Koenig, H.G. 2011. *Spirituality and Health Research: Methods, Measurement, Statistics and Resources*. West Conshohocken, PA: Templeton.

Myers, G.E., and Roberts, S. eds. 2014. *An Invitation to Chaplaincy Research: Entering the Process*. New York: HealthCare Chaplaincy Network. Accessed August 17, 2020, http://www.healthcarechaplaincy.org/docs/publications/templeton_research/hcc_research_handbook_final.pdf

Rowntree, D. 2018. *Statistics without Tears: An Introduction for Non-Mathematicians*. London: Penguin.

Watt, R., and Collins, E. 2019. *Statistics for Psychology: A Guide for Beginners (and Everyone Else)*. London & Thousand Oaks, CA: Sage.